CHINA'S ROLE IN WORLD AFFAIRS

CHINA'S ROLE IN WORLD AFFAIRS

MICHAEL B. YAHUDA

ST. MARTIN'S PRESS   NEW YORK

Copyright © 1978 Michael B. Yahuda

All rights reserved. For information write:
St. Martin's Press Inc., 175 Fifth Avenue, New York, N.Y. 10010
Printed in Great Britain
Library of Congress Catalog Card Number: 78-19218

ISBN 0-312-13358-8

5 May 79

First published in the United States of America in 1978

Printed and bound in Great Britain

CONTENTS

PREFACE

This book analyses China's foreign policy within a framework suggested by the conceptualisation of the outside world and China's place within it, as articulated and acted upon by China's leaders. Following an introduction which explains why this mode of analysis is peculiarly appropriate for arriving at an understanding of China's position in world affairs, the book is divided into two parts. The first concerns China's experience as a formal ally of the Soviet Union, and the second discusses China's behaviour as a fully independent country in world affairs. The main focus of the book is more on the intellectual themes which have dominated China's foreign policy than on the detailed activities of China in world affairs.

My thanks are due to Mr John Gittings and Dr Michael Leifer for their useful comments on a chapter each of the book. I am also grateful to Mrs K. Beggs and Miss Hilary Parker for typing certain chapters. But a special debt of gratitude is due to Ms Susan Swan for the typing and retyping of successive drafts of the manuscript.

February 1978   Michael B. Yahuda
London

LIST OF ABBREVIATIONS

AALA	Asia, Africa and Latin America
ASEAN	Association of South-East Asian Nations
CPC	Communist Party of China
CPSU	Communist Party of the Soviet Union
CQ	*China Quarterly*
FLP	Foreign Languages Press, Peking
FNLA	National Front for the Liberation of Angola
ICBM	Inter-Continental Ballistic Missile
JCP	Japanese Communist Party
JPRS, I and II	Joint Publications Research Service, Washington, D.C. *The Miscellany of Mao Tse-tung Thought*, Vols. I and II
KMT	Kuomintang
MPLA	Popular Movement for the Liberation of Angola
NCNA	New China News Agency
OAU	Organization of African Unity
OPEC	Organization of Petroleum-Exporting Countries
PKI	Communist Party of Indonesia
PLA	People's Liberation Army
PLO	Palestine Liberation Organization
PRC	People's Republic of China
SALT	Strategic Arms Limitation Talks
SCMM	Selections from Chinese Mainland Magazines (US Consulate, Hong Kong)
SCMP	Selections from Chinese Mainland Press (US Consulate, Hong Kong)
SPRCM	Selections from the People's Republic of China's Magazines (US Consulate, Hong Kong)
SW	*Selected Works of Mao Tse-tung*, Vols. I-V (Foreign Languages Press, Peking)
SWB/FE	(BBC) Summary of World Broadcasts/Far East
UN	United Nations
UNITA	National Union for the Total Independence of Angola
Wan Sui	*Mao Tse-tung Ssu Hsiang Wan Sui* (*Long Live Mao Tse-tung Thought*), China, 1969

1 INTRODUCTION

The questions this book is seeking to answer are, what have China's leaders had to say during the different phases of China's external relations about the kind of role that the new and socialist China should play in world affairs? And what have been the main factors which have led China's leaders to move from one phase to another?

Since the establishment of the People's Republic of China in 1949, the Chinese people and their leaders have been concerned with revolution and socialist economic construction at home and with a foreign policy which serves those causes abroad. How they have understood their achievements, problems and future tasks in the context of the relationship between the domestic and external dimensions is crucial with regard to the determination of foreign policy in China. The pursuit of these questions should facilitate the task of exploring the mainsprings of Chinese foreign policies and the reasons for the changes which have occurred since 1949. It should also help to cast light on what China's leaders, especially Chairman Mao Tse-tung, have considered to be the main forces at work in international society.

China's International Position

China's international position is unlike that of any other power. At a strategic level China is the only country which claims the ability to defend itself successfully from attack by both or either of the two superpowers. Moreover, since its foundation the People's Republic of China (PRC) has been a critical independent factor in the balance of world forces. As a former American Secretary of Defense, James Schlesinger, pointed out in 1975, the most important strategic change which has occurred to the benefit of the United States since the end of the Second World War was not any major technological change or weapons development but rather the shift of China from being an ally to becoming an adversary of the Soviet Union. This has caused the diversion of roughly a quarter of the military might of the Soviet Union to north-east Asia. Schlesinger's observation in itself is highly suggestive of China's strategic importance in global terms.

As a corollary to this it should be appreciated that, outside the superpowers, China is the only country which has a fully independent nuclear strategy and strike force. Those of the British and even the

French in the final analysis are linked with the United States. China currently has the beginnings of a second-strike capability, i.e. the ability to absorb an initial nuclear strike against it, and then still have the possibility of striking back with a few remaining missiles. But of course this cannot be compared with the devastating panoply of nuclear power which, say, the Soviet Union has arrayed against China. The disparity in power also leads to very different strategies. Clearly the devastation which the Soviet Union could wreak upon China is out of all proportion to the limited damage which China could cause in return. Thus China's strategy has sometimes been compared to that of a bee sting. Moreover, unlike the nuclear deterrence relationship between the two superpowers, China's nuclear posture is based upon uncertainty. The nuclear deterrence between the two superpowers is based upon the certainty of knowledge regarding their respective capabilities and deployments. This is essential if the deterrence situation based upon the common acceptance of mutual assured destruction is to be sustained. China's posture is precisely the opposite. No one can be quite certain as to what kind of a second-strike capability the Chinese might have by now and therefore there can be no clear assessment of the kind of damage which China could inflict upon the adversary. Moreover, the Chinese government has repeatedly declared that it will never be the first to use nuclear weapons and has claimed that its own nuclear force is purely for the purpose of self-defence. At least so far, the Chinese have not used the language and concepts of deterrence theory. There is little that is known about Chinese nuclear procurement policy and what kind of nuclear force they are seeking to acquire and deploy.

There are other factors which combine to make China's position in world affairs so special. As China's leaders have repeatedly pointed out, economically the country is still relatively backward despite many impressive achievements. It is true that in terms of gross national product China ranks very high (among the top ten in the world), but if calculated on a *per capita* basis the ranking is low (around the 90-100 mark). As for logistic capabilities, patterns of transportation and communication, China does not compare very well with the advanced industrialised countries. Yet paradoxically this relative backwardness is a major factor in China's capacity to defend itself, which in turn is critical for China's position as an important independent power in world politics. This relative underdevelopment is conducive to China's capacity to fight a people's war. The very factors which militate against China's capacity to sustain prolonged offensives beyond its borders (like its poor logistics) strengthen its ability to fight a people's war. The cellular economy with decentralised management (within a centralised planning framework) and the largely self-sufficient communes, the dispersed grain stores etc., a militia force, a people's army and so on all suggest a situation in which popular resistance and warfare could be carried on even if the main communications systems were in enemy hands. The relatively unmodernised features of China would work in favour of the defending forces and against the invaders.

If China's global significance is linked with the fact of its general economic backwardness and therefore with the fact of its membership of the Third World, it should be noted that China is a very peculiar member of the Third World. For one thing, the PRC is the only Third World country to have a permanent seat at the Security Council of the United Nations. For another, it is self-reliant and it has no real external trade or aid dependencies. The PRC is the only member of the Third World whose domestic economy is affected only marginally, if at all, by the international economic system. Uniquely, the PRC has hardly been affected by the changes in the international economic system in the 1970s. To be sure, China engages in foreign trade, but like all great continental countries this takes up considerably less than 10 per cent of her GNP. At the same time, the PRC has no foreign investments or foreign economic interests. China has become one of the largest individual country donors of aid to Third World countries. But the terms of Chinese aid are highly distinctive. In addition to consisting largely of intermediate technology, all Chinese aid projects are given without 'strings', and since 1964 without interest. Chinese workers are paid at local rates, they train their local equivalents and the general aim is to leave projects in such a way that they can be locally managed, operated and maintained so that even the spare parts could be locally produced.

Likewise the PRC has not imposed dependency relations either on its smaller socialist allies, such as North Korea or Albania, or on its immediate and smaller neighbours. Consider the example of North Korea: the war in Korea in the end was fought primarily by Chinese forces. In 1958, five years after the armistice, all the Chinese troops were withdrawn. American forces, however, remained in the south. It was not until 1977 (24 years after the armistice and 19 years after the Chinese withdrawal) that an American President pledged their eventual total withdrawal. The year 1958 was hardly one of reduced Sino-American tensions and yet the PRC was under no American or Soviet pressure to withdraw its forces. Indeed according to the accepted rules, as it were, of great-power behaviour, given the exigencies of the local and international situation, no one would have questioned the Chinese right to maintain forces in what had become a buffer area. The consequence of the Chinese withdrawal was that North Korea became very independent of China. In fact, during the Cultural Revolution in China relations with the North Koreans became very strained indeed. But the general result of China's policy has been that the Chinese have not been beset with the kinds of problems that the Russians or the Americans have had with dependent smaller allies who then find that dependence institutionalised, which in turn enables the smaller countries to play something of a role in the domestic politics of the country concerned. Dependency relationships bind both parties in complex ways.

This consideration of China's international position suggests very much a picture of a country whose political system is perhaps one of the most autonomous in the world, and of a country which internationally is untrammelled by the kind of interdependencies and alliance systems which limit the freedom of manoeuvre of other major powers. It is a picture of a country which plays an important part in the shaping of the patterns of international politics, which at the same time is being idiosyncratically withdrawn from the complex multi-levelled configurations of interdependencies which characterise the foreign relations of all other major countries. China's leaders, therefore, are able to go in for what Liddell-Hart once called the 'grand strategy', as contrasted with the more fissured patterns of foreign relations which are the norm for other countries. Because China is withdrawn a little from the world, the leaders who control to a very large extent the character of the PRC's external relations at all levels have been able not only to analyse general international trends and orientations, but have been able to act upon them. Thus Chinese general pronouncements about international affairs, even on the planes of conceptual theoretical analysis, tend to have a direct and immediate bearing upon China's foreign policy actions at all levels from the strategic to those concerned with trade and diplomacy.

Since all major governmental action in China is explained and legitimated by authoritative ideological statements, these statements tend to assume the functions of organising devices for authoritative action. On international questions authoritative conceptualisations become one of the major devices by which is worked out deductively what is routine within foreign policy decision-making and that which requires resolution by a higher level, if not the highest. Examples of this on the grand scale are the 'lean to one side' doctrine of 1949 which led to the Sino-Soviet alliance, and the 'three worlds' theory of the 1970s. On a smaller scale, consider this lesser-known example: during the Cultural Revolution North Korea had been stigmatised in China as a revisionist country and relations between the two became virtually frozen. Once the Cultural Revolution was over, the North Korean government was keen to re-establish good relations. On the occasion of the twentieth anniversary of the establishment of the People's Republic of China on 1 October 1969, a senior North Korean leader flew out to China. The Chinese airport authorities, however, refused permission for the plane to land, on the grounds that it was revisionist. In the end the question was sent for resolution to Mao personally. He then welcomed the North Korean and, to signal publicly the change in Sino-Korean relations, Chairman Mao arranged for the leader to stand next to him on the Tien An Men rostrum.

China's independence, largely deliberately chosen, has enabled the Chinese leaders to define China's relationship to the outside world seemingly with relatively more freedom of manoeuvre than any other country. Thus, for example, China emerged out of the isolation of the Cultural Revolution to pursue a foreign policy of almost opposite dimensions. While the former was introverted, the latter was open and expansive; the Cultural Revolution period stressed revolutionary purity, the latter stressed international diplomacy at its most sophisticated levels; in the former period little regard was displayed for diplomatic norms and niceties, while in the latter period these were observed with scrupulous attention to form and detail. So abrupt sometimes have been the changes in Chinese foreign policy that it would seem almost as if China's leaders could ring down the changes at will.

Such an impression, however, would be exaggerated. A country which has perceived itself to have been perpetually under threat by one or other of the two superpowers simply does not have that kind of freedom of manoeuvre. China is the only country to have been threatened with nuclear attack by both the superpowers. Since its establishment the PRC has been challenged by powers militarily superior to itself. All China's initiatives and changes have been in large part responses to and interactions with the perceived changes and moves of others. However special China's international position may be, China is still a member of the international system and it is deeply affected by substantive changes in that system, particularly in the political and strategic spheres.

Within the framework of contingency adjustments to international pressures and changes, however, China's relative autonomy has allowed it perhaps more than any other state (with the possible exception of the two superpowers) to evolve independently its own analysis of the main forces at work in international society and of China's place within it. Moreover, China's leaders have been able to act more effectively and independently upon their autonomous perceptions and analyses than possibly the leaders of any other major power. Thus although from the outset the PRC has been faced with adversaries more powerful than itself, its leaders, and especially Chairman Mao himself, have always sought to seize, and make sure of holding, the initiative. This was true of his leadership of the revolution before 1949 and he tried to continue it in China's foreign relations after 1949.

Perhaps the concept which best illustrates Chinese thinking on this question of seizing and holding the initiative, despite apparent relative weakness, is Mao's 'paper tiger' thesis. The concept that all reactionaries and imperialists are paper tigers and that indeed the atom bomb is also a paper tiger explained that what was truly decisive in the long term in determining the outcome of struggle in history was whether or not the contending forces had genuine popular support. This meant that while in the short term it was absolutely crucial to take account of the overall strength of a reactionary enemy, a revolutionary force which concentrated upon awakening and mobilising popular support should, within the context of a long-term strategy, continually challenge the enemy at its vulnerable points so as to bring into play the decisive factors which would finally decide the outcome. It was this way of thinking which underlay Mao's strategy in the War of Resistance against Japan and indeed in the Civil War which toppled Chiang Kai-shek and brought Mao to power. It is this, too, which has given the Chinese leaders and people since 1949 the necessary confidence to face over-whelmingly more materially powerful adversaries than themselves. Thus in the 1950s the PRC initiated crises in Sino-American relations within a general context in which the Chinese were essentially reacting to the threats and challenges by a much stronger superpower. Far from being impressed by the growth of American military bases throughout the world in the 1950s, Mao saw this as a source of weakness: 'They put their bases everywhere, just like an ox with its tail tied to a post, what good can that do?'[1] At the height of the offshore islands crisis in September 1958 when China had been threatened by nuclear attack, Mao addressed his colleagues in the following terms:

Who is more afraid of who? . . . I think that Dulles fears us a bit more . . . It's a question of strength, it's a question of popular support. Popular support means strength, and we have more people on our side than they do. Between the three isms of communism, nationalism and imperialism, communism and nationalism are rather closer to each other. And the forces of nationalism occupy quite a large area, the three continents of Asia, Africa and Latin America . . . It is the multitude of the people who grasp the truth in their hands, and not Dulles. The hearts of the Americans are hollow; ours are more sincere. For we rely on the people, and they prop up those reactionary rulers.[2]

A significant characteristic of Chinese foreign-policy-making which is intimately linked with domestic politics is indeed the function of authoritative conceptualisations and the symbolic acts of key leaders (especially those of Chairman Mao in his lifetime) as organising devices for authoritative action. Examples of the latter are the significance attached to highly publicised meetings by Chairman Mao with various foreign visitors at key turning-points in China's foreign policy. Thus in the late 1950s and in 1960, as the Sino-Soviet dispute escalated, Mao's meetings with people from Asia, Africa and Latin America provided one of the first indications of where the priorities of China's foreign relations were to be directed. Likewise, his summoning of the late Edgar Snow in 1970 to be photographed alongside him on the rostrum of Tien An Men at the mammoth grand rally for National Day signalled the Chairman's intention to open out towards the United States.

China's Three International Constituencies

China has perhaps three natural constituencies in world politics to which it may be considered to belong. The first is the constituency of socialist states and Communist revolutionary movements. Since the Sino-Soviet split it would be more proper to speak of the 'genuinely' Marxist-Leninist variety as opposed to those considered by the Chinese to be revisionist or worse. The second is the constituency of the Third World, of countries which have but recently emerged from the domination of colonialism or semi-colonialism and which are seeking to develop their economies from a relatively low or negligible industrial base. The third is the constituency of the small or medium powers.

It is, however, with the socialist and the Third World constituencies that the Chinese have identified most. These have always been prominent in the international preoccupations of China's leaders, although in different ways at different times. Already in November 1949 one Chinese leader identified China's revolution as being a model peculiarly appropriate for other Asian countries to emulate:

The path taken by the Chinese people in defeating imperialism and its lackeys and in founding the People's Republic of China is the path that should be taken by the peoples of the many colonial and semi-colonial countries in their fight for national independence and people's democracy.

This naturally linked the two constituencies. By 1954 and 1955 they had become clearly separated: China belonged to the socialist camp headed by the Soviet Union on the one hand, but it also belonged to the emerging countries of Asia and Africa as instanced by its attendance at the Bandung Conference. Nevertheless China's leaders continued to identify the principal contradiction in the world as being between the socialist camp headed by the Soviet Union on the one hand and the imperialist camp headed by the United States on the other. By the middle 1960s China's leaders had shifted their position. Although the principal contradiction still involved opposition to imperialism headed by the United States, it was judged to be less centred in the socialist camp than in the developing countries of Asia, Africa and Latin America. Yet another ten years later in the middle 1970s, China's leaders had identified the Third World as the revolutionary motive force propelling the world historically forward, but at the same time care was taken to cultivate relations on a party-to-party basis with the remaining few countries still viewed as socialist and with what were regarded as genuine Marxist-Leninist organisations, however minuscule, in other countries. By this stage the socialist camp had long since been declared out of existence. Thus, throughout its existence the People's Republic has identified itself with these two constituencies while perceiving the relationships in different ways in different periods. Indeed, one of China's continuing problems is to prevent spillage from one constituency to the other. Thus many in the Third World are guarded and suspicious about China's revolutionary credentials and aspirations. Chou En-lai's celebrated remark in early 1964 that 'Africa was ripe for revolution' gave rise to considerable suspicion and resentment among certain African leaders. It is quite clear, however, that at the time he was referring to what in Marxist terms would be described as the democratic, rather than the socialist, revolution. In another context, more than eleven years later, the government of Malaysia officially protested to the Chinese about their official support in the *People's Daily* for the Communist Party of Malaya, which the Malaysians regarded as interference in their internal affairs which went against the terms of the mutual recognition between the two states. The Chinese explanation that a distinction had to be drawn between state-to-state relations and party-to-party relations was not regarded as satisfactory by the Malaysian government. In another vein, China's embrace of a Third World identity and the attempts to discredit the Soviet Union in Africa led to Russian accusations in the early 1960s of a racist quality to China's positions on world affairs.

China's socialist identity involves not only the question as to with whom the People's Republic would choose to be linked, but also raises the question of the relationship between the pursuit of socialism within China and the conduct of relations with an outside world which is largely non-socialist. At one level this involves seeking to pursue the kind of foreign policy which facilitates the independent development of socialism, that is, the kind of policy which, since the break with the Soviet Union, has required that the rest of the world be held at one remove, so that the internal aspect of self-reliance would not be unduly affected. At another level, Chinese claims as to the universalism of their experience is also an important element in the conscious thinking about the place of China in world affairs. For example, the Chinese claim to have pioneered the way to showing how a socialist state can prevent its own degeneration into revisionism and hence the restoration of capitalism. Curiously, while the Chinese claim a universal significance to their struggles in the political sphere beginning with the Cultural Revolution, they have not demanded that those countries recognised by them as socialist should follow their example. The Chinese do not even require these countries to accept the main outlines of the Chinese view of the structure of the world and of the main currents of international affairs. The Chinese, however, have not always taken such a relatively modest position. During the Cultural Revolution the Chinese maintained that Mao Tse-tung thought was binding equally on all revolutionaries, whether in China or elsewhere in the world.

Three Approaches to Role Definition

Over the years, then, China's leaders have taken up a number of different positions on these issues affecting China's perceived role in world affairs. Yet the Chinese leaders have liked to argue that the principles governing their conduct of international affairs have always been consistent. If there have been changes, they argue, these have been due to the changing policies of others. They hold (as may be seen, for example, from Chou En-lai's Political Report to the 10th Congress of the Communist Party of China in August 1973, or indeed from Hua Kuo-feng's Political Report to the 11th Party Congress four years later) that

China's foreign policy may be seen as operating at three levels. First, with regard to the 'genuine Marxist-Leninist and other organisations' (i.e. whom the Chinese regard unreservedly as full-blooded revolutionaries); second, with regard to the 'oppressed peoples and nations' (i.e. the victims of 'imperialist aggression, subversion, interference, control or bullying'); and third, with regard to the imperialist powers themselves, especially the two superpowers. The three levels may be said to call for the following types of policy respectively: unity, solidarity and opposition. The major difference with the 1950s on this list is the shift of the Soviet Union from the first level to the third; that is, the shift from being considered to be the leader of the socialist camp to being regarded as the more dangerous of the two superpowers.

This view of their own policies may have much to commend it, but from the point of view of foreign policy this formal appeal to consistency obscures more than it clarifies. This is especially true with regard to the different phases through which Chinese foreign policy has passed. As has already been suggested, a better way to understand how the Chinese operationally view their relationship with the outside world is to examine the kind of roles which China's leaders at different times have sketched out for China, arising out of their varying analyses of the main characteristics of the world situation at important turning points.

Since 1949, basically three very different ways of analysing international affairs and placing China within the world have been developed in China. The first might be regarded as the traditional Communist/Soviet one of dividing the world into two main groupings, with the proletarian socialists on the one side and the bourgeois capitalists on the other. Those in between may be regarded as essentially more or less progressive, to be cultivated and encouraged; or as largely reactionary, to be isolated and pressurised. In this view China's main role was perceived as a member of the socialist camp led by the Soviet Union. Since 1960 no Chinese leader has openly advocated this role. Up until 1966 there were those in China who thought of its role as a country linked to the socialist camp but in a critical way. After that time Chairman Mao's view of the Soviet Union as having turned revisionist and as having ceased to be a socialist country is the only one to have been overtly articulated in Peking. It will be recalled, however, that *in extremis* the outmanoeuvred Lin Piao in September 1971 chose to flee in the direction of the Soviet Union when he died in the aircraft crash on the way. The manner of his death showed in a very graphic way that the link with the Soviet Union was still an option considered by senior Chinese leaders in the 1970s.

The second mode of analysis was that prevalent during the Cultural Revolution, when China was regarded as the 'bastion of socialism' alone with the 'people of the world' defying the 'anti-China, anti-socialist alliance of the US imperialists and the Soviet revisionists'. This isolationism of revolutionary purity, unsullied by compromises with the outside world or by foreign influences within China, is particularly associated with the Cultural Revolution period of 1966-8. Shades of this view, which at times had a xenophobic quality, could be detected in the outlook of the 'gang of four' and their acolytes in Chinese politics up to the death of Chairman Mao.

The third basic approach, and perhaps the most complex, was that based on Maoist analysis of contradictions and the intermediate zones in world affairs. Central to this approach is the view, first developed at length by Chairman Mao in 1946, that the future of the world is determined on the one hand by the struggle between the United States and the Soviet Union for control over the vast intermediate zone between them, and on the other hand by the struggles of the people in these countries to resist imperialist attempts to control them. According to this view the dangers of a new world war and of an attack on China by imperialist powers are inversely related to the success of genuine revolutionary struggles and the emergence of truly independent countries in this intermediate zone. The role specified for China by this approach has in fact varied over time. During the period of the close Sino-Soviet alliance this approach was barely mentioned. Although it came to the fore during the Great Leap Forward in 1958, in fact this mode of analysis only began to fully shape policy once the Sino-Soviet break became complete from 1963 onwards. Because of the difference in China's foreign policy approach and indeed conception of its world role before and after the Cultural Revolution, it is useful to distinguish between the two phases. Although both phases emphasised the importance of united front politics, the first, from 1963 to 1965, specified a clear line for the united front which excluded many Third World countries, which allowed for interventionist policies in their affairs and which had China steering clear of entanglements with either the Soviet Union or the United States. The second phase, after the Cultural Revolution, required China to take a more expansive view of the united front so that all countries except the two superpowers could be included, and it called for rigid respect of the sovereignty and independence of all countries to the exclusion of interventionism (other than the kind of moral support for Marxist-Leninist organisations mentioned earlier).

At the same time this second phase required China to take advantage of the differences and problems or contradictions between the two super-powers. This provided the basis for China's improved relations with the United States and for its direct involvement in the considerations of power politics which led its leaders to support the US link with Japan, for example. Thus it is useful to distinguish between the two aspects of China's international role within the general approach of contradictions theory as the revolutionary united front role and as the state-based united front role.

These three approaches involve quite different and conflicting views as to the nature of socialism and as to how China should be related to them. The period in which China was associated most closely with the Soviet view of world affairs was also the period in which economically China's pattern of development most closely followed the Soviet one. The Cultural Revolution period, when China's international role was defined as a bastion of socialism, was also one marked by a highly idiosyncratic political process. The period which has stressed the contradictions mode of analysis is one that has stressed the autonomy and independence of the Chinese political system faced with two main tasks of continuing class struggle and building up the country. There are obvious links between the external and internal dimensions of being linked internationally to the Soviet Union and of following domes-tically a variant of the Soviet model as there are between pursuing revo-lutionary purity at home and abroad during the Cultural Revolution.

The links between the pursuit of an internationalist united front abroad (whether or not overt power-political considerations are in-volved) and the general nature and direction of the domestic system cannot be so easily established. Indeed, one aspect of the united front approach, as was evident in the domestic struggles with Chiang Kai-shek's forces in the 1930s and 1940s, was simply to ensure that the Communist side could still retain its revolutionary identity, its own army and its own independence and freedom of manoeuvre. In those years the Communist Party varied its policies with regard to land requi-sition and rent reduction, depending on how widely the net of the united front was cast. Thus during the War of Resistance against Japan the Communist Party sought to appeal to all the patriotic rural classes and hence rent reduction was emphasised. But in the final Civil War period of 1946-9 landlords were seen as belonging with the enemy and the emphasis changed to stress land requisition.

So it has been internationally. When the emphasis was upon taking a firm line against the United States, particularly for its actions in Indo-China, while at the same time excluding the Soviet Union, the internationalist united front net was cast in such a way as to exclude all those who did not follow that line. In 1965 that also included the whole non-alignment movement and also some revolutionary and national liberation movements often in opposition to their established governments. After the Cultural Revolution the internationalist united front was directed against both the superpowers and particularly the Soviet Union, so that all other states were welcome to join..

Crucial to both periods and both interpretations of the united front was that Chinese domestic affairs were totally autonomous. Nevertheless certain links can be identified. Intra-leadership conflict has often included a foreign affairs dimension. The struggle with Lin Piao from 1969 to 1971 focused on whether or not it was preferable to open out towards the United States as well as upon domestic concerns. Certainly in Chinese eyes there was a linkage between the internal and external dimensions of the affair. Another and a more systematic link revolves around the question of self-reliance. If China is to play a critical role in the putative internationalist united front against the two superpowers and if China is to lead the Third World by example in the struggle for a new international economic order, it follows that China's economy should be run without becoming tied down in dependency kinds of external economic relations. There has been argument in China as to what are the foreign trade limits beyond which the principle of self-reliance is affected. It is clear, nevertheless, that a basically self-reliant economy and military strategy are required if China is to play the role of a leading member of an internationalist united front.

Historical Influences

If, as has been argued, China's position in world politics is distinctive as a relatively autonomous actor so that the PRC leadership has been able to a very considerable extent to determine China's relationships with the outside world, it is important at the outset to identify the main historical experiences and ideas which have combined to shape the international outlook of the PRC leadership.

The dominant historical experiences of the leaders who founded the PRC were, first, those of the nationalist awakening of the Chinese people attendant upon the collapse of the traditional order and, second, the revolutionary struggles which ultimately brought those leaders to supreme power.[3]

To be sure, the legacy of the imperial or feudal past is far from negligible. There are of course a wide variety of attitudes and values which have survived from that past which permeate Chinese society at all levels. But it is important to take account of the wide-ranging and deep revolutionary transformations through which the Chinese people have moved in the last hundred and fifty years. The imperial legacy and the continuities from that past cannot but have been distilled and modified by that experience. The traditional order, whether considered in terms of the economy, the society, the politics or the ideology, collapsed to be totally transformed and restructured. The problems posed in tracing the present continuities from the more ancient past are immense and they cannot be resolved simply by searching for parallels between present and past. Considered in this light, there is little value in observations which assert that China today is simply the past writ large with sufficient accommodations to modern realities to make it viable.[4]

Certainly every attempt after the fall of the last imperial house to restore the imperial idea or Confucian ideals has failed. Thus the conscious attempt by Chiang Kai-shek during the period of Kuomintang rule in China to draw upon these rules and attitudes as a basis for strengthening the legitimacy of his regime through the so-called 'New Life Movement' was virtually foredoomed to failure. The attempt to revive and breathe life into Confucianism, once the underlying social structures and global outlook which had given it meaning and substance no longer existed, could not but result in an authoritarianism and a kind of Fascism in modern conditions.[5]

It is interesting to consider that although Chairman Mao was in his early teens when the last-ever tribute was paid to the imperial 'Son of Heaven' in Peking in 1908 (by Nepal), there is no evidence to suggest that he was even aware of the event. On the other hand, there is evidence of his consciousness of China's deep humiliations and of the need for change even at this early date.[6]

Nevertheless the legacy of the 'Celestial Empire' cannot be discounted. China is the oldest state in the world today with a continuous history as an independent political entity stretching back to the ancient past. Thus in their territorial disputes with the Soviet Union the Chinese today make great play of the fact that since time immemorial China has always been a multi-nationality state.[7] Traditionally, Confucian historiography depicted China as the centre of the world, 'the Middle Kingdom' — the repository of the only true civilisation and virtue — whose ruler was the 'Son of Heaven' mandated to rule over 'all that was below Heaven'. All other rulers were theoretically subordinate to him. China's physical isolation from other great centres of civilisation gave shape and coherence to this myth. And in practice tribute was periodically paid by peoples and countries on China's periphery. These were principally the 'barbaric' nomadic groups to the north, Korea and the small principalities in south-east Asia and the Himalayan states. To this day, China's relationships with these countries are marked by this historical experience. Arguably, China's leaders have a deeper and closer understanding of the social and political processes of those countries on China's periphery (especially if they too, like Vietnam, Korea or Japan, had been deeply affected by Confucian influences) than of those with whom they have claimed a special affinity, like the East European countries in the 1950s or, say, the African countries in the 1960s and 1970s.

Recent research, however, has shown that the tributary relationships were often far more complex than the Confucian historians and writers suggested.[8] Moreover, the notion of hierarchy which was central to the traditional Chinese Confucian concept of world order has been consistently rejected by the leaders of the PRC. Indeed few other leaders have been more insistent on the need to base international relationships in practice as well as in legal theory upon the principles of sovereign equality. To be sure, the legacy of the past is important in terms of the Chinese sense of identity and dignity as a nation. China's readiness to stand aloof to a large extent from the outside world, proud and certain in the correctness of its independent vision of the essential character of world politics, cannot be understood without deference to its ancient legacy. Likewise the didactic style of much of China's foreign policy pronouncements and indeed of its diplomacy owe a great deal to certain Confucian traditions. Yet the actual analyses of the forces at work in international society, the specific choices made in China's foreign policy and the formulations made of China's changing role in world affairs are better understood within the historical framework of nationalism and revolution of the modern period.

Nationalism

Even where it is possible to identify specific continuities with the traditional past these have become totally transformed by modern conditions so that the problems are totally transformed. Thus, the emphasis on unity has been a feature of Chinese patriotism down the ages, but it took on specific features in the modern nationalist era which distinguish it from the earlier periods. In the modern era it has been concerned not just with a unified Chinese political entity as before, but with unity within clearly defined borders. Since nationalism emerged during the last years of the Ching imperial dynasty the emphasis has been on identifying China's borders with the maximum extent of the areas under notional control of the dynasty at the height of its powers in the seventeenth and eighteenth centuries. However, by the foundation of the PRC in 1949 China's new leaders had come to accept the independence of the former tributaries like Korea, the small Himalayan countries and those in south-east Asia. But as we shall see, they still raised questions about the Mongolian People's Republic which had formerly been the Chinese province of Outer Mongolia. However, like earlier Chinese nationalists, China's Communist leaders also perceived that the national minority areas on the periphery of what might be called Han China have only sought to break away from the Chinese state at the instigation and the direct support of foreign powers. The establishment of Mongolia's independence in 1924 was the result of Soviet machinations. The Soviet Union too was behind attempts to detach Sinkiang.[9] The Tibetan rebellion of 1959 was also encouraged and supported from the outside. These considerations are of obvious significance with regard to Peking's attitude towards the Taiwan question, which probably would have been solved in 1950 but for the American intervention. Of course the Taiwan question is further compounded by the fact that it is a rival government and it is part of an uncompleted civil war. Chinese on both sides of the Taiwan Straits are conscious of analogous situations in China's distant past when rival dynasties divided China. But there are no ancient parallels to the modern international system, and the concepts of nationhood, sovereignty and territorial integrity are alien to the ancient past.

The nationalist reaction to the alien presence on Chinese soil in the Treaty Ports and the external dependencies of Chinese administration on foreign aid, foreign military supplies, the foreign international economic system, foreign culture, etc., goes right to the heart of much of the attitudes of the leaders of the PRC in international affairs. If Confucian statesmanship of the nineteenth century regarded the foreign enclaves as objectionable but tolerable ways of containing and hopefully controlling the alien presence, the nationalism of the twentieth century regarded them with abhorrence as a stigma of Chinese humiliation. The source of the PRC's insistence on establishing new border agreements with its neighbours as between equals — often with little substantive difference from those established under the aegis of the foreign imperial powers — stems from this. It is the desire to purge China's borders of the contamination of the imperialist legacy which is crucial here. The new agreements may be seen as expressive of the Chinese people who have 'stood up' to define on equal terms the bases of their relationships with their neighbours. It may be seen as the important symbolic gesture of a liberated people to deny the legitimacy of the acts performed by their erstwhile alien oppressors and exploiters. The slate is wiped clean and a new beginning is made.

China's special insistence upon equality as between states, the importance attached to sovereignty and the special view of the nature of true independence can be traced back to the nationalist experience. No other country today upholds the importance of statehood and the inviolability of sovereignty more than China. Any notions of interdependency or limited sovereignty are rejected angrily by Chinese spokesmen. The PRC even refuses to recognise the legitimacy of United Nations peace-keeping forces. Chinese spokesmen at the relevant UN Security Council meetings which decide on the provision of such forces regularly explain that China does not veto the resolutions since the sovereign states concerned voluntarily accept the stationing of such forces on their territories. The PRC government, however, simply takes no part in the voting over such resolutions. It does not even abstain. That would be to sanctify the proceedings, albeit in a negative way. By refusing to take part in the vote the PRC government is able to maintain the purity of its principled position without at the same time forcing its will on the sovereign governments who accept the legitimate claims of such forces to operate on their soil.[10]

The maintenance of such a pure uncompromising position on questions of sovereignty has obvious relevance to the declared aims of China's revolutionaries to pursue the construction of socialism and the permanent revolution within China to the exclusion of foreign incursion. They are insistent that the Chinese people should be free to develop their own way ahead without succumbing to foreign pressure. Likewise they wish to be free of alien pressure to modify their endeavours except in ways that they themselves choose to do so. This is clearly related to contemporary Chinese concepts of independence and self-reliance.

Independence for China's revolutionary leaders and especially for Mao Tse-tung has always meant more than the formal trappings of international recognition in law of an independent government. After all, as a semi-colony China never fully lost its formal independent government recognised as such by the foreign powers. The fall of the Ching Dynasty in 1911 was followed by various Republican governments, often as empty shells controlled by whichever warlord clique happened to be in control of the capital, and then by the Chiang Kai-shek government, which right to the end had been beholden to foreign powers. For Mao, independence meant the popular liberation of a free people able to display their creativity and initiative without foreign pressures and controls, however indirect. It meant economic independence and the ability to determine priorities without being beholden to external dependent relationships. There was, therefore, a special irony, as we shall see, in the dependent alliance that Mao Tse-tung freely and personally entered into with the Soviet Union. But a major cause of the beginnings of the Sino-Soviet split centred precisely on the question of the dependency relationships which the Soviets sought to preserve.

One area where these dependency relationships with foreign powers were most evident to Chinese revolutionaries and which has closely affected their views on the question ever since has been that of aid, foreign investment and the foreign concessions of the open door. Commenting in 1923 bitterly on the so-called 'amity' of the foreigners, the radical nationalist and burgeoning Communist Mao Tse-tung observed:

> The 'Council of Ministers' of the Chinese Government is really both accommodating and agreeable. If one of our foreign masters farts, it is a lovely perfume. If our foreign masters want to export cotton, the Council of Ministers thereupon abolishes the prohibition of the export of cotton; if our foreign masters want to bring in cigarettes, the Council of Ministers thereupon 'instructs the several provinces by telegram to stop levying taxes on cigarettes'. Again, I ask my 400 million brethren to ponder a little. Isn't it true that the Chinese Government is the counting-house of our foreign masters?[11]

Regarding aid and capital investment, Western studies have confirmed that although the total foreign investment up to the 1930s was in the order of US$3.5 billion, China was in fact a net exporter of capital. Apart from a brief period from 1894 to 1901 when China had a net inflow of capital of US$1.5 million, C.F. Remer has shown that China exported capital to the tune of US$22.3 million a year for the 1902-13 period and at the annual rate of US$56.1 million for the years 1913-30. If to these figures are added the payments of the Boxer indemnity, the net outflow for the period 1902-30 comes to the figure of US$1,335.7 million.[12]

If one breaks down the figures of foreign loans to determine their utilisation, the picture is even less appealing. Of the foreign loans, 60 per cent was spent on administrative and military requirements and loan services, 34 per cent on railways and only 6 per cent on manufacturing industry.[13] The familiar depressing scene of much of post-war aid and foreign loans to formally independent Third World countries was enacted in China several decades earlier. Loans begat more loans to pay off the earlier ones. In practice they served the interests of foreign powers and business combines together with the interests of the local ruling elites. Contemporary Chinese historians note the damage done to local capitalistic enterprises and industries. They have noted the ruinous effects on domestic cash crop producers of being exposed to the vicissitudes of the international economic system.[14] The author Mao Tun detailed graphically the ravages inflicted on a silkworm-producing village in the Yangtse basin as a result of the impact of the great depression in his famous story, 'Spring Silkworm'.[15]

One need go no further than these experiences to locate the origins of the PRC's unique position on the granting of foreign aid which seeks to establish no special 'strings' or to acquire privileges for the technicians sent out. Nor is there any attempt to create long-term protected outlets for China's exports. In addition to stressing intermediate technology, China's aid seeks to leave the recipients in full control and command of the relevant project with full independent access to re-supply and maintenance requirements. The aid is agreed upon according to the needs and aspirations of the recipient as specified by the government concerned. Since 1964, moreover, aid, which has been estimated at over US$5 billion,[16] has been free of interest charges.

When China's revolutionary leaders sought to appeal to Third World countries it was to their national experiences that they turned. Thus the common history which they stress is of having been objects for European expansion, colonialism and imperialism. The Chinese have sought to draw common patterns for external penetration. But, more importantly, they have also sought to demonstrate common patterns of resistance and uprisings by the peoples in the Third World against their imperialist oppressors and exploiters. This was regarded as of such political significance that historical articles on these themes were published prominently in the *People's Daily* and the *Red Flag*. For example, in 1972 four articles were published under the pseudonym of Shih Chun which attempted to place China's new foreign policy of combining with the Third World and opening to the US within international historical perspectives. The first article explained these aims as follows:

Victorious in revolution, socialist China must strive to make greater contributions to mankind. Since the Chinese Revolution is part of the world revolution, all the revolutionary tasks we undertake are closely linked to the revolutionary struggles of the world's people. To have the world at heart, it is necessary to understand it. The world today is a development of the world of yesterday. The contemporary struggles of the world's people against imperialism and its lackeys are a continuation and development of their past and long struggles against class oppression, oppression by foreign rulers and colonial rule. To study world history will enable us, by acquiring knowledge of the entire process of world history and drawing on historical experience, to better understand the special features of the present world situation, foresee its general trend, strengthen our confidence in the victory of the proletarian patriotism and internationalism.[17]

Revolution

The ideas and the experiences of the Chinese revolution under Mao's leadership have had a decisive impact on the thinking and the conduct of China's external relations.[18] The Chinese leadership has consistently reached back to this pre-1949 experience as a source for explanations and indeed inspiration in dealing with international politics. It is almost impossible to underestimate the influence this experience has had on Mao's thinking on war, on the correct way to carry out revolution, on united fronts, on how to assess power, the relationship between class and nation, how to move from weakness to strength, and so on. Much has been written on these and related themes.[19] Here I shall discuss briefly certain aspects of Mao's thinking about international affairs within the context of China's revolutionary experience.

Perhaps the most significant aspect of the revolutionary experiences relevant here is simply that China's revolution has always been considered an integral component of a universalist movement. The sense of being in the van of history as a world-wide movement with a universalist ideology has been critical to the legitimacy of the revolution. The ideology, of course, came from outside China and no amount of the application of its general principles to the specific conditions of China, nor the extent of Mao's creative contributions to its treasure house, can alter that simple fact. Sino-centricity is not a viable option (at least on the intellectual level) for a Chinese Marxist-Leninist. China's international position may be peculiar to itself, yet even in the eyes of the most xenophobic of Chinese revolutionaries China's place is necessarily within this world and not as a self-contained unit outside it.

One important aspect of Mao's leadership of the Chinese Revolution has been the way he has linked the pursuit of revolution within China to the problem of dealing with the external imperialist threat. This whole question has been one of the most enduring issues both before and after the advent to power. As early as 1928 Mao outlined a view relating the prospects of developing the revolution in China directly to the impact of external forces in China.

There were others who saw reason for pessimism in the fact that the revolutionaries were contending with swirling, shifting warlord forces militarily more powerful than that of the revolutionaries. They quailed at the numerous array of imperialist foes and external influences in China and they were envious of the supposed good fortunes of those revolutionaries in fully fledged colonies with only one imperialist oppressor with which to contend. Mao, by contrast, rebuked this pessimism and saw reason for optimism precisely because of this situation. In his view, red political power could exist in the China of those days precisely because there were several warlord cliques and, beyond them, several imperialist countries. This was so because they were divided. Their divisions related directly to the systemic causes of their activities. The imperialists were engaged in capitalist rivalry with each other and the divisions among the white forces in China were the domestic reflections of this. In a word, there were contradictions between them. As Mao explained it:

> The contradictions and struggle among the cliques of warlords in China reflect the contradictions and struggles amongst the imperialist powers. Hence as long as China is divided among the imperialist powers, the various cliques of warlords cannot under any circumstances come to terms, and whatever compromises they may make will only be temporary. A temporary compromise today engenders a bigger war tomorrow.[20]

Mao went on to assert that the continued existence of areas under red political power completely encircled by a white regime was a unique occurrence in world history. He gave several reasons for this. His first, and the one we are concerned with, dealt with the international context: 'it cannot occur in any imperialist country or in any colony under direct imperialist rule, but can occur only in China which is economically backward, and which is semi-colonial and under indirect imperialist rule.'[21]

The implications for Mao's later analyses of world forces and trends and of China's place within them are very great. The general approach is not from the universal to the particular. It is not from universal principles

of Marxism or of general laws and development of imperialism world-
wide to China. Rather it is generalising within a Marxist-Leninist
framework from the particularities of China. It is a question of looking
at the world from the perspectives of Chinese problems, which in turn
are seen as problems of universal significance. An official Central Committee note on the above went on to argue that this view 'on the
question of establishing independent regimes in colonies under
imperialist rule has changed as a result of the changes in the situation'.
What had changed the situation, in the view of the committee, was the
popular Communist-led struggles against the Japanese invasion during
the Second World War, which meant that after the war those colonial
peoples who had built their armed strength refused to return to the old
ways. Having noted the internal change the note went on to draw
attention to the profound changes in the external imperialist system as
the result of war devastation, Soviet strength and 'finally because the
imperialist front was breached in China by the victorious Chinese revolution'.[22]

This may be seen as a further application of the principles of analysis
as established by Mao in 1928. While the internal confidence and
strength drawn from the experience of the revolutionaries is primary,
the secondary aspects of the external environment are crucial too.

A further development in China's revolutionary experience of profound future international significance was briefly hinted at in that
Central Committee note. Again it is typical that the revolutionary
optimist Mao should be alert to it while many of his comrades were full
of pessimism. In his talk with Anna Louise Strong in 1946 Mao Tse-
tung provided an explanation of international affairs which has dominated Chinese Communist thinking on international questions ever since.
The famous paper tiger thesis was advanced here for the first time. But
more germane to this analysis is his view of the nature of the US
imperialist threat and how it can be thwarted. As John Gittings has
pointed out, Mao's views on the question were fundamentally different
from those of Stalin and the Soviet Union at that time.[23] Indeed, the
divergence of views has persisted since then. It was submerged tempor-
arily during the period of the Sino-Soviet alliance, but it has surfaced
since and it is one of the crucial bases for the very different way in
which Soviet and Chinese leaders have approached international politics
ever since.

The Soviet Union at that time was moving towards the 'two-camp'
thesis which argued that the world was divided into two antagonistic
blocs and that the purpose of the imperialist bloc headed by the United

States was to attack the Soviet Union, the head of the socialist camp. As a variant of Stalin's 'socialism in one country' thesis, it followed that every Communist movement should pay careful attention to avoiding provocative acts against the United States lest this gave rise to an attack on the Soviet Union, which would be the start of World War III. This was one of the considerations which led Stalin to oppose the path of revolutionary armed struggle in China's civil war.

Mao, by contrast, maintained that the question of an American anti-Soviet war was 'propaganda', 'a smokescreen put up by the US reactionaries to cover many actual contradictions immediately confronting US imperialism'. He went on to explain:

> The United States and the Soviet Union are separated by a vast zone which includes many capitalist, colonial and semi-colonial countries in Europe, Asia and Africa. Before the US reactionaries have subjugated these countries, an attack on the Soviet Union is out of the question.

Mao acknowledged that the US had anti-Soviet military bases in many countries but observed:

> At present, however, it is not the Soviet Union but the countries in which these military bases are located that are the first to suffer US aggression. I believe that it won't be long before these countries come to realise who is really oppressing them . . . It turns out that under the cover of anti-Soviet slogans they are frantically attacking the workers and democratic circles in the United States and turning all the countries which are the targets of US external expansion into US dependencies. I think the American people and the peoples of all countries menaced by US aggression should unite and struggle against the attacks of the US reactionaries and their running dogs in these countries. Only by victory in this struggle can a third world war be avoided; otherwise it is unavoidable.[24]

Apart from making it almost the internationalist duty of the Chinese Communists to undertake armed struggle against the Kuomintang, this analysis was pregnant with meaning for China's future world role. It brought out the significance of the intermediate zone and of the struggle of what are now called Third World countries against being dependencies of imperialist forces as the crucial factor in holding back imperialist expansion and ultimately in preventing a new world war. It also alluded to the international application of Mao's concepts of united fronts and on how to exploit contradictions.[25] Here one can also see the germs of later Maoist ideas on the correct way to apply proletarian internationalism; not in the Russian pattern of being linked with the Soviet Union and following its experience and sheltering under its protective umbrella, but rather by popular independent revolutionary activity.

On the question of how to conduct relations with reactionaries and imperialists, the PRC leaders were later to look back to Mao's explanation on allying and negotiating with the Kuomintang and the Western democracies. The alliance was called for following the Japanese attack on China, when it was stressed that among the various contradictions it was necessary to focus upon the principal one and the principal aspects of that so that the others could be subordinate to it for as long as it continued to be the principal contradiction. Thus the Japanese were the principal enemy and therefore the struggles with the Kuomintang and the other imperialist powers should be subordinated to that for the time being. Later in 1945 Mao also provided a theoretical rationale for negotiating with Chiang Kai-shek in Chungking at the end of the war.[26] With its frank analysis of the various factors and forces at work in such delicate negotiations with an enemy, this has provided the ideological framework for the complex range of negotiations held with foreign adversaries after 1949, including President Nixon's visit in 1972.

The pre-1949 Marxist-Leninist experience in China as expressed through Mao Tse-tung Thought has not only shaped much of the PRC leadership analyses on international politics at the conscious level but at other levels as well. The conflicts within the Chinese leadership between the more orthodox Leninist Communist Moscow-dominated views of organisation, politics and internationalism on the one side and those of a more populist, Yenan 'democratic' China-centred view on these questions have found their expression in the upper reaches of the CPC in the decades both before and after 1949. Indeed, so fundamental is this dualism that it finds its expression in Mao Tse-tung Thought itself, where at different times both strands can be identified. For example, just as many rousing populist calls to the masses can be found in Mao's writings along the lines in which they were called to rise up against many of the party leaders during the Cultural Revolution, so many articles and exhortations can be found calling for a self-conscious, highly organised elite vanguard which seem very much orthodox Leninism.[27]

At another level, the source of the confidence of the PRC leaders in China's ability to withstand the threats of enemies overwhelmingly more powerful militarily than themselves can be traced to their experiences in the 1930s and the 1940s. Who could have thought that the 30,000 men and women who survived the Long March to outer Yenan in 1935 would be in control of China fourteen years later? Certainly not Mao, who as late as 1947 was not expecting victory before the early 1950s. The Maoist theories as to the source of true power as emanating from a people embarked upon their own liberation are derived from those experiences. That is why, in the most profound sense, the Chinese do not believe that revolution can be exported. There is no Maoist equivalent to Lenin's march on Poland in the aftermath of the revolution. For Mao, therefore, a small country truly can defeat a large one and the weak can defeat the strong. But, as he has often stressed, the road is long, tortuous and daunting. If this has the aspect of a moral drama it is because the victory of the Chinese Revolution itself has something of that aura, too.

Notes

1. Cited in John Gittings, *The World and China 1922-72* (Eyre Methuen, 1974), p. 224.
2. Ibid., p. 225.
3. For the best account of this period of China's history in the context of China's evolving position in international affairs see Wang Gung-wu, *China and the World Since 1949: The Impact of Independence, Modernity and Revolution* (Macmillan, 1977), Chapters 1 and 2, pp. 1-26.
4. The best known presentation of this view is by C.P. Fitzgerald, *The Chinese View of Their Place in the World* (Oxford University Press, 1969). Consider especially his conclusion: 'The Chinese view of the world has not fundamentally changed; it has been adjusted to take account of the modern world, but only so far as to permit China to occupy still the central place in the picture' (p. 71).
5. For a brief but penetrating analysis of the anachronistic attempt by Chiang Kai-shek to resuscitate Confucianism from the late 1920s onwards, see Mary C. Wright, *The Last Stand of Chinese Conservatism: The T'ung Chih Restoration 1962-1974* (Stanford University Press, 1975), Chapter XII, pp. 300-12.
6. Edgar Snow, *Red Star Over China* (Pelican Books, 1972), pp. 161-6.
7. See, for example, articles in the journal *Li Shih Yen Chiu (Historical Research)* in 1974 and 1975. In particular, 'New Land Explorers or Gangsters Invading China?' and 'Refute the Fabricators of Lies – On Several Questions Concerning the Sino-Soviet Border'. Both are in issue No. 1, 20 December 1974, translated in selections from the People's Republic of China's Press (SPRCP), No. 809, pp. 4-23 and SPRCP, No. 805, pp. 1-9 respectively.
8. See the essays in J.K. Fairbank (ed.), *China's Traditional World Order* (Harvard University Press, 1967).
9. Allen S. Whiting and Sheng Shih-tsai, *Sinkiang, Pawn or Pivot* (Michigan University Press, 1958).

10.   This has become standard Chinese practice at the UN since first assuming their rightful seat in 1971. For example, the Chinese did this over the Security Council voting on the cease-fire agreement of the Middle East in 1973.

11.   Stuart R. Schram, *The Political Thought of Mao Tse-tung* (Penguin Books, revised and enlarged edition, 1969), p. 210.

12.   See C.F. Remer, *Foreign Investment in China* (Macmillan, 1933), cited by Jerome Ch'en in 'Modern Chinese History', paper delivered to Toronto Conference, 'Another Past Another Future', August 1976, on 'Criticize Lin Piao Criticize Confucius'.

13.   Ch'en, 'Modern Chinese History'.

14.   See the analysis in *The Opium War* by the Compilation Group for the History of Modern China series (FLP, 1976), pp. 1-18.

15.   Mao Tun, *Selected Works* (in Chinese) (People's Literature Press, Peking, 1961), pp. 3-25.

16.   For the figures on the extent of China's aid see Carol H. Fogarty, 'China's Economic Relations with the Third World' in *China: A Reassessment of the Economy*, a compendium of papers presented to the Joint Economic Committee, Congress of the United States of America, July 1975, p. 730 ff.

17.   Drawn from the series of articles by Shih Chun on studying world history in the *Peking Review*, Nos. 21, 24, 25, 26 and 45 (1972).

18.   For a useful but slightly dated analysis see Tang Tsou and Morton H. Halperin, 'Mao Tse-tung's Revolutionary Strategy and Peking's International Behaviour' in *American Political Science Review*, Vol. 59, No. 1 (March 1965).

19.   For the latest book on these themes and their impact on China's foreign policy see J.D. Armstrong, *Revolutionary Diplomacy* (University of California Press, 1977).

20.   Mao Tse-tung,'Why is it that Red Political Power can exist in China?', 5 October 1928, in *Selected Works* (hereafter *SW*) Vol. I, p. 63.

21.   Ibid., p. 63.

22.   Ibid., note 7, p. 71.

23.   See Gittings, *The World and China,* pp. 141-50.

24.   Mao Tse-tung, 'Talk with Anna Louise Strong', August 1976 in *SW*, Vol. IV, pp. 99-100. For a fuller and more vivid version see A.L. Strong, 'World's Eye View from a Yenan Cave', *Amerasia* (April 1974).

25.   The standard work on united fronts in Mao's experience during the pre-liberation period – see Le Van Slyke, *Enemies and Friends* (Stanford University Press, 1967). See also Armstrong, *Revolutionary Diplomacy*, for the foreign policy applications of united fronts.

26.   *SW*, Vol. IV, 'On the Chungking Negotiations'.

27.   As Schram has pointed out, one of the main preoccupations of Mao has been concerned with the contradictions between centralism and democracy or leadership and the mass line. During the high storms of the Cultural Revolution Mao is said to have chided Chang Ch'un-ch'iao and Yao Wen-yuan with 'extreme anarchism' in calling for the doing away of 'heads' (or bosses – in Chinese, 'chang'). Mao commented: 'In reality there will still always be "heads".' See Stuart Schram (ed.), *Mao Tse-tung Unrehearsed* (Penguin Books, 1974), p. 277.

PART ONE

CHINA AS AN ALLY OF THE SOVIET UNION 1949-1963

INTRODUCTION

For the first thirteen to fourteen years of its existence the PRC was seen by its leaders as an integral part of the socialist camp. Such independence of outlook, initiative and action undertaken by China's leaders in international affairs during this period was subsumed within the framework of the socialist camp. To be sure, the PRC membership of the camp went through many phases during these years. From being a junior ally (but never a pawn or a satellite) of the Soviet Union to becoming an independent and almost equal partner, the PRC finally became a major ideological critic and nation-state adversary. The structural and operational characteristics of the socialist camp itself were always at best somewhat vague and ill-defined. To a large extent these could be seen as the sum of the relationships between the Soviet Union and each of the other member states in turn. Certainly, for China's leaders membership of the camp meant principally (but not exclusively) the alliance with the Soviet Union.

It was not until 1963 that China's leaders began to identify a role for the PRC which was more or less free from alliance considerations. As will be shown later, even after that date there continued to be a current among some of China's leaders which sought to reactivate the alliance and which still identified China's international role within a framework shaped by the socialist camp. Indeed the final break in party relations between China and the Soviet Union did not take place until 1966. Up until then it is possible to quote leaders on both sides claiming that in the event of an American attack each would come to the defence of the other. This would suggest that alliance considerations may have held good even as late as that. Nevertheless 1963 is taken here as the effective cut-off point because henceforth China sought to exclude the Soviet Union from all its foreign policy initiatives. The nuclear Test-Ban Treaty signed in Moscow in July 1963 by the representatives of the Soviet Union, the United States and Britain was seen by the Chinese as an attempt by the two superpowers to combine together to bring pressure to bear against China. It was the final proof of the revisionist character of the Soviet leadership who were perceived to have chosen alliance with the Americans to attack the interests of socialist China. Mao, especially, was prominent in the search for a new framework of relationships within which to cast China's foreign policies. Thus it is from 1963 that it is possible to identify a number of different options or international roles being considered by China's leaders.

Looking back in 1962 over the alliance, Mao himself divided the period into two stages: the first up to 1957, with China as a passive uncritical imitator of the Soviet Union, and the second from 1958, when the Chinese began to display independent creativity in pioneering their own way.[1] Here our perspective is more international and the period will be divided differently. Up until the death of Stalin in 1953 China was in many ways a dependent ally. As it turned out, China's role became far less independent than envisaged by Mao, even in the summer of 1949. Nevertheless in certain respects China was still able to operate a foreign policy that had important independent dimensions. But from 1953 up to 1957 the PRC had become an independent great power and equal ally of the Soviet Union within the socialist camp. The period 1958 to 1963 is best seen as the process of the break-up of the alliance. It was only in 1962 that Mao claimed finally in an inner party speech that 'the leadership of the Soviet Union has now been usurped by revisionists.'[2]

The views that China's leaders took of the PRC's role in world affairs developed and changed during these fourteen years. To give but one example taken from the early years of relative subordination, the approach to the other newly independent countries of Asia changed dramatically in 1951. The realisation that countries like India and Burma were not simply still under the control of their former colonial masters and that their neutralism was not without content meant that the thinking about China's pattern of revolution as being the model for Asian countries seeking liberation (which at this stage was regarded by China's leaders as the only true form of independence) needed to be reconsidered. Moreover, this caused China's leaders to think again about the whole nature of the post-war world.

Generally, however, the dominant characteristic of the place that China's leaders defined for the PRC in international affairs was as an ally of the Soviet Union. China's leaders were committed to transforming China into a socialist country with an advanced economy. In addition to relying upon Soviet help and example in those endeavours, the Chinese also relied strategically upon their stronger partner as a major factor in the ultimate deterrence of the United States. In that sense the Soviet Union provided the strategic cover under which the defence of PRC national security interests could be managed by the Chinese themselves.

In the first instance the Chinese relied upon their own strength and their own efforts, as demonstrated by their intervention in the war to aid North Korea and to defend China's national security. The burdens and sacrifices were shouldered by the Chinese (and of course by the Korean) peoples, but not by the Soviet people. Nevertheless the Sino-Soviet alliance was undoubtedly the most important factor in preventing the United States from enlarging its military conflicts with China (i.e. other than the Korean War itself and the 1954 and 1958 clashes over the offshore islands). This ensured that the vastly superior American panoply of power would not be brought to bear against China. As we shall see, the Chinese certainly maintained in the 1950s that it was the strength of their Soviet ally which kept the Korean War a limited one and which prevented the Americans from really attacking Manchuria in earnest. At the same time the Chinese also claimed to have made a tremendous contribution to the defence of the socialist camp. They argued that China was in the front line and that the Soviet Union was in the second line or in the rear. This meant that China had provided in a very real sense protection for the Soviet Union and the socialist camp.

In a speech of 12 September 1953 (i.e. after the end of the war) which was not published until 1977 in Volume V of his *Selected Works*, Mao argued that it was China's military prowess based on popular support combined with the political and economic costs of the war which compelled the Americans to come to terms. He claimed, 'This time we have taken the measure of the US armed forces. If you have never taken them on, you are liable to be scared of them.' He went on to deduce from the experience of the Korean War that China had made a tremendous contribution in shaping the immediate future of world affairs: ' . . . a new imperialist war of aggression against China and a third world war have been put off.'

With the historical perspective of twenty years later Chou En-lai enlarged upon this point when he argued at the 10th Party Congress in 1973 that the Korean War was a watershed in the history of America as a global expansionist imperialist power. From that point on, Chou maintained, the United States had begun to decline. The clear implication is that China's forces had turned the scales of world history.

Few would deny the tremendous significance of the Chinese military achievements in the Korean War. For the first time in modern history Chinese forces had successfully fought a major war with the greatest Western military power. In itself this showed that the new China was a major force to be reckoned with on the world stage. Moreover it was the first war that the United States had fought without emerging victorious. There is much to be said therefore for the above-quoted views of Mao and Chou. The question which needs to be considered is the significance to be attached to the Sino-Soviet alliance as a factor in shaping the course of the war. As will be pointed out later, the Chinese certainly had a grievance regarding the tardy delivery of Soviet military aid which also was not always of the highest quality. Moreover, the Chinese not only bore the brunt of the fighting, but they also had to undertake the economic costs of the war on the Communist side. They even had to pay for the Soviet military supplies. Nevertheless there can be little doubt that it was the Soviet factor which ensured that the war remained a limited one and that China proper was not subjected to direct American attack.

The strategic significance of the Sino-Soviet alliance should not be under-estimated. Caution is required in taking Chinese statements at face value, either during the time in which the alliance was very much operational when the significance of the alliance is likely to be over-stated, or after the Sino-Soviet split when its importance is likely to be downgraded if not ignored altogether. Thus the relevant American decision-makers during the Korean War consciously felt their options constrained by the Soviet factor. Indeed, even once the Sino-Soviet split had become evident in the early 1960s, American decision-makers were by no means certain that Soviet strategic protection of China had been totally withdrawn.

Notes

1. 'Talk at an Enlarged Central Work Conference', 30 January 1962 (also known as 'the 7,000 cadre speech' in Stuart Schram (ed.), *Mao Tse-tung Unrehearsed* (Penguin Books, 1974), p. 176.
2. Ibid., p. 181.

THE FORMATION OF THE ALLIANCE 1949-1950

Before embarking for Moscow to negotiate the alliance in December 1949, Mao had sketched out a role for China that saw it as a member of an international united front rather than as an ally. It was to be a China which would assert its sovereign rights, its territorial integrity and equality in inter-state relations. The new China would join the forces of 'peace and progress' headed by Moscow from whom it would learn about socialist construction, but it would also seek extensive trade and credit arrangements with Western imperialist countries. The new China would have an important regional role as having shown a new way of revolution to the peoples of the East. It was a rather chastened Mao who returned from Moscow weeks later in February 1950. In his speech on the Ten Major Relationships of 25 April 1956, Mao recalled:

> At the time of the War of Liberation Stalin first enjoined us not to press on with the revolution, maintaining that if civil war flared up, the Chinese nation would run the risk of destroying itself. Then when the fighting did erupt, he took us half seriously, half sceptically. When we won the war, Stalin suspected that ours was a victory of the Tito type, and in 1949 and 1950 the pressure on us was very strong indeed.[1]

China's struggle for liberation was nothing if it was not independent. As we have seen, already in 1946 Mao had outlined a view of international politics altogether different from that emerging in the Soviet Union. At that time he did not see the world as essentially divided into a peace camp headed by the Soviet Union and an imperialist camp headed by the United States with there being an imminent danger of a world war to be started by an American attack. Those who saw the world in those terms undoubtedly feared that a successful revolutionary war of liberation in China might have provoked the Americans to do precisely that. By arguing that a vast intermediate zone lay between the two great powers and that American actions would first be directed towards trying to gain mastery of that zone, Mao was able to maintain that there was no imminent danger of a world war. Moreover, if China could be successfully liberated a crucial part of that zone would be denied to the Americans and that would make a world war even less likely. From this perspective there can be little doubt that the most important strategic gain acquired by the Soviet Union and the international Communist movement since the Second World War was the victory of the Chinese Revolution. But of course that was not the way it was seen in Moscow. Apart from fears of American retaliation, there were clear indications that the victory of the Chinese Communists was not welcomed universally. There is considerable evidence to show bad feeling between the Chinese and Soviet sides in Manchuria.[2] In 1946, probably with the full knowledge of the Soviet authorities, the Soviet-dominated People's Republic of Mongolia instigated an attempt by the 'Inner Mongolian Revolutionary Party' to split off that province from China, perhaps in the way that Outer Mongolia had been split off from China in 1924 to become the People's Republic. But apparently the attempt was foiled by Mao's forces.[3] There were signs that Stalin would have preferred the Chinese Communists to have stayed north of the Yangtse. In April 1949 the Soviet Ambassador was the only one to go south with the retreating Nationalist government to Canton and there he negotiated a five-year extension of Soviet rights in Sinkiang.

How and why then did China's leaders, and especially Mao, willingly subordinate China to an alliance and a dependency relationship with the Soviet Union?

It was not until the winter of 1948-9 that first Mao Tse-tung and then Liu Shao-ch'i began to follow the Soviet-inspired view of the two-camp thesis and to affirm specifically that the new China would adhere to the Soviet-led anti-imperialist camp.[4] By 18 March 1949 (i.e. before the crossing of the Yangtse and the conquest of the south), an authoritative Chinese analysis of international affairs accepted the Soviet thesis that the most important problem in the world was the danger of a new world war.[5] Various factors combined to cause China's victorious leaders to bend so much to the Soviet view. The very fact of their impending victory changed the needs and perspectives of the Chinese revolutionaries. They no longer represented the apparently weaker and smaller forces caught up in a civil war but were soon to represent China as a whole. They were going to have to enter into what for them was the new uncharted territory of building up a complex economy from a new centre of gravity in the cities. They were also internationalist revolutionaries, Communists; they would have to lean to the side of the Soviet Union now that the Cold War was at full blast. Chou En-lai reportedly told American representatives, 'We shall have to lean to one side, but how far we lean depends upon you.' As John Gittings has argued, right through 1949 the United States steadfastly turned its back

on all overtures from the Chinese Communist side and presented a
posture of unredeemed hostility and enmity to the new China.[6] Although Mao was to call on the Chinese people to side with and learn
from the Soviet Union he showed considerable signs of independence of
outlook that suggested a very special role for China.

In his celebrated essay on the People's Democratic Dictatorship of
30 June 1949 which set down the guidelines for the structure and
policies of the new China, Mao argued that it was the experience of
China's modern history which demonstrated conclusively that 'all
Chinese without exception must lean either to the side of imperialism
or to the side of socialism. Sitting on the fence will not do, nor is there
a third road.' It is interesting to note, however, that in this forcibly
argued case for leaning to the Soviet Union Mao did not mention
specifically either a peace camp or a socialist one. He defined China's
future role in terms of united fronts:

Up to now the principal and fundamental experience the Chinese
people have gained is twofold:
1. Internally, arouse the masses of the people. That is unite the
working class, the peasantry, the urban petty bourgeoisie and the
national bourgeoisie, form a domestic united front under the leadership of the working class, and advance from this to the establishment
of a state which is a people's democratic dictatorship under the
leadership of the working class and based on the alliance of workers
and peasants.
2. Externally, unite in a common struggle with those nations of the
world which treat us as equals and unite with the peoples of all
countries. That is, ally ourselves with the Soviet Union, with the
People's Democracies and with the proletariat and the broad masses
of the people in all other countries, and form an international united
front.[7]

The phraseology and indeed the concepts here can all be traced back
to the Chinese revolutionary experience. They are not derived from
Soviet terminology. Indeed the concept of a domestic united front with
the bourgeoisie was alien to Soviet practice in Eastern Europe at this
time, as was, of course, the special terminology used to define the new
Chinese state.[8] Mao also in typical trenchant style asserted that special
regard would be paid to Chinese sovereign equality with all other states
and that there would certainly not be a meekness of spirit in the
attitude towards reactionaries and imperialists: 'We must not show the

slightest timidity before a wild beast.' On the other hand, Mao also looked forward to 'doing business' with and possibly obtaining credit 'on terms of mutual benefit' in the future from Britain and the US, but only 'because their capitalists want to make money and their bankers want to earn interest to extricate themselves from their own crisis'. 'Genuine and friendly help' could only come from the side of the Soviet Union.

Mao refuted the view that the liberation of China had been possible without international help. It was not so much a question of direct material aid (in fact no mention was made of that); rather it was the consequence of the existence of the Soviet Union as a socialist state and the victories and struggles of the masses of people throughout the world — 'If not for all these in combination, the international reactionary forces bearing down upon us would certainly be many times greater now.' By these terms all revolutionary victories and struggles were mutually supportive, but not by their being linked by a coherent strategy and tactical approach as in the days of the Comintern, or as Stalin was imposing in Europe through the Cominform. They were mutually supportive simply by their carrying out their own independent struggles against domestic reactionaries and external imperialists who were necessarily the common foes of all. In this sense Mao was continuing to be an internationalist in the only way that he had been throughout his life, and that is by combining it with Chinese patriotism and by placing the Chinese experience within a universalistic context. In no sense was Mao declaring the subordination of the new China to the Soviet Union.

Another important theme in Mao's seminal essay was the need for economic reconstruction and development. The war had been won, but now new tasks lay ahead: 'We shall soon put aside some of the things we know well and be compelled to do things we don't know well.' Mao pictured the imperialists as 'standing by and looking on, awaiting our failure'. He continued: 'We must overcome difficulties, we must learn what we do not know. We must learn to do economic work from all who know how, no matter who they are.' This latter remark was a reference to former Kuomintang people and capitalists who stayed on at their posts. Mao later pointed to the example of the Soviet Union as a success both in making revolution and in construction work: 'The Communist Party of the Soviet Union is our best teacher and we must learn from it.'

As far as the question of state-to-state relations was concerned, China's new leaders had already declared in 1947 that they would not be bound by any treaties or agreements signed on behalf of China by the Kuomintang (KMT). The new independent China would start with a clean slate. In this 1949 essay Mao made it clear that the new China would seek to establish relations with 'all foreign countries on the basis of equality, mutual benefit and mutual respect for territorial integrity and sovereignty'. These concepts were later to form the core of the 'Five Principles of Peaceful Coexistence' first announced by Chou En-lai and Pandit Nehru in 1954 and which then became the cardinal principles guiding China's diplomatic relations.

All this was codified in the Common Programme adopted by the Chinese People's Political Consultative Conference on 29 September 1949 which, together with other documents adopted then, provided the constitutional and political framework for the new PRC to be established by Mao Tse-tung himself two days later. Articles 54-60 of the programme dealt with foreign policy. One of its important points concerned the commitment of the new government to do its utmost to protect the proper rights and interests of Chinese residing abroad.[9] But in fact so little attention was paid by China's leaders to this that it was not until 1954 that Premier Chou En-lai defined for the first time China's attitude to the question of the nationality of overseas Chinese. He rejected the concept of dual nationality. Overseas Chinese had to take up either Chinese or local nationality. In either case they were enjoined to follow local laws. But it was only henceforth that the PRC leadership was able to identify with sufficient clarity what were 'the proper rights and interests' of the relevant categories of people it had committed itself to defend in the 1949 Common Programme.[10]

The definition of China's national identity implicit in this context also called for a reassertion of Chinese control of all the outlying regions near the borders. The aspiration of Chinese nationalists since the 1890s to transform China's frontier areas into clear and specific boundaries was now to be completed. Henceforth boundaries were to be the clear demarcation line between the sacred motherland of the Chinese people and the outside world. This meant that the outer provinces like Tibet and Sinkiang, inhabited largely by other nationalities, were to be brought firmly within the control of a centralised modern state for the first time in history. It meant that such genuine autonomy as they may have been moving towards was to be firmly curtailed. To be sure, such autonomous tendencies as could be identified in these provinces had begun to emerge only with the advent of imperialist pressures. Regions which had existed for centuries as frontier areas on the margins of the Chinese administrative empire were now considered in a new light because of the advent of the modern state system. For the Chinese — Communist and Nationalist alike — the main problem centred on the need to remove the vestiges of imperialism from China's outer reaches and to reassert control over lost lands. The question that arose, of course, was which lands should be considered as legitimately belonging to the Chinese state. This problem was never posed before the nineteenth century. Up until then there was the China ruled directly by the official bureaucratic system, and then beyond that there were the frontier areas designed as some kind of buffer regions to protect China proper from nomadic invaders. This was particularly true of the north and west.

Elsewhere there was a complex series of tributary arrangements. Some Chinese maps published since the 1920s have claimed all these vast territories including virtually the whole of Soviet Asia, Mongolia, the small Himalayan states, Burma, Indo-China and Korea as belonging to China, or, at any rate, as having been unjustly taken from China by imperialism. One such map was published in a school textbook in Peking in 1954.[11] But it is important to note that no map like that was ever published for official use. Moreover, in practice no modern Chinese government has laid claims to these vast lands. The PRC claims, as we shall have occasion to examine elsewhere in this book, have been confined to the two western provinces of Tibet and Sinkiang, Manchuria (or the north-east provinces), Taiwan and groups of islands in the South China Sea. Such claims as Mao had entertained regarding Outer Mongolia in 1936[12] were given up, as we shall see, in the treaty of 1950 with the Soviet Union.

From the perspective of China's Communist leaders the main problems regarding these areas were outside intervention and the legacy of imperialism. There had been a long history of Tsarist and then Soviet involvement in Sinkiang.[13] The British had been active in Tibet since the end of the nineteenth century. Manchuria had long been a 'cradle of conflict' (to use Owen Lattimore's distinctive phrase[14]) between Russia and Japan, while Taiwan had been under Japanese control since 1895 and had now become the last resting place of Chiang Kai-shek and the battered remains of his forces. Thus each of these border provinces was being pushed in the separatist direction by external powers. This was not a case of an internally motivated search for self-determination. It was rather the result of imperialist designs upon China. This largely explains the uncompromising zeal to re-establish control over these areas. The patriotic sentiment of correcting historical wrongs and of unifying China was allied with the Communist perspective of fearing further attempts by imperialists to make trouble by seeking out the feudal leaders of national minority peoples in the border lands.

The desire to cleanse China from all imperialist vestiges found its clearest expression in the attitude that the PRC leaders were to take up regarding the question of borders. Since the existing borders had been largely settled (and in many cases only sketchily so) by the unequal treaties imposed on China by the imperial powers in the nineteenth century, the new China sought to arrive at new border agreements. The new leadership keenly desired that China and each of the twelve states with whom a common border is shared in this area should establish agreements based on the principles of equality and mutual benefit and so wipe away the stigma of the past. Not all the twelve states shared the same passionate hatred for the imperialist character of existing border arrangements. Indeed, both India and the Soviet Union were later to base their claims on precisely colonial derived borders. These, however, were problems for the future.

It is clear that China's leaders conceived of the PRC as an entirely new China which would settle China's accounts with the legacy of imperialism so that the Chinese people could proceed with the main task, which was domestic; that is, the consolidation of victory and the building towards socialism on the basis of a new revolutionary unity of the Chinese people.

In order to complete this brief survey of the international role claimed for the nascent PRC, we must consider the claims made by China's new leaders for the international significance of their path of revolution and indeed of the view taken of the other newly independent countries in Asia. The most widely noted aspect of the CPC divergence from the CPSU during the early days of the People's Republic concerned the CPC claim to have pioneered independently a new road of making revolution very different from that of the Bolshevik Revolution. What is more, that road, 'the way of Mao Tse-tung', was said to be peculiarly suited to Asian countries. Thus Liu Shao-ch'i in a celebrated passage told the Conference of Asian and Australasian Trade Unions in Peking in November 1949:

> The path taken by the Chinese people in defeating imperialism and its lackeys and in founding the People's Republic of China is the path that should be taken by the peoples of a great many colonial and semi-colonial countries in their fight for national independence and people's democracy.

This view challenged directly Soviet authority over the Communist parties of Asia. It was also indicative of Chinese contempt for the 'feeble-minded bourgeoisie of the East' and their claims to lead independent governments in former colonial Asia. In the same month Mao publicly declared that the people of India (which had become an independent state two years earlier in 1947) were living 'under the yoke of imperialism and its collaborators' and he averred that 'in many respects [India's] past fate and its path to the future resemble those of China'.[15] In sum, the role that China's leaders specified for it in the world situation was to be an independent member of the camp headed by the Soviet Union. As such, it had a special status arising out of Mao's independent contributions to Marxism-Leninism and because China's way of revolution was better suited to Asian circumstances than the Russian Revolution itself. But, as we have seen, China's new tasks were directed towards economic reconstruction. Within the Soviet-led united front new China would hope to have equal, independent and also commercial relationships with all countries, including the US.

If the Chinese leaders were prepared to have businesslike relations with the capitalist world and if they had displayed many signs of an independence of outlook from Moscow, the United States leadership was not prepared to act upon these. To the contrary, by the summer of 1949 the United States leadership was already committed to the containment of China while privately expressing the hope that conflict would arise between Mao and Stalin.[16] Meanwhile, contradicting the findings of his own department's White Paper on China regarding the independent quality of its revolution, the US Secretary of State, Dean Acheson, declared in his letter of transmittal to Congress of 30 July 1949:

> We continue to believe that, however tragic may be the immediate future of China and however ruthlessly a major proportion of this great people may be exploited by a party in the interest of a foreign imperialism, ultimately the profound civilisation and the democratic individualism of China will reassert themselves and she will throw off the foreign yoke. I consider that we should encourage all developments in China which now and in the future work toward this end.[17]

The main consequence of this attitude was to drive Mao further into Stalin's embrace and help to reduce much of the independence of outlook and actions sought by China's leaders.

The Dependent Ally 1950-53

There are two vivid passages from Mao's unofficial writings which graphically and pungently describe his humiliating experience of negotiating the treaty of alliance with Stalin. Mao himself characterised the negotiations as a 'struggle' in which he had to give way whenever Stalin insisted. The depth of Mao's feelings can be gauged from his curt description of Soviet demands upon Manchuria and Sinkiang as constituting colonialism. Furthermore, Stalin's evident distrust of Mao's independent quality inevitably soured the Sino-Soviet relations right from the outset and it was undoubtedly a factor in the casting of China into the role of a rather uneasy dependent ally. This was to change decisively after the consolidation of Communist power in China, the victory in Korea and the death of Stalin. However in 1958, at a time when Mao was leading the Chinese people away from the Soviet model and towards self-reliance, he finally revealed his unhappy experience with Stalin:

> In 1950 I argued with Stalin in Moscow for two months. On the questions of the Treaty of Mutual Assistance, the Chinese Eastern Railway, the joint-stock companies and the border we adopted two attitudes: one was to argue when the other side made proposals we did not agree with, and the other was to accept their proposal if they absolutely insisted. This was out of consideration for the interests of socialism. Then there were the two 'colonies', that is the Northeast and Sinkiang, where people of any third country were not allowed to reside . . . [18]

Four years later in 1962, at another critical turning-point in his attitude towards the Soviet Union, when he had finally concluded that the Khrushchev leadership was irredeemably revisionist, Mao returned to this theme:

> They did not permit China to make revolution: that was in 1945. Stalin wanted to prevent China from making revolution, saying that we should not have a civil war and should cooperate with Chiang Kai-shek otherwise the Chinese nation would perish. But we did not do what he said. The revolution was victorious. After the victory of the revolution he next suspected China of being a Yugoslavia, and that I would be a second Tito. Later when I went to Moscow to sign the Sino-Soviet Treaty of Alliance and Mutual Assistance, we had to go through another struggle. He was not willing to sign a treaty.

After two months of negotiatons he at last signed. When did Stalin begin to have confidence in us? It was at the time of the Resist America, Aid Korea campaign from the winter of 1950. He then came to believe that we were not Tito, not Yugoslavia.[19]

The Treaty of Alliance and Mutual Assistance was signed on 14 February 1950 – St Valentine's Day. The treaty was closely modelled on that signed with Nationalist China five years earlier. By its terms: (1) the Soviet Union was to maintain its special privileges in Manchuria with regard to the Chinese Changchun Railway (or Chinese Eastern Railway), Port Arthur and Dairen until a peace treaty was signed with Japan or until 1952, whichever came sooner; (2) the Soviet Union would advance to China credit of $300 million over five years; (3) the independence of Mongolia was recognised; and (4) certain property acquired by the Soviet Union from the Japanese in Manchuria would be returned to China without charge, as would some property in Peking. On 27 March further agreements were signed concerning the establishment of joint-stock companies to exploit petroleum and non-ferrous metals in Sinkiang and Manchuria, as well as a civil aviation company. On 19 April 1950 a trade agreement was signed. It was later revealed that both sides agreed to exchange information on important questions of international affairs affecting them both.[20] And as we have seen from the above quotations by Mao, it had been agreed to forbid residents of third countries to reside in Sinkiang and Manchuria because of the Sino-Soviet joint-stock companies.

Perhaps the most important provision in the treaty was the first article which unambiguously declared:

In the event of one of the contracting parties being attacked by Japan or any state allied with it and thus being involved in a state of war, the other contracting party shall immediately render military and other assistance by all means at its disposal.

This provision played a critical role for China as the ultimate deterrent against an American attack through all the Sino-American conflict situations of the 1950s and the early 1960s. There can be little doubt, for example, that but for this position the Americans might have carried the Korean War to the Chinese mainland. Certainly Chinese commentaries upon the treaty all emphasised the importance of this provision.

The treaty allotted the Soviet Union very special positions in areas traditionally desired by Russia as special spheres of influence in Sinkiang and Manchuria. At the same time the treaty clearly specified that these would be temporary in nature. The economic aid was not great — certainly not when Chinese needs are considered. On the other hand, China needed access to Soviet experience and know-how perhaps even more than specific grants. Furthermore, during Stalin's lifetime China received aid for the construction of at least forty major heavy industrial plants. Considered in these terms, Soviet aid was not as limited as it may have seemed on first consideration of the treaty. But above all, from a Chinese perspective, the treaty provided the promise of a secure international environment in which to concentrate on the primary domestic economic tasks ahead.

From a strategic point of view, it was easy to see how China stood to benefit, but from a Soviet perspective the gains were less clear. After all, the major strategic benefit to the Soviet Union from a liberated China derived less from any formal obligations or mutual defence agreements than from the very fact of the denial to the United States of such an important country in world affairs. The treaty did not bring China under Soviet control and yet the Soviet Union was formally tied to act on behalf of China should it become involved in military conflict with the United States. Moreover, from a Soviet perspective, so total a victory by the Chinese revolutionaries could not but raise tensions with the United States even more sharply. Yet at the back of Stalin's mind was the possibility, as not a few Westerners suggested at the time, that Mao might become another Tito.

It is worth noting that before the Korean War the new China displayed many signs of vigorous independence as the major liberated power in Asia with peculiar revolutionary responsibilities. Nothing in the practice of revolution, the writing of China's leaders or in the actions of the PRC suggested that this role would be interpreted in terms of spreading revolution by force of Chinese arms. The vision of China's role in this regard has to this day remained fundamentally a supportive and didactic one. In no sense was China's role to take over, or play the main part in, a foreign revolutionary movement or in a struggle for national liberation. On the other hand, China would be vigorous in its diplomatic support and, where practicable, in terms of its aid to struggle seen to be on the right road. The revolutionary war in Vietnam was seen in that light; but the Malayan struggles were seen differently. Thus even while Mao was in Moscow, China became the first 'Communist' state to extend recognition to the Vietminh as the Democratic Republic of Vietnam, in January 1950. This, of course, led to considerable disquiet in the Western powers and reversed any French

thoughts of recognising China. The Russians and the People's Democracies followed the Chinese example reluctantly a little later. The
struggles in Malaya, however, were not seen in Peking as genuinely
national in character since exclusive reliance was placed on ethnic
Chinese in the revolutionary ranks. Chinese support, therefore, was
minimal and the struggles were not much mentioned in the Chinese
Press or by Chinese leaders.[21] If American policy had made the PRC
early in 1950 lean even further to the Soviet side than its leaders would
have wished, their actions by the end of the year had led to what Mao
later characterised as 'dependence' on the Soviet Union. Truman's
decision to intervene afresh in China's civil war by interposing his
Seventh Fleet between Taiwan and the mainland on 27 June (two days
after the outbreak of the Korean War) was followed by the American
refusal to heed Chinese warnings over their northward march in Korea.
This led to Chinese intervention in the war. The decision to intervene
was not an easy one: the Chinese had never before been able to fight
successfully against determined Western armies. Moreover, consolidation
of the revolutionary victory was incomplete. There is evidence to
suggest that the Chinese leadership was divided over the question.[22]

The armed conflict also led to a more rigorous enforcement of the
US trade embargo with China. Although the Chinese were clearly committed to increasing their trade with the Soviet Union and the People's
Democracies, it may be doubted whether they had intended that trade
to increase as a proportion of their total trade from barely 8 per cent in
1949 to 61 per cent in 1951 and to 70 per cent in 1952. It is interesting
to note that before falling away completely in 1951, the US proportion
of China's foreign trade in 1950 was 23 per cent (coming second to the
Soviet Union as China's largest trading partner by only 0.36 per cent).[23]

Thus, within the space of a few months in the second half of 1950,
China's chosen path to independence in international affairs had been
totally transformed. The prospect of completing the civil war and re-
unifying the country by the liberation of Taiwan had of necessity
receded when it had earlier seemed imminent.* Instead of proceeding in
time to full international recognition on the terms laid down by Mao in
1949, the PRC was now to be relatively isolated diplomatically. The die
was cast in Sino-American relations. China's options had been much
reduced and the PRC had been forced by events into a growing depen-

---

*By one of the strange twists of history, the invading force being prepared by
China earlier in the year had been struck down by schistosomiasis (the disease
carried by water snails) and the date of liberation was postponed. Otherwise the
entire course of recent history might have been very different.

dence upon the Soviet Union. What made matters even worse was that considerable uncertainty still remained about the reliability of the Soviet Union in this situation. Not until the latter stages of the war did the Soviet Union issue significant statements of strategic support for China. Soviet military aid was not forthcoming until late summer 1951, presumably because Stalin feared that greater Chinese success might have led the Americans into desperate measures which might have even led to a Soviet-US war.[24] As if to point up that China alone was carrying the burden of the war and to signal the consequences for China's claims as an independent Communist power, the thirtieth anniversary of the CPC on 1 July 1951 was celebrated with renewed emphasis upon the independent creativity of Mao Tse-tung as a theorist. The significance of the Chinese Revolution in Asia and of China's ability to defeat the Western forces because of the revolutionary spirit of its people were also stressed.[25]

Speaking a little over a year later on 4 August 1952, Mao noted that in contrast with the previous year when the expenditure on the war 'more or less equalled' that for national construction, this year the war burden had been halved, the troops had been reduced in number and they were 'better equipped'. That presumably reflected the results of the inflow of Soviet aid, even though this is not mentioned in the speech itself as made public in 1977.[26] Nevertheless, the Chinese were not entirely satisfied with the quality of the Soviet military equipment. Moreover they complained that after the war they were also required to pay the Soviet Union for this assistance, even though the Chinese had good cause to argue that they had been fighting not only to defend China and Korea but in the interests of the socialist camp as a whole.[27] Certainly the Chinese have always maintained that such military assistance as they have given to others – even non-socialist countries – has been free of charge. Yet as may be implied from Mao's observations in 1952, Soviet aid made quite a difference.

Despite the constraints of the framework of the Sino-Soviet alliance, China's leaders continued to maintain a foreign policy that was still largely independent. There seems little doubt that without reference to Moscow, China's leaders themselves revised their view regarding India and Burma and hence the category of states representative of newly independent former colonies led by national bourgeois governments. Hitherto, as we have seen, their people were regarded as being 'under the yoke of imperialism and its collaborators'. But once the Indian and Burmese governments refused to sign the United States-Great Britain draft peace treaty with Japan and had even refused to attend the San

Francisco Conference, the Chinese took an entirely different view. The *People's Daily* front-paged the Indian refusal note of 23 August and issued an editorial stating that this 'proved that the age is past when imperialist governments can do whatever they please'. Far from meekly suffering further inroads of imperialist penetration, these countries were now to be seen as centres of resistance to imperialism. Mao was later to remark:

> In the initial period after the founding of our state, some people, including myself . . . , took the view that the parties and trade unions of Asia and the parties of African states might suffer serious damage. It was later proved that this point of view was incorrect.[28]

The Chinese had rejected the draft peace treaty with Japan for excluding China and the Soviet Union and for attacking their fundamental interests. Chou En-lai castigated the peace treaty, the bilateral US-Japan Security Treaty, the US treaties with the Philippines and then with Australia and New Zealand as 'instruments with which the United States aims to oppress and enslave the Asian people and to prepare for unleashing another aggressive war in Asia'.[29] Chinese commentaries repeatedly argued that the Americans were treading in the shoes left by the Japanese militarists and that this was a latter-day version of Japan's old Co-Prosperity Sphere for Asia. Therefore great significance was attached to the refusal of some of the Asian countries to join in with this American design. Although the Indian Ambassador had played an important role in Sino-American diplomacy before the Chinese crossing of the Yalu, this did not bring about any substantial change in the Chinese estimation of the basic Indian position. Indeed it can be argued that Mao's 1949 views were confirmed in his eyes when the Indian government sought to dissuade the Chinese authorities in 1950 from sending the People's Liberation Army (PLA) into Tibet on grounds that could only have been treated with contempt. The argument of the Indian government was that if China did not stay the hand of the PLA, a bad impression would be formed by the Western powers at the UN. The notion that China should reduce her sovereignty simply to curry favour with the former oppressors of China and the current leading imperialists went against everything for which Mao stood. A Tibetan delegation was dragging its heels in India rather than go to negotiate in Peking and China's leaders in the end responded officially to Indian criticisms of their actions in Tibet on 30 October 1950:

With regard to the viewpoint of the Government of India on what it regards as deplorable, the Central People's Government of the People's Republic of China cannot but consider it as having been affected by foreign influence hostile to China in Tibet and hence expresses its deep regret.[30]

A year later China's view changed totally and that in turn meant that a re-evaluation had been made of the pattern of events in Asia and China's place within them. No longer was China's road to revolution to be promoted as the only proper path for other Asian countries to follow if they were to taste the fruits of independence. Instead Chou En-lai declared on 23 October 1951:

The unity of the Chinese people and the peoples of Asia will certainly create a powerful and matchless force in the Far East which will rapidly push forward the great wheel of history in the movement for the independence and liberation of the peoples of the Asian countries.[31]

Mao himself, on the same occasion, went even further. He drew the conclusion that 'the forces of the whole system of imperialism have been very much weakened'. In his speech he struck an optimistic tone. His mode of argument was typical of the period of the Sino-Soviet alliance. China was placed firmly in the 'camp of peace and democracy headed by the Soviet Union', right was on China's side — as were the people of the world whose 'level of consciousness [had] been raised'. Moreover, 'the power of the Soviet Union, our closest ally, has been greatly strengthened.' He averred that there was no need to fear a new world conflagration as the outcome could only be a defeat for the imperialists, since the aggressors of the Second World War had had even more favourable circumstances and still they had failed. The situation in former colonial Asia, far from being still dominated by the forces of imperialism, was henceforth regarded as favourable to the resistance to the Western powers. The Chinese also found evidence of this new mood in the Middle East.[32]

By 1951-2 China's new leaders' self-confidence had deepened. They had successfully held the largely American forces at bay in Korea while domestically the economy had been largely rehabilitated and the victory consolidated. At an international economic conference held in Moscow in April 1952 the Chinese delegation successfully concluded trade agreements with businessmen from Britain, France, Belgium, The

Netherlands, Switzerland, Finland and Italy from Western Europe, as well as Ceylon, Indonesia and Pakistan, to the value of US$223 million. The Vice-Minister of Trade publicly declared China's hope of increasing its trade with capitalist countries during the following 'two to three years' to a level of between $3,750 million and $4,750 million.[33] China was clearly anxious to diversify its trade outlets, to break out of the American trade embargo and from the close Soviet embrace so as to assume the more independent role in world affairs sketched out by Mao in 1949. A sign of the new self-confidence was given by Chou En-lai when he claimed: 'No problem of international importance today can be solved without the participation of the Soviet Union and the People's Republic of China.'[34]

China was now seen as one of the world's great powers, not just with a right to be heard but also with sufficient influence to be a necessary participatory party to any settlement of 'problems of international importance'. Significantly, however, Chou En-lai's view of China's exalted status in world affairs was of a China coupled with the Soviet Union. It is interesting to note in passing that the Soviet Union tended to confine China's great-power status to Far Eastern questions only. Earlier in 1951 the Soviet Foreign Ministry had proposed a four-power conference on the German problem which would have excluded China and which went against the Soviet-orchestrated propaganda for a five-power conference for world peace.

It should be pointed out that China's dependence upon the Soviet Union went much deeper than the instrumental and strategic aspects suggested so far. That dependence, however, arose out of domestic rather than international considerations. It was caused to a large extent by the lack of familiarity of China's Communist leaders with the organisational, technological and economic skills necessary to run a state geared to the development of socialism. At the same time these leaders, conscious that the Soviet Union had already traversed that road, maintained that the Soviet Union should be regarded as China's teacher and elder brother. Whole sectors of China's economy, state administration, welfare services, education and so on were just modelled directly upon the Soviet pattern. Some idea of the extent of the attempt to popularise the Soviet model can be seen from the figures given by the General Secretary of the Sino-Soviet Friendship Association on 16 November 1952. In September 1952 the association was made up of 1,896 regional associations at provincial, city and county levels and 119,978 branch associations with a total membership of 38.9 million people. In the year September 1951 to August 1952 the association had published 74 different kinds of periodicals and more than 1,100 books; 22,000 rallies had been held; 32 million people had seen 18,000 film shows and 49 million had visited photographic exhibitions. In the words of the General Secretary,

> through these activities the people not only gain a better understanding of the Soviet Union, they rid themselves of narrow nationalist thinking and see the actual life of the people of the socialist Soviet Union, that is to say, get a glimpse into their own future.

Po Yi-po, the influential Finance Minister, in a report on the national budget declared quite simply on 17 February 1953: 'The Soviet Union of today will be the new China of tomorrow.' Mao himself ten days earlier had stated: 'We must set going a tidal wave of learning from the Soviet Union on a nationwide scale in order to build up our country.'

In March 1958, when Mao was calling for more self-reliance and independent creativity, he looked back critically to these years (in fact he regarded his strictures as applying up to 1957):

> In the period following the liberation of the whole country, dogmatism made its appearance both in economic and in cultural and educational work. A certain amount of dogmatism was imported in military work, but basic principles were upheld, and you still could not say that our military work was dogmatic. In economic work dogmatism primarily manifested itself in heavy industry, planning, banking and statistics, especially in heavy industry and planning. Since we did not understand these things and had absolutely no experience, all we could do in our ignorance was to import foreign methods. Our statistical work was practically a copy of Soviet work; in the educational field copying was also pretty bad, for example, the system of a maximum mark of five in the schools, the uniform five years of primary school, etc. We did not even study our own experience of education in the liberated areas.[35]

Shortly before Stalin's death further indications of China's subordinate status became evident. Although it was announced on 15 September 1952 that the Chinese Changchun Railway was to be handed back to China, a note was also published from Chou En-lai requesting the postponement of the withdrawal of Soviet troops from Port Arthur. As China was preparing for its First Five-Year Plan due to commence in 1953, several Chinese economic delegations were being delayed in

Moscow as they were asking for more help. It was not until after Stalin's death that they were to get satisfaction. Likewise it was only after Stalin's demise that the huge millstone of the Korean War was lifted off China's back by the signing of the cease-fire agreements at Panmunjon.

In sum, although China had retained a good measure of independence as a dependent ally of the Soviet Union, that dependence was still in evidence. To be sure, a good part of it, particularly in the domestic sphere, was voluntarily, if not eagerly, embraced. Nevertheless the expectations of Mao in the summer of 1949 had not been realised. He had then sketched out a role for China as an independent member of a large international united front centred on the Soviet Union, trading freely with the Western world while posing as a unique revolutionary model to the peoples of the East. Moreover, it was to have been a China with its sovereignty, unity, territorial integrity and essential dignity restored. It was within such a framework that Mao had envisaged taking place, first, the consolidation of victory and, second, the building towards socialism. Instead China had become a junior ally of the Soviet Union with the Soviets exercising special rights in Sinkiang and Manchuria reminiscent of imperial practices of an era that was thought to have passed from Chinese history. Moreover, the American intervention on the Taiwan question meant that the unification of China could not be realised soon. This, together with the trade embargo and the erection of the containment cordon around China, was to cast a very long shadow over China's foreign options and indeed its role in world affairs for many years to come. It also effectively condemned China to operate on the margin of the international diplomatic community. The actions of both the Soviet Union and the United States had resulted in China's freedom for manoeuvre being closely circumscribed.

The military success, however, in repulsing and then holding at bay the largely American forces in Korea brought a significant change in China's self-confidence and international image. For the first time in modern Chinese history Chinese forces had repelled a determined Western military assault. As we have seen, Mao argued at the time that this meant not only that China would be respected, but that it had made a new world war less imminent. Chou En-lai twenty years later was to claim that the Korean War was the turning-point in America's role in world affairs as its decline was said to have begun then. As early as 1952 Chou had first asserted China's claim to have acquired global and not just regional significance when he stated that the solution of major international problems required the participation of China as well as the Soviet Union.

At the same time China's leaders also showed themselves to be willing and able to adjust quickly and comprehensively to any of their conceptions of the world shown to be false. Thus as soon as the newly independent bourgeois governments of India and Burma showed that they were not still dominated by their former colonial masters, the Chinese leaders were prepared to make the necessary ideological change. The acid test on this matter was the question of willingness to participate at the San Francisco Conference of 1951, which drew up not only the peace treaty between the Western powers and Japan (to the exclusion of China and the Soviet Union) but was also an important instrument used by the United States in the erection of the containment structures around China. By refusing to participate, India and Burma had showed that they had joined the opposition to imperialism at a time and on an issue that mattered. Henceforth the image of Asia held by China's leaders was to change considerably. No longer was Asia to be divided into three categories: the socialist 'paradise' of Soviet Asia, the liberated countries of Asia (like China) which were building towards socialism, and the dark misery of exploited and oppressed Asia dominated by colonialism, whether formally independent or not. From now on the newly independent countries of Asia elsewhere were to have an important place in China's leaders' view of the anti-imperialist forces in world affairs.

Thus within the framework of the subordinate ally of the Soviet Union China's leaders had evolved a changed role for the PRC. Its readiness to use force to defend its frontiers and to prevent a US military presence on its borders had been vindicated. The alliance with the Soviet Union was regarded as the main factor in deterring the United States from escalating the war beyond levels with which the Chinese could deal. Thus by uniting with the camp of peace and socialism, China's national interests could be defended. At the same time it meant that by defending these interests against imperialist pressure the interests of the whole camp were also advanced. China's international problems and their solution were seen as part of global problems. Thus decisive shifts in China's foreign policy (like those on Asian neutralism) arose out of the identification of new general tendencies rather than out of a series of bilateral relationships. It was not the service that the Indian Ambassador had performed as a go-between between China and America that had mattered. It was the perception that India, together with other newly independent countries, could and did stand up to imperialism that was decisive. They were soon to have a place in the array of forces in the peace camp that in the Chinese view could hold imperialism at bay.

Notes

1. Published officially for the first time by NCNA on 26 December 1976 (the first birthday after Mao's death) in *Peking Review*, No. 1 (1977). See *Selected Works*, Vol. V, p. 304. For the slightly different version published by Red Guard sources see Stuart Schram (ed.), *Mao Tse-tung Unrehearsed* (Penguin Books, 1974), pp. 61-83.

2. See, for example, John Gittings, *Survey of the Sino-Soviet Dispute* (Oxford University Press, 1968), Chapter 1, pp. 27-42; and John Gittings, *The World and China 1922-1972* (Eyre Methuen, 1974), pp. 148-50. For a Soviet account see O.B. Borisov and B.T. Koloskov, *Soviet-Chinese Relations 1945-1970*, edited with an introductory essay by Vladimir Petrov (Indiana University Press, 1975), pp. 52-62.

3. Article in *Unen* of 19 August 1974 broadcast on Mongolian radio. See BBC, *SWB*, Part 3, The Far East, No. 4684.

4. Mao Tse-tung, 'Revolutionary Forces of the World Unite, Fight Against Imperialist Oppression', November 1948, *Selected Works*, Vol. IV, pp. 283-6. Significantly the article was written for the Cominform journal on the 31st anniversary of the Bolshevik Revolution. See also Liu Shao-ch'i, 'On Nationalism and Internationalism', NCNA (London), Special Supplement No. 12, 28 December 1948.

5. NCNA editorial, 18 March 1949.

6. This conclusion is drawn from Gittings, *The World and China,* Chapter 8, pp. 163-99.

7. Mao Tse-tung, 'On the People's Democratic Dictatorship', 30 June 1949, *Selected Works*, Vol. IV, p. 415.

8. See Benjamin I. Schwartz, *Ideology in Flux* (Harvard University Press, 1968), Chapter 1, pp. 47-65 for an analysis of the ideological issues involved.

9. *The Common Programme and Other Documents of the First Plenary Session of The Chinese People's Political Consultative Conference* (FLP, 1950).

10. For a comprehensive analysis which also debunks the myth of China's supposed use of the overseas Chinese as a fifth column see S. Fitzgerald, *China and the Overseas Chinese* (Cambridge University Press, 1972).

11. Lin P'ei-hua (ed.), *Chung-Kuo Chin-tai Chien-shih (A Short History of Modern China)* (Peking, 1954) cited in Alastair Lamb, *Asian Frontiers* (Pall Mall Press, 1968), on which much of the discussion on border questions relies.

12. In July 1936 Mao told Edgar Snow: 'When the People's Revolution has been victorious in China, the Outer Mongolian Republic will automatically become a part of the Chinese federation, of its own will.' See Edgar Snow, *Red Star Over China* (Penguin Books (revised and enlarged edition), 1972), p. 505.

13. See Allen S. Whiting and Sheng Shih-Ts'ai, *Sinkiang, Pawn or Pivot* (Michigan State University Press, 1958).

14. Owen Lattimore, *Manchuria, Cradle of Conflict* (Macmillan, 1932).

15. See S.R. Schram, *The Political Thought of Mao Tse-tung* (Penguin Books, 1969), pp. 378-9 for the text of the published telegram.

16. See note 6.

17. Cited in R. MacFarquhar (ed.), *Sino-American Relations 1949-1971* (Praeger for the Royal Institute of International Affairs, 1972), p. 69.

18. Speech of 10 March 1958 at the Chengtu Conference in Schram, *Mao Tse-tung Unrehearsed*, pp. 101-2.

19.   Speech at the Tenth Plenum of the Eighth Central Committee, 24 September 1962, ibid.,p. 191.
20.   See *Izvestia* editorial 4 June 1964, reproduced in Gittings, *Survey*, pp. 48-9.
21.   For an analysis from the Malayan side see Anthony Short's authoritative study, *The Communist Insurrection in Malaya 1948-60* (Muller, 1975). Despite access to Malayan security files no direct evidence was found of Chinese external controls or indeed of attempts to control the Malayan Communist Party. As to be expected, however, Malayan Communists did draw inspiration from the Chinese revolutionary experience to the north.
22.   The classic study of the Chinese decision to intervene is A.S. Whiting, *China Crosses the Yalu* (Michigan University Press, 1960).
23.   For these and other relevant figures see articles in *People's China*, Vol. III, No. 7 (1 April 1951), pp. 5-7 and *People's China* No. 20 (1952) (16 October 1952), pp. 16-17, continued on pp. 33-5.
24.   See Gittings, *The World and China*, pp. 185-6 and by the same author, *The Role of the Chinese Army* (Oxford University Press, 1967), pp. 119-27.
25.   See Collection of Commemorative Articles on the 30th Anniversary of the CPC in *People's China*, Vol. IV, No. 1 (1 July 1951).
26.   Mao Tse-tung, *Selected Works*, Vol. V, p. 78.
27.   See remarks by the 'rightist' Lung Yun published in NCNA, 18 June 1957, cited in R. MacFarquhar (ed.), *The Hundred Flowers* (Praeger, 1960).
28.   'Speech at the Tenth Plenum' in Schram (ed.), *Mao Tse-tung Unrehearsed*, p. 191.
29.   Premier Chou En-lai's Political Report to the National Committee of the CPCC, 23 October 1951, Supplement to *People's China*, Vol. IV, No. 10 (16 November 1951).
30.   See Chinese reply of 30 October 1950 to Government of India, *People's China*, Vol. II, No. 11 (1 December 1950), Supplement, p. 12.
31.   See note 29.
32.   See *People's Daily* editorial 31 October 1951, 'The Just Struggle of the Peoples of Iran and Egypt'.
33.   *People's China*, 1 May 1952, p. 27.
34.   'Foreign Minister Chou En-lai's Statement on the USSR Peace Proposal', *People's China*, Vol. IV, No. 11 (17 November 1951), p. 37.
35.   'Talk at Chengtu: On the Problem of Stalin' in Schram (ed.), *Mao Tse-tung Unrehearsed*, p. 98.

3 THE INDEPENDENT EQUAL ALLY 1954-1957

This phase of the alliance was the most productive for the PRC. The self-confidence which had begun to emerge in 1952 and 1953 was to be fully expressed during these years. Externally China developed an independent and active role in world affairs while internally Mao Tse-tung fashioned a distinctively Chinese pattern of socialist development which began to diverge sharply from the Soviet model. The Sino-Soviet alliance, however, remained the cornerstone around which these independent initiatives were carried out. Thus Soviet help was critical for the successful implementation of China's First Five-Year Plan, the terminal date of which was the end of 1957, while China's new policies towards the countries of Asia and Africa were seen in this period as an *extension from*, rather than *replacement of*, the core essentials of the socialist camp and the Sino-Soviet alliance. To use Maoist terminology, the principal contradiction was still that between the camp of socialism headed by the Soviet Union and the camp of imperialism headed by the United States.

At the same time, some of the important issues in the Sino-Soviet dispute began to take shape during this period. Disagreements ranged from the more apparently ideological problems of how to handle the question of Stalin, what emphasis to give to the emergence of revisionism and whether or not class struggle continued through the socialist period to the seemingly more strategic problem of the proper way to tackle imperialism. Moreover, by the end of 1957 Mao was beginning to stress once again that the main target of American imperialism was the oppressed nations. With regard to Sino-Soviet relations, as we shall see, Mao began to identify the source of the problems in Russian great-nation chauvinism and in the Soviet tendency to emphasise their material accomplishments at the expense of revolutionary principles. At one point he relates how he had instructed Chou En-lai to give them a 'good dressing down'. Nevertheless at this stage Mao did not suggest the relationship was irreparable. On the same occasion he observed that this kind of 'wrangling' was inevitable in the international Communist movement. He compared it to differences within a single Communist party.

This was a period in which the new China assumed great-power status at the Geneva Conference in 1954 and in which it began to play a new and unprecedented diplomatic role — first, with the national governments of the newly independent countries of Asia and Africa and, second, in the international relations of the socialist camp in Eastern Europe. Moreover, China's leaders were even laying claims to the right to pronounce in public on ideological questions for the camp as a whole, including the Soviet Union, when they attempted to lay down the correct guidelines for handling the question of Stalin and the relationship between unity and diversity within the socialist camp. Nevertheless, whatever independence of judgement and policy the Chinese leadership might display, the PRC continued to be constrained by its relative weakness *vis-à-vis* the United States and the Soviet Union.

Despite the alliance tensions which developed throughout this period the basic viability of the Sino-Soviet alliance itself was not yet questioned. The Chinese subsequently traced the origins of the Sino-Soviet dispute to the Soviet Party's 20th Congress in February 1956, but this did not stop them from placing their security firmly within a system headed by the Soviet Union. Moreover, the Soviet leadership would hardly have agreed in October 1957 to provide China with a sample atomic bomb and with other aspects of nuclear technology if it had been suspected that the Chinese leaders were beginning to operate a strategy incompatible with that of their major ally. It should be noted, however, that because the transfer of the nuclear technology was to be spread over a period of years, the Soviet leaders in practice could still seek to maintain some control over the transfer. Perhaps even then they sought means of restricting China's independent capacity to pursue foreign policy lines inimical to Soviet interests. But at the time of the agreement it was by no means clear that such divergences as did exist between the two sides were no more than differences of emphasis and national priorities which could be contained within the alliance framework.

Another illustration of the closeness of the alliance at the end of this phase is that as late as March 1958 Mao still thought sufficiently highly of Khrushchev to praise him in a speech on internal affairs to a domestic inner party audience behind closed doors as a vigorous element who had come to the centre from the provinces and who was, therefore, a worthy model for Chinese provincial leaders to emulate.[1]

From a Chinese perspective the period as a whole was characterised by a relaxation of international tensions in which all international disputes could and should be settled by negotiation. But from about the summer of 1957 the Chinese leaders began to identify a significant change in the position of the United States. The United States was seen to be developing an increasingly offensive and aggressive posture towards the Afro-Asian countries, and towards China in particular. The Americans were perceived to be rapidly replacing the less dangerous British and French in the Middle East and had arrogated to themselves an interventionist role there with the announcement of the Eisenhower Doctrine of January 1957. The following month Mao and his colleagues learned of a White House decision to deploy nuclear-tipped surface-to-surface Matador missiles on Taiwan — a decision which was duly carried out in May. Nuclear weapons were also deployed in South Korea. The real turning-point was the speech by Dulles in San Francisco on 28 June 1957, when any prospects of improved Sino-American relations which had emerged after the Geneva and Bandung Conferences were rejected in words reminiscent of Dean Acheson eight years earlier:

> We can confidently assume that international communism's rule of strict conformity is, in China as elsewhere, a passing and not a perpetual phase. We owe it to ourselves, our allies and the Chinese people to do all that we can to contribute to that passing.[2]

Until then China's leaders shared Khrushchev's view of the United States, namely that 'within the US ruling circles', according to Chou En-lai, in addition to the monopolist warmongers,

> there are also some more far-sighted persons who have gradually come to realise that the use of war and the threat of war, the advocacy of going to the 'brink of war', and the continued adherence to a rigid policy of reliance on 'strength' can only isolate the United States further. Therefore, they are asking for a more sober policy based on the recognition of realities. There are also quite a few people in American industrial and commercial circles, who are dissatisfied with the US policy of embargo and demand development of normal international trade. All this is welcome.[3]

Later on the Chinese were to ridicule Russian claims to have identified 'sober' circles in the American leadership. But the Chinese could claim consistency in their argument that any softening of the American position was the result of the determination and strength of the revolutionary forces coupled with contradictions with America's allies rather than because of any change of heart in American ruling circles. Moreover, the Chinese, unlike the Russians, always claimed that the more moderate circles did not exercise control of America's foreign policy. China's leaders maintained that the decisive factor in thwarting the war-

mongers was the solidarity and preparedness of the peace forces headed
by the socialist camp. After the summer of 1956 they gradually
dropped references to such cleavages in American ruling circles and they
then ceased to take any cognisance of what Khrushchev called the
'sober-minded' groups in the American 'ruling circles'. But despite these
and other differences the Chinese and the Soviet leaders were still able
to maintain their differences within a tangible alliance framework at the
Moscow Conference of November 1957; from 1958 onwards the
Chinese became increasingly self-reliant in their defence endeavours and
Soviet aid was not largely increased for the Second Five-Year Plan. The
divisions between the two countries began to grow until the gulf became
unbridgeable.

China's New International Status

> For the first time as one of the Big Powers, the People's Republic of
> China joined the other major powers in negotiations on vital inter-
> national problems and made a contribution of its own that won the
> acclaim of wide sections of world opinion. The international status
> of the People's Republic of China as one of the big world powers has
> gained universal recognition. Its international prestige has been
> greatly enhanced. The Chinese people take the greatest joy and pride
> in the efforts and achievements of their delegation at Geneva.[4]

This was regarded by the *People's Daily* editorial as one of the more
significant outcomes of the 1954 Geneva Conference on Korea and
Indo-China. China's leaders clearly perceived China's role in global
rather than in purely regional terms. Although China's military capabilities have been of regional rather than world-wide significance, China's
foreign policy has always been cast within the wider international
setting. In this period the wider orientation found expression, for
example, in the activist role China played in the politics of Eastern
Europe in 1956.

Pride in China's new-found status, however, was not without its
problems and ambiguities. The new China did not wish to be considered
as yet another great power which followed the accepted pattern of
requiring control over adjacent territories for the sake of national
security interests. Its leaders firmly sought to reject the policies of great-
nation chauvinism or indeed great Han chauvinism. An early indication
that the new China was not going to follow even Soviet examples of
great-power behaviour was Chinese policy towards Korea after the
Geneva armistice. China's forces were progressively withdrawn until

they had all left Korea by the summer of 1958.[5] Yet US forces remained in the south and indeed from early 1957 onwards their military capability was continually reinforced. By the accepted norms of great-power behaviour as practised by the Americans or by the Russians, the Chinese would have been expected to maintain a military presence in North Korea. Hundreds of thousands of their young men (including a son of Mao himself) had died in defence of China's national security on the Korean battlefields. The Cold War and the tensions between North and South that originally had led to the outbreak of war back in 1950 were still very much in evidence. Had the Chinese remained in North Korea, even with a reduced force as a precautionary measure and as a means of exercising control over the North Korean administration, few would have questioned their right to do so. Their total withdrawal was a graphic illustration of China's leaders' intentions not to act as great-power Han chauvinists while still claiming great-power status.

At the Geneva Conference, however, where this new status had received recognition, China may be said to have acted like a great power in the more traditional sense of the term. The Chinese negotiators had been instrumental in persuading their smaller and relatively dependent neighbours, the Vietminh, to withdraw from their area of effective control near the 20th Parallel back north to the 17th so as to make the agreement possible. It should be noted, though, that at the time this was thought to be a prelude to the reunification of Vietnam through elections two years later, which even President Eisenhower was convinced that the Communists would win handsomely. It would be less than fair on the basis of this example alone to regard China as just another great power prepared to impose its will on its weaker neighbours for its own purposes. The Chinese leaders in this period were concerned to take advantage of and perhaps promote still further the easing of international tensions which they had detected soon after the end of the Korean War.

Thus, following the Indo-Chinese agreements Chairman Mao congratulated President Ho Chi Minh of the Democratic Republic of Vietnam, noting *inter alia* that they 'will help promote collective peace and security in Asia and further relax international tension'. Mao's hopes were not based, as might have been expected, on the conclusion that the Western powers, having been humiliated on the battlefields, were henceforth bound to be on the retreat in Asia. His hopes were based rather on the contradictions which had been detected between the Western countries. Britain and France had shown in Geneva that they had no wish to see the United States involved in adventurist actions in

Asia. Two other reasons were advanced in the *People's Daily* editorial on the conference: first, the attitudes of the parties to the Geneva Conference were said to show that there was growing international support for the concept that 'countries with different social and political systems in Asia and the rest of the world can coexist peacefully, that any international dispute can be settled by negotiation, and world peace can thus be assured'; and, second, that the American 'policy of strength' had suffered 'another ignominious setback'.

China's interest in the prospects of a period of international calm was because of the need to concentrate upon the development of the economy in accordance with the First Five-Year Plan (which, incidentally, was not published until 1955). Thus Premier Chou En-lai addressed a meeting on the PRC's Fifth Anniversary (1 October 1954) attended by Soviet and other Eastern European leaders, saying:

> We need a peaceful international environment in order to build our country. The aim of our constructive efforts is to raise the living standards of the people and strengthen our national security. This determines the fact that the only objective which our country can have in all its activities in international affairs is the preservation of world peace. It can have no other policy. We firmly believe that countries with different social systems can coexist peacefully, and that all international disputes can be settled peacefully.[6]

Alone of the great powers, China belonged to the Afro-Asian world of newly independent countries. It was within that context that China had played the key role in formulating a new set of principles for international diplomacy – the Five Principles of Peaceful Coexistence. Thus in his speech Chou went on to draw the attention of fellow socialist camp members to China's special regard for the 'efforts in the cause of peace of such principal Southeast Asian nations as India, Indonesia and Burma'. Chou drew attention to the importance of the Five Principles of Peaceful Coexistence (a concept which as we shall see owed nothing to the Soviet Union) and said that these 'should be the basic principles guiding relations between nations' (presumably including the whole world and, therefore, the Soviet Union too).

Chou then stated: 'We are, of course, also willing to coexist peacefully along with the United States.' But he immediately excluded the question of Taiwan: 'Up to the present the United States is still occupying our territory, Taiwan. They are attempting to prevent the Chinese people from liberating it, and using the traitorous Chiang Kai-shek clique to threaten our country with war.'[7]

Chinese publications spelt out why Taiwan was a special and a pressing problem. Not only was it a question of China's unity being incomplete, but American military harassment of the mainland was noted and particular attention was drawn to the military activities of Chiang Kai-shek's forces supported by the United States. One article counted 41 different raids between 1950 and August 1954, employing in all some 28,000 men. Chiang's air force from July 1950 to September 1954 flew 977 bombing, strafing and reconnaissance missions in 1,427 sorties over the coastal areas of the mainland, including even Shanghai. More than 470 PRC vessels were seized at sea. This excluded the incessant flow of secret agents. Meanwhile the Americans were seen as being engaged in feverish activities to include Taiwan in the system of bases extending round China's maritime periphery so as to set up a North-East Asian Treaty Organization to be linked with SEATO. The article concluded that this did not provide the necessary environment in which the Chinese people could carry on their peaceful construction.[8]

This provided the overt rationale for the so-called 'first offshore islands crisis'. The PRC liberated the Ta Chen islands off the Chekiang Province coast which had menaced Shanghai, but not Amoy or Matsu off Fukien. Interestingly, the capture of the islands was effected without a military struggle. Following a Chinese military build-up and a propaganda campaign, the Americans and the KMT forces concluded that it was best to vacate the Ta Chens. The remaining offshore islands were critical for the KMT as they were adjuncts of the mainland and part of Fukien Province. They symbolised the continuing link between the KMT on the island of Taiwan and the Chinese mainland which they were pledged to conquer. Obviously it could be argued that Peking shared a similar perspective but in reverse: KMT possession of these islands showed that Taiwan was still part of China and that would be a real obstacle to any attempt to detach Taiwan from China.[9]

In December 1954 the Americans duly signed the Defence Treaty with Chiang Kai-shek, but the so-called North-East Asian Treaty Organization long mooted in American circles (and a subject of understandable concern to the Chinese[10]) did not materialise. It seems that the PRC-engineered crisis thwarted the plan. In March 1955 President Eisenhower let it be known that US forces would have tactical nuclear weapons at their disposal in the Formosa Straits. Meanwhile Taiwan and the offshore islands were reinforced, so that by the middle of 1955 the Chinese felt the need to improve their own defence preparedness and increased their military spending. Although the four-power (USA,

USSR, UK and France) summit conference in Geneva of 18-23 July was deemed by Chou En-lai on 30 July to have resulted in 'a definite degree of relaxation' in international tension, he was still anxious that China was vulnerable to a surprise attack because of the tight American military cordon around China. He concluded therefore:

> Under these circumstances, we must preserve our vigilance, we must strengthen our country's necessary defence forces. Only in this way can we protect the fruits of our socialist construction, guarantee the integrity and security of our nation's sovereignty and territory, and moreover be of service to enterprises safeguarding world peace.[11]

By the beginning of 1956 Mao and Chou En-lai took a more relaxed attitude towards the United States and were more confident of China's ability to defeat armed intervention from any quarter. It should be noted too that by this stage, following the initiative of Chou En-lai at Bandung in 1955, Sino-American ambassadorial talks had begun to take place in Geneva. Moreover, Mao had referred in January to the reduction of American forces by 100,000.

China's interest in attempting to reunify the country was reflected in Sino-Soviet relations too. During the 1954 Khrushchev and Bulganin visit Mao raised the question of Soviet dominance of the Mongolian People's Republic. Ten years later he related:

> In accordance with the Yalta Agreement, the Soviet Union, under the pretext of assuring the independence of Mongolia, actually placed the country under its domination. Mongolia takes up an area which is considerably greater than the Kuriles. In 1954, when Khrushchev and Bulganin came to China, we took up this question but they refused to talk to us.[12]

A *Pravda* editorial later commented:

> They [the Chinese] would like to deprive the Mongolian People's Republic of independence and make it a Chinese province. It was precisely on this point the People's Republic of China's leaders proposed the 'reaching of agreement' to N.S. Khrushchev, who naturally refused to discuss this question and told the Chinese leaders that the destiny of the Mongolian people was determined not in Peking and not in Moscow but in Ulan Bator, that the question of Mongolia's statehood could be settled only by the country's working

people themselves and by nobody else.[13]

Regardless as to whichever version is correct it is clear that Mao had raised the question of the status of Mongolia and that Khrushchev and Bulganin had refused to discuss it. In his memoirs Khrushchev recalled that Chou En-lai had sounded him out as to the likely Soviet attitude if Mongolia were to be part of the Chinese state. Khrushchev remembered replying as follows:

> Our attitude would depend on the attitude of the Mongolian com-
> rades, but I can give you my personal opinion: I very much doubt
> that the Mongolians will welcome your suggestion. Besides, Mongolia
> is about to become a member of the United Nations and has recently
> established diplomatic relations with a number of states. The Mon-
> golians would lose that recognition if they were absorbed into China.
> However, I certainly don't want to speak for the Mongolian
> leaders.[14]

Back in 1936 Mao had told Edgar Snow that Mongolia would seek to be incorporated into the new China which would eventually emerge. Perhaps Mao felt that China's new-found international status and the recognition of the PRC's equality and full independence accorded by the Soviet leaders provided the right opportunity to ease Moscow out of its dominance of Mongolia preparatory to linking it with the PRC.

Thus the primary obstacles to the full reunification of China were Russia in the north and America in the east. With regard to Taiwan, Peking established early on the principles which were to guide its policy: in the discussions with the Americans Chou En-lai distinguished between an American military withdrawal from the island (which was negotiable) and the method by which Taiwan might be liberated (which was not). To the end the Chinese side refused to publicly commit themselves to peaceful liberation (although they considered it was possible and indeed attempts were to be made later in this period to do so) since that would be an unequivocal public recognition that China's sovereign claims were limited. China's position was eventually to be vindicated by the Shanghai Communiqué of February 1972, agreed by President Nixon and Premier Chou En-lai. The question of Mongolia was more compli-cated since the Chinese had already recognised its independence and exchanged mutual recognition. Moreover, in 1952 the Mongolian leader Tsedenbal paid an official visit to Peking and trade agreements were signed. Later in 1960 a border agreement was also made. The only basis on which Mongolia could be incorporated within the PRC would be as a result of a voluntary request. For this to take place Soviet predominant influence would have to be removed from the country. Mongolian suspicion of Chinese eventual aims has ensured that the country has never wavered in its adhesion to Moscow.

However great its international status as a power had become, China still clearly lacked the final necessary power to challenge either superpower when the latter was determined not to give way. Among the reasons for the priority given to domestic economic construction by China's leaders was that once the PRC was to acquire sufficient economic and military strength China would be free of the external pressure upon it and its demands would be met. Thus in December 1955 Mao argued: 'We should take advantage of the truce to speed up the tempo and accomplish the overall task . . . If we can fulfil the overall task during the transition period ahead of schedule, taking care of the battlefield should be easy.'[15]

In May 1958 Mao put it even more clearly:

Though we have a large population, we have not yet demonstrated our strength. One day when we catch up with Great Britain and the US, Dulles will respect us and acknowledge our existence as a nation. Our policy is that we will not invite him as a guest, but if he should knock on our door, we would entertain him.[16]

But one area where China's new-found status was directly reflected in a changed pattern of international relationships was the socialist camp. Doubtless the extent of the change was exaggerated by the weakness and division of the Soviet leadership until Khrushchev's consolidation of his power in the summer of 1957. Had the succession to Stalin been smoother the increase of Chinese influence would have been commensurably smaller. In the event, however, Sino-Soviet relations became almost as between equals.

The relative equality of Sino-Soviet relations within the socialist camp after Stalin's death was demonstrated by the fact that the new Soviet leaders, Khrushchev and Bulganin, visited Peking for the PRC's Fifth Anniversary celebrations on 1 October 1954 and then proceeded to give up all the remaining special privileges in China claimed by the Soviet Union. Thus Soviet rights to partial control of the Chinese Eastern Railway and to exclusive use of the naval facilities in Port Arthur and Dairen were all returned to Chinese hands, as were the 50 per cent Soviet shares in the four joint-stock companies. Henceforth

Sino-Soviet relations were not to be marked by such vestiges from a by-gone colonial era. Moreover, Soviet economic aid (all of which had to be paid for) was dramatically increased. The Soviet Union was now to equip China with 141 heavy industrial plants. In 1956 the figure was increased to 156. At the anniversary meeting Khrushchev went on to cede all the points regarding Chinese claims for the particular distinctions within the framework of Marxism-Leninism which Stalin had striven so hard to deny. Thus he conceded that China's revolution was a model for the peoples of the colonial and dependent countries and that China's special form of government, 'the people's democratic dictatorship', was a creative application of doctrine. Khrushchev also endorsed China's great-power claims, ' . . . today it is impossible, without the participation of the PRC, to solve international problems, ease international tensions or find a peaceful solution of disputed questions.'[17]

It is true that Khrushchev did not consult his Chinese comrades before his 'de-Stalinisation' speech and his revision of Leninist orthodoxies on war and revolution at the 20th Party Congress in February 1956. But the Chinese leaders in turn responded by presenting their own ideological appreciation of the Stalin question. It should be noted that the Chinese analysis was not directed towards only Chinese realities, but it was cast on a universal plane and it sought to provide answers relevant to the entire Communist movement.[18] The implication clearly was that if the Russians could seek to lay down the line on a matter which affected all members of the socialist camp — and what is more, do it badly — then the Chinese could do so too, but do it well. Before a year passed China's leaders were to make an independent impact on the politics of the East European camp members, even with regard to their relations with the Soviet Union. Despite the great disparities in power and in terms of their relative accessibility to the region, the Soviet leaders did not challenge the right of their Chinese colleagues to act in this way. Indeed there are signs that they may have encouraged such an intervention, despite the evident unease of having to rely upon the Chinese to bolster their position.[19]

It is important to note that however pleased China's leaders were with China's new-found recognition as a great power in its own right, Mao continually warned against becoming imbued with great-nation chauvinism. As we shall see, this was one of the many flaws which he detected in Soviet behaviour. Thus in a speech on the draft of the Constitution on 14 June 1954, Mao discussed the objective of building China into a modernised great socialist country. He went on to note that as China could not produce a single motor car, plane, tank, or tractor there was no room for bragging or being cocky. He continued:

> Of course I don't mean we can become cocky when we turn out our
> first car, more cocky when we make ten cars, and still more cocky
> when we make more and more cars. That won't do. Even after fifty
> years, when our country is in good shape, we should remain as
> modest as we are now. If by then we should become conceited and
> look down on others it would be bad. We must not be conceited even
> a hundred years from now. We must never be cocky.

Two years later Mao returned to this theme when he urged modesty upon the Chinese people: 'In international relations, the Chinese people should rid themselves of great nation chauvinism resolutely, thoroughly, wholly and completely.'[20]

Interestingly, the only aspect of China's foreign policy which Chou En-lai later came to regret was indeed an aspect of its great-power be-haviour at the Geneva Conference. Thus he told Harrison Salisbury of the *New York Times* in June 1972 that 'never again' would he 'put pressure' on Hanoi to accept an international settlement of the war patterned on the model of the ill-fated Geneva Conference of 1954. 'He felt himself personally responsible for urging the Vietnamese to go along with the agreement. He would not be party to any similar effort in the future.'[21]

The Bandung Phase

China's policies towards the newly independent countries of Asia had already begun to change in 1951, but it was not until 1954-5 that this dimension of China's foreign policy became fully developed. It culmin-ated in the Afro-Asian Conference of 29 countries at Bandung, Indo-nesia, in 1955.[22] This conference has since symbolised an important current of Chinese foreign policy which was marked by a readiness to resolve any differences by negotiations at the governmental level with all countries (including the US) in the moderate reasoned tone of diplo-matic language and by a willingness to recognise a commonality of purpose and interest between socialist China and the national bourgeois governments of Afro-Asian countries. The Bandung Phase was also one in which China's common identity with former colonial countries was developed totally independently of the Soviet Union. At the time the Chinese leaders described the Afro-Asian aspect of their foreign policy as an addition to the 'camp of peace and democracy' and therefore as an adjunct to the socialist camp. But as the Sino-Soviet dispute unfolded, the Chinese leadership began to attach increasing importance to Afro-Asia as the primary centre of the anti-imperialist struggle and as the part of the world with which the Chinese were to identify most.

On 23 April 1954, India and China concluded an agreement on trade and intercourse between the Tibet region of China and India which gave rise to the famous 'Five Principles of Peaceful Coexistence'.* At Geneva the Chinese delegation reached an agreement with their British counterparts to establish a Chinese Chargé d'Affaires in London. On his return from Geneva towards the end of July 1954, Chou En-lai stopped over in India and Burma where the 'Five Principles' were reaffirmed and their relevance was extended beyond Asia to the world as a whole. Meanwhile trade was beginning to expand with the West European countries, including West Germany.[23] Thus the essential characteristics of the Bandung diplomacy had been established before 1955, but nevertheless the Bandung Conference marked an important landmark. The Afro-Asian countries were establishing for the first time their common collective ideals and objectives in the post-war world and China was to play an important part in this new dimension of international politics.

Chou En-lai's posture towards the other 28 countries was most conciliatory; in addition to stressing the primacy of the two points which China shared with them all (i.e. a common history of colonial dominance and a desire to consolidate further the hard-won independence by economic construction), Chou went out of his way to try to resolve the outstanding differences. Thus in his prepared speech he singled out two countries which were linked by military alliance with the United States to make the point: 'There is no reason why the relations between China and Thailand, The Philippines and other neighbouring countries cannot be improved on the basis of these five principles.'[24] Moreover, it was at the conference that Chou was able to establish understandings with several such countries — notably Pakistan — and was assured that their part in the military alliances was not trained against China. In a supplementary speech Chou sought to reassure his listeners that they had nothing to fear regarding the nature of China's political system. He ad-

---

*These were: (1) mutual respect for each other's territorial integrity and sovereignty; (2) non-aggression; (3) non-interference in each other's internal affairs; (4) equality and mutual benefit; (5) peaceful coexistence. These may be compared with Mao's three principles laid down in his 'On the People's Democratic Dictatorship' and in the 1949 Common Programme: 'Equality, mutual benefit and mutual respect for each other's territorial integrity'.

mitted to being an atheist but he denied that religion in China was being suppressed. He also denied that China engaged in subversive activities. Chou pointed out that China's revolution was indigenous and hard won. It was not imported and China had no wish to export it to others. He pleaded: 'We are against outside interference: how could we want to interfere in the internal affairs of others?' Chou showed that the new China had no desire to take advantage of the dual nationality principle with regard to the overseas Chinese. It was the Kuomintang who exploited this issue, not the PRC. Chou likewise rejected the argument that by setting up a Chuang (people of the same ethnic identity as the Thais) autonomous region China was threatening others. There were good domestic reasons for recognising the special position of national minorities in China. Chou referred delegates to the example of Sino-Burmese relations where, despite the existence of minorities on both sides of the border and despite the disruptive activities of the Kuomintang remnant armed forces on the borders, friendship was flourishing. Chou countered the subversion charge against China by showing that if any country was a target for subversion it was China; the US was still trying to subvert the Chinese government in many ways.[25]

Nevertheless there were special problems which applied to China's relations with her neighbours in south-east Asia which even Chou En-lai's diplomatic skills could not surmount. Clearly it was not just a question of China's attitudes. Very few of the governments of the area could have been regarded as presiding over stable political systems. If from China's point of view the primary interests were those of national security and if these were not threatened there was no reason why 'problems left over from history' could not be solved, the perspectives of the more fragile governments in much of south-east Asia were different. Four particular sets of problems may be identified (not necessarily in order of importance):

(1) Most of them faced insurgencies of one kind or another which drew inspiration from the PRC. In its declaratory statements the PRC has always offered support to those led by indigenous Communist parties. After all the only revolutionary armed struggles taking place in the world under the leadership of Communist parties were in this area. Clearly it was always open to the Chinese Communists to transform their symbolic and limited practical aid into something more substantial. From the point of view of the neutralist Burmese government, it was obviously important that the PRC's active

support for the Burmese Communist Party (White Flag) armed struggle had been negligible. The PRC had not seriously intervened in Burma despite the fact that the White Flag had modelled its activities upon the Chinese revolutionary experience, nor had the PRC been provoked by the presence of Kuomintang forces in North Burma, which by 1953 had reached the figure of 13,000 soldiers before half of them were repatriated to Taiwan.[26] Yet the calculations of the Burmese government were inevitably affected by the capacity of their giant neighbour to apply considerable pressure at any time of its choosing. From the point of view of most of China's south-east Asian neighbours the significant point was simply that the PRC leaders openly endorsed movements subversive of the local governments. The distinction which the Chinese drew between state relations (determined by the 'Five Principles of Coexistence') and party relations (determined by the principles of proletarian internationalism) was of greater significance to the Chinese themselves. Most of these governments were more conscious of the identity between Chinese party and state leaders, who after all were 'dangerous' Communists.

(2) The presence of overseas Chinese throughout south-east Asia was a complicating factor of considerable importance. They were frequently regarded as potential fifth columnists, giving China points of access to the countries concerned. Many of the overseas Chinese not only took pride in China's new-found international status but many also had various links with the PRC. Their fundamental loyalty was often in doubt. Moreover domestic inter-racial tensions between these Chinese and the local populations provided China with a potential interest in seeing that the overseas Chinese (especially those who held Chinese nationality) should not be persecuted or maltreated.[27] The fact that the local fears of the overseas Chinese as potential fifth columnists belonged to the realm of myth alone did not alter the reality of those fears.

(3) A similar mythical fear which was none the less real arose out of the historical fact that at times in the distant past many of the countries in the area had paid tribute to the Chinese Celestial Court. They were concerned lest the new vigorous and united China should seek to reassert some claims for dominance or suzerainty. China was a major local power and now that the two- or three-century interlude of European imperial presence was declining rapidly, there was the

possibility that traditional patterns might re-emerge under the cover of new guises.

(4) Last but not least, the American presence in the area since the Second World War had come to be that of the dominant external power. Its anti-Communism posture was locally focused upon hostility to the PRC. All the local governments therefore had to take a position regarding American blandishments. The residual colonial interests of the West Europeans had not disappeared. For example, the British were still important for the security arrangements of Malaya (Malaysia) and Singapore. But ultimately it was the American presence which was the one that counted. Potentially, the American dimension provided a linchpin around which the previously listed three points could be linked in an anti-PRC alliance. At the same time the local governments were also stirred by anti-colonialist and anti-imperialist themes. Apart from the American dependencies of South Vietnam and Taiwan, the local governments had little to gain from being so identified with the American position as to gain the total enmity of the PRC. Thus they had reason to join with non-aligned countries like India in seeking a reduction in Sino-American tensions.

Four days after his arrival and following intensive lobbying by fellow delegates, Chou En-lai on 23 April 1955 made a statement on the relaxation of tension in the Far East which showed that the Chinese posture was more than just a rhetorical one:

> The Chinese people are friendly to the American people. The Chinese people do not want to have a war with the USA. The Chinese Government is willing to sit down and enter into negotiations with the United States Government to discuss the question of relaxing tension in the Far East, and especially the question of relaxing tension in the Taiwan area.[28]

Chou's moderate stand was only reluctantly reciprocated by the United States. His statement eventually led to ambassadorial meetings in Geneva between the two countries. As the historian of these talks, who was also a former American Ambassador and a chief representative at them, has made clear, the principal reason for the failure of the negotiations to make much headway in the 1950s may be located in the obstructive attitude of the American administration.[29] But with regard to the newly independent countries of Asia and Africa, China's new stand in Bandung paved the way for extending China's relations to a much wider range than hitherto. Egypt in particular became the diplomatic centre from which the Chinese established contacts not only in the Middle East, but also with the newly emerging independence movements in Africa.[30]

This phase of China's foreign policy was reflected also in relations with Western Europe and the socialist bloc. It even led to a new appraisal of the United States. First, Chinese experience at Geneva confirmed their leaders in the belief that contradictions existed between the United States and its European allies. The British were seen to have been a restraining influence on the Americans. It was with the Conservative Eden that Chou negotiated the establishment of the office of Chargé d'Affaires in London, but it was the Labour Party leadership that visited China later in 1954.[31] The Chinese were also gratified by the emergence of the Mendès-France government during the Geneva Conference. The hard-line Bidault government had been replaced because of popular discontent with the French prosecution of the Indo-China War: Chinese analysts concluded that the popular reaction meant that the governments of America's allies were being pushed away from close involvement in America's 'policy of strength'. Hence the American administration was becoming more isolated.[32]

The mode of analysis and the perspective on international affairs shown by the Chinese at this juncture demonstrated a remarkable similarity to those Soviet concepts of united front tactics in Europe in which the moderate reformist left is seen as playing a positive international role. In later years the Chinese were to move away from such concepts. A further illustration of the proximity of Chinese and Soviet modes of analysis was shown by the way the Chinese identified a division in American 'ruling circles'. The Political Report of the CPC Eighth Congress of 27 September 1956 which analysed the various pressures operating on American imperialism which limited its capacity for offensive actions identified as the main danger 'the aggressive cliques in the United States which persist in the policy of arms expansion and war preparations'. Although the Report noted that 'the danger of war still exists' it asserted that 'the world situation is tending towards a relaxation of tension, and a possibility of *lasting* world peace has now begun t materialize' (emphasis added).[33] Chou En-lai in an official report to the National People's Congress on 28 June 1956 observed, 'even within the United States ruling circles, some people who are more sober-minded are beginning to realize that there is no future for the policy of cold war and the policy of strength.' He went on to describe an ongoing debate between them and those other persons still 'in a powerful position, particularly those who actually handle foreign policy who are still obstructing this change'.[34] Where the Chinese analysis came to differ from that advocated by Khrushchev was that in the Chinese view any pacific intentions of certain groups in the American leadership were not the result of enlightenment about the dangers of nuclear war, but that in fact this was the result of countervailing pressure by the socialist camp, the newly independent countries and the contradictions within the imperialist camp. Thus the passage of Chou's Report cited above concluded that this 'internal debate showed the United States ruling circles are in an acute dilemma in which both peace and war are difficult alternatives'.

The Socialist Camp

The Sino-Soviet alliance continued to provide the essential framework within which China's national security could be safeguarded. Soviet economic help was still vital in the establishment of big plants for China's heavy industry. The Chinese armed forces were significantly modernised with Soviet aid, but Soviet protection did not extend to giving Peking full unqualified support for its position on Taiwan. Moreover, other signs of suspicion and tension in the Sino-Soviet relationship were shown by Khrushchev's informing West European leaders like Adenauer and Macmillan in 1955 about his long-term fears regarding China.[35] Moreover, Harrison Salisbury in Moscow on 'one sultry night in the summer of 1954' witnessed the following interchange between Chou En-lai and Soviet leaders after Chou had offered a toast in English to Mikoyan:

> Mikoyan said through an interpreter, 'Why don't you speak in Russian, Chou — you know our language perfectly well.'
> Chou rejoined saucily: 'Look here Mikoyan, it's time you learned to speak Chinese. After all, I have learned to speak Russian.'
> Chou's remarks had to be interpreted into Russian for Mikoyan, who sulkily grumbled: 'Chinese is a difficult language to learn.'
> 'No harder than Russian', Chou snapped back. 'Come down to our Embassy in the morning. We'll be glad to teach you Chinese.'
> Kaganovich then intervened with a rude remark in Russian, but Chou, continuing to speak in English, said: 'There's no excuse for you people.'[36]

Nevertheless, throughout this period (until perhaps from the summer of 1957 onwards) the Chinese and Russian leaderships, in public at any rate, shared a common view on the question of how to treat the United States, its allies and the newly independent countries of Asia and Africa. Even after the Soviet 20th Party Congress in February 1956 and the Polish and Hungarian uprisings, Mao addressed the All-China Federation of Industry and Commerce as follows:

> Do you think that socialism will succeed? Do you have doubts about its success? Do you fear that the socialist camp will collapse? In my opinion, even if it should collapse, there will be no big danger. But I don't think it will collapse, not at all. The principal components of the socialist camp are the Soviet Union and China. China and the Soviet Union stand together. This is a right policy. But there are still people who have doubts about this policy. They say, 'Don't stand together.' They think that China should take a middle course and be a bridge between the Soviet Union and the US. This is the Yugoslav way, a way to get money from both sides. Is this a good way? I don't think it is good at all for it does no good to the nation. For on one side is powerful imperialism under whose oppression China has been for a long time. If China stands between the Soviet Union and the US, she appears to be in a favourable position and to be independent, but actually she is not. The US is not dependable. She would give you something but not much. How could we expect imperialism to give us a full meal? It won't . . . Just today I received a Brazilian representative. Brazil is a large country with a population of 60 million and an area as large as China's. It has been under the oppression of US imperialism all these years. Illusions of securing a bridge between the Soviet Union and the US and Britain for profit — this kind of thinking is wrong. We do not know how to design a big plant. Who would design large plants for us — such as chemical industry, steel industry, petroleum industry, tanks, airplanes and manufacture of automobiles?

Mao went on to argue that Britain and the US were only now helping India's heavy industry because the Russians did so. He concluded:

> Imperialism wants to keep its technology secret. No imperialism has ever designed anything for us* . . . When we lean to one side, we are

---

*Interestingly, in February 1964 (as we shall see later) Mao complained that Soviet products were 'heavy, crude, high-priced, and they always keep something back'. That is, they kept their technology secret. Mao concluded that it was better to deal with the French bourgeoisie, 'who still have some notion of business ethics'.

with the Soviet Union and on an equal footing with her. We won't encounter problems such as those Poland and Hungary have faced. We are followers of Marxism but we do not blindly copy Soviet experience.[37]

Indeed even before the Soviet Congress Mao had indicated in speeches to the Political Bureau that a new spirit of independence was required in those matters on which the Chinese had hitherto relied absolutely upon the Soviet Union. China's agricultural policies had always followed an independent path and during collectivisation many lessons from Soviet failures had been drawn. It is also true that the socialisation of China's remaining industries and handicrafts in 1956 did not follow Soviet patterns either. But planning and many aspects of economic life were modelled directly upon the Soviet experience. Thus in December 1955 Mao compared China favourably with the Soviet Union.

> Our country as compared with the Soviet Union: 1) Ours has been evolved from over twenty years of experience in the base areas and three revolutionary wars . . . Before victory we already had experience in every field. After casting about several times we quickly founded the nation and accomplished our revolutionary task. (The Soviet Union was a newly developed country; it went through the October Revolution and had neither army nor government, and party members were few.) 2) We have the assistance of the Soviet Union and other democratic nations. 3) Our population is large and our position is favourable . . . *Chinese peasants are even better than the workers of Britain and America.* Hence, they can achieve greater, better and faster results in reaching socialism. We should not always compare ourselves with the Soviet Union. By being able to produce 24 million tons of steel after three Five Year Plans, *we will be faster than the Soviet Union.*[38]

Three months earlier Mao had said: 'It will probably be in about fifty to seventy years, or roughly between the 10th and the 15th Five Year Plans, that *we shall succeed in our efforts to catch up or overtake the United States.*' (Emphasis added to both extracts to show the extent of Mao's ambition.) In an earlier part of this speech Mao provided the rationale for linking China's international and domestic concerns:

> We should take advantage of the time to speed up the tempo and accomplish the overall task . . . If we can fulfil the overall task during

the transition period ahead of schedule, taking care of the battlefield
should be easy. If fighting is to resume, we will be in a better
position to fight . . . [39]

These quotations from Mao Tse-tung's unofficial speeches and
writings show that not only was he exhorting his colleagues to chart an
independent course but he was encouraging them to look ahead to a
time when China could occupy the first place in all the main fields of
human endeavour. Thus in January 1956 Mao told the Politbureau:

Our country's territory is extensive, the population is large, the
position too is not bad and the coastline is very long (even if we do
not have steamships); our country ought to develop so that it would
become first in the world in terms of culture, science, technology
and industry.[40]

Even Mao's celebrated remark that China's poverty and 'blankness'
were advantageous was made before the Khrushchev changes of line at
the 20th Congress. A public version of this was first released during the
early stages of the Great Leap Forward in 1958, when it was widely
regarded as being a major departure from the spirit of Soviet Marxism
and as a factor in the Sino-Soviet split. Yet it was introduced by Mao
during a period in which the Sino-Soviet alliance was very much alive.
Thus in the speech just quoted Mao declared:

China has an advantage: first it is poor, and second it is 'blank' —
lacking knowledge — but it is good like this sheet of white paper.
This side had been written on and so one can't write any more fine
words on it. After several decades, then we shall be able to overtake
other countries.

These extensive quotations show that well before the storms broke
over the Soviet 20th Party Congress and over the uprisings in Poland
and Hungary later in 1956, Mao had already embarked upon a Chinese
route to development and he was charting China's course in international affairs with greater confidence and independence than in the
early days of the Sino-Soviet alliance.

How then did the events of 1956, which shook the socialist camp,
affect the Chinese position? In later years the Chinese side were to trace
the origins of the Sino-Soviet dispute to the 20th Congress of February
1956, and especially to the modification of Lenin's stands on the inevit-

ability of war, the possibility of a peaceful transition from capitalism to socialism and that the essential conflict between the imperialist and socialist forces would be based henceforth on peaceful competition. These were later dubbed the 'three peaces' (peaceful coexistence, peaceful transition and peaceful competition), and indeed there was a certain logical link between them. Once it is maintained that mutual nuclear deterrence can prevent global war and that steps should be taken to minimise the risk, then a high premium is necessarily placed upon avoiding armed revolutionary conflicts. It could also be argued that as the result of a deterrence situation with the greatest imperial power it, too, could be prevented from intervening in civil wars or aiding the reactionary side. In either case the door is opened to peaceful transition. The link which the Chinese were later to identify was the turn away from revolution to revisionism and reformism. There is some public contemporary evidence to show that at the time the Chinese disliked these modifications of Leninist doctrine.[41]

With the publication of Volume V of the *Selected Works of Mao Tsetung* in 1977, more evidence has come to light of Mao's contemporary observations in 1956 and 1957. Thus in his speech at the Second Session of the Eighth Central Committee of 15 November 1956 Mao commented on the 20th Congress of the CPSU as follows:

I think there are two 'swords'; one is Lenin and the other is Stalin. The sword of Stalin has now been discarded by the Russians . . . This sword has not been lent out, it has been thrown out. We Chinese have not thrown it away. First we protect Stalin, and second, we at the same time criticize his mistakes . . .

As for the sword of Lenin, hasn't it too been discarded to a certain extent by some Soviet leaders? In my view, it has been discarded to a considerable extent. Is the October Revolution still valid? Can it still serve as an example for all countries? Khrushchev's report at the 20th Congress of the CPSU says it is possible to seize state power by the parliamentary road, that is to say, it is no longer necessary for all countries to learn from the October Revolution. Once this gate is opened, by and large Leninism is thrown away.[42]

. . . During the October Revolution, the masses in the cities and the villages were fully mobilized to wage class struggle. Those who are now sent by the Soviet Union as experts to various countries were but children or teenagers at the time of the October Revolution, and many of them have forgotten about this practice. Comrades in some countries say that China's mass line is not right, and they are

only too happy to pick up the paternalistic approach. There is no
stopping them if they want to do so; in any case, we adhere to the
Five Principles of Peaceful Coexistence, with non-interference in
each other's internal affairs and mutual non-aggression. We have no
intention of exercising leadership over any country save our own,
that is the People's Republic of China.[43]

This shows that not only were the criticisms of the Soviet line on
peaceful transition being aired behind the scenes in Peking, but the
paternalistic attitude of the CPSU towards other parties was also
singled out for attack. Both themes were to become prominent in the
Chinese public critique of the CPSU in the early 1960s. At the time,
however, China's main public preoccupation was with the Stalin
question and then the Polish and Hungarian affairs rather than with the
questions of Lenin and of peaceful transition. Indeed, as Mao told his
Central Committee in the aforementioned speech in late 1956: 'We
don't approve of some of the things done in the Soviet Union, and the
Central Committee has already said this to the Soviet leaders several
times: some questions which were not touched upon will be taken up
later.'
  The Chinese reaction to Khrushchev's ill-considered denunciation of
Stalin (which Mao described as his assassination by bullet) was to
publish a careful, theoretically polished analysis of the Stalin question
which appraised him positively as a Marxist-Leninist revolutionary
whose proletarian merits outweighed his errors by the order of 70:30.[44]
The implications for China had been wide-ranging and not the least of
them was the impact of the attack upon the cult of personality on
Mao's position in the political system. The Chinese ideological response
was highly significant from our perspective. The Chinese Political
Bureau in effect had challenged the traditionally accepted orthodoxy
that Moscow alone had the right to define the universal theoretical and
practical bases for action for all members of the socialist camp and the
international Communist movement. China's special contribution
henceforth was no longer to be significant only to its own region or to
Asia, but it was to be universal in nature. A reconsidered view was
issued later in the year following the Polish and Hungarian uprisings
which sought to give an authoritative final analysis of the intra-bloc
problems of 1956 and which *inter alia* also introduced the concept of
there being contradictions between the government and the people in
socialist countries.[45] The Soviet leaders have always rejected this.
  In 1956 the Chinese leaders, seeking greater independence within the

socialist camp themselves, supported others who struggled for the same purpose. It bothered the Chinese little that in Poland the move away from the Stalin pattern led to the decollectivisation of agriculture. Thus at the CPC Eighth Congress in September, Mao is said to have urged Ochab (then First Secretary of the Polish United Workers' Party) to 'follow absolutely the search for an autonomous internal policy and develop their own social system as Yugoslavia had done'.[46] In his speech to the Congress Ochab spoke of the 'intimate feelings' which existed between Poland and China. The chief Soviet delegate to the Congress, Mikoyan, felt snubbed in Peking and he therefore left Peking hurriedly before the end of the Congress.[47] The Chinese later claimed that they had advised the Russian leaders not to intervene in Poland when Khrushchev had intended to do so and that they had prodded the Russians to send back their armed forces into Hungary when they were reluctant to do so.

Evidence is lacking as to the correctness of these claims, but contemporary accounts point to the consistency of the Chinese position that the essential difference between Poland and Hungary was that the latter sought to withdraw from the Warsaw Pact. Thus on 1 November 1956 an official Chinese statement on the Soviet statement of two days earlier referred to 'recent happenings in Poland and Hungary' as examples of 'misunderstandings and estrangements' in inter-camp relations (in other words, the Soviet Union was not without blame). On receiving news of the declaration of neutrality by the Nagy government the Chinese statement was issued with the word 'Hungary' deleted.[48] A *People's Daily* editorial of 4 November confirmed that the announced withdrawal from the Warsaw Treaty was the critical difference between Poland and Hungary. Privately, however, Mao's assessment of Poland hardened as well. Thus in his speech of 15 November 1956 cited previously, after saying 'the sword of Stalin has now been discarded by the Russians', Mao went on to observe: 'Gomulka and some people in Hungary have picked it up to stab at the Soviet Union and oppose so-called Stalinism.'

At the same time the *public* Chinese attitude towards Yugoslavia changed. Instead of being considered as sharing with China the struggle for greater autonomy within the socialist camp, it came to be seen as being prepared to see the actual break-up of the camp itself, and it was also being viewed as a baleful domestic influence on other camp countries – including, as we have seen, China. The threat to the cohesiveness of the camp was serious from a Chinese perspective. Not only would the basis upon which China's national security rested be undermined, but it would have drastically weakened the forces holding at bay the aggressive elements in the US. This in turn, according to the logic of Chinese arguments, would have dramatically increased American military pressure upon China and thus set back the domestic and external objectives so actively sought.

On 25 April 1956 Mao had outlined new guidelines for the development of the Chinese economy in a celebrated inner party speech, 'The Ten Major Relationships'. This classic of Maoist developmental theory set out for the first time the view which was to become basic to the Chinese model — in order to develop heavy industry prior attention should be paid to agriculture and light industry. The speech also surveyed the whole range of state activities, thus providing a framework within which China would develop politically and culturally along autonomous lines. Thus Mao looked forward to China's development of nuclear weapons; and his guidelines for relations with foreign countries showed a strong determination to carry out an approach which would have led China further and further away from dependence upon the tight relationship with the Soviet Union. Those in China who followed the Soviet pattern blindly were criticised scornfully. The Chinese were exhorted to learn science, technology and even factory management and culture from the capitalist countries. Mao appealed to the Chinese people 'to bestir ourselves, enhance our national confidence and encourage the spirit typified by "scorn US imperialism" which was fostered during the movement to resist US aggression and aid Korea.' (The unofficial version of the speech here quotes approvingly from Mencius, 'when speaking to the mighty, look on them with contempt.')[49]

It was the urge for greater autonomy and creativity independent of the Soviet Union coupled with the emphasis on unshackling the intellectuals and others from tight party control by appealing to their patriotism which had brought the restive East European countries and China together in 1956 and the first half of 1957. The 'Hundred Flowers' campaign in China was more than an issue of cultural liberalisation. It involved a challenge to the party apparatus engineered and encouraged by Mao. It has been persuasively analysed as a kind of forerunner in certain respects to the Cultural Revolution.[50] The campaign was swiftly brought to a close early in June 1957 and in its wake came the 'anti-rightist movement' which once and for all swung China away from the reformist currents in Eastern Europe.

China's closeness to these East European currents should not be exaggerated. As we have already seen, Mao's attitude to the Poles also underwent a change after the Hungarian incident. In that same speech of 15 November 1956 cited earlier, Mao offered a trenchant analysis of the situation in both Poland and Hungary which differentiated it sharply from the situation in China and which also provides an interesting gloss on his thinking on the eve of launching the Hundred Flowers movement:

> The fundamental problem with some East European countries is that they have not done a good job of waging class struggle and have left so many counter-revolutionaries at large; nor have they trained their proletariat in class struggle to help them learn how to draw a clear distinction between people and the enemy, between right and wrong and between materialism and idealism. And now they want to reap what they have sown, they have brought the fire upon their own heads.

Until that point, however, China's leaders had been very active in the politics of the relations between Moscow and its East European allies. Liu Shao-ch'i is thought to have been in Moscow during the critical period of the Hungarian uprising and its crushing by Soviet tanks.[51] Chou En-lai interrupted an Asian tour to visit the Soviet Union, Poland and Hungary in January 1957, where he signed a series of joint communiqués involving the three countries and where he criticised Khrushchev's handling of the Stalin question while simultaneously stressing the importance for the Soviet leadership of the socialist camp because of its greater experience and strength. At the same time P'eng Chen was also engaged in an extensive tour of Eastern Europe.

Volume V of the *Selected Works of Mao Tse-tung* relates how during Chou En-lai's visit to Moscow Mao telephoned him to say, 'These people are blinded by their material gains and the best way to deal with them is to give them a good dressing down . . . ' Mao then went on to observe,

> When a man's head gets too swelled, we have to give him a good bawling out one way or another. This time in Moscow, Comrade Chou En-lai did not stand on ceremony and took them on, and consequently they kicked up a row. This is good, straightening things out face-to-face. They tried to influence us and we tried to influence them. However, we didn't come straight to the point on every question, we didn't play all our cards but kept some up our sleeves. There will always be contradictions. As long as things are tolerable on the whole, we can seek common grounds and reserve differences, to be

dealt with later. If they insist on having everything their own way, sooner or later, we will have to bring everything into the open.[52]

Just as China for the first time was making a direct impact on the affairs of Eastern Europe, so were these in turn making an impact upon China. The Hungarian events made a deep imprint on the minds of China's leaders, and on Mao especially. From time to time he would refer to the Hungarian Petöfei Club (which was regarded as having prepared the necessary intellectual ferment for the uprising to take place) as an institution which might find Chinese parallels. The need to avoid a Chinese 'Hungary' was undoubtedly a factor in the launching of the Hundred Flowers campaign.

The Chinese attitude towards the Soviet Union in this period was highly critical. The Chinese were obviously dissatisfied with the quality of the Soviet leadership. But at the same time Mao and his colleagues recognised the importance of the part the Soviet Union played in sustaining both China's external relations and the domestic economic construction. Mao clearly came to see himself as the principal guardian and extender of the Marxist-Leninist heritage. But he too was not immune from the effects of de-Stalinisation, as witnessed by the relative dimming of his personal political aura at the CPC Eighth Congress in September 1956.[53] Nevertheless, following the Hungarian events the Chinese leaders increasingly began to emphasise the importance of Soviet leadership of the camp. Despite Chinese dissatisfaction with the internal affairs of the socialist camp, the resistance to American imperialism was clearly regarded as more important. Even before the Hungarian affair the Chinese leadership argued that 'peace can be preserved only by determined resistance to aggression.' If the prospects for a continued relaxation of international tensions were good this was only because the forces for peace throughout the world, backed by the might of the socialist camp headed by the Soviet Union,were growing while the reactionary aggressive forces were becoming increasingly isolated and fraught with internal conflicts or contradictions.

Finally, it should be noted that Volume V of his *Selected Works* records only two talks of Mao to sets of visitors in which the significance of China's distinctive revolutionary experience is urged upon them as relevant to their struggle. Interestingly, both talks are to people from Latin America and they both took place after the beginnings of the Sino-Soviet dispute. The first took place on 14 July 1956 and the second on 25 September 1956. The first was directed towards 'two Latin American public figures' on whom Mao urged the relevance of

China's analysis of US imperialism as a paper tiger, especially as to how the weak will become strong and the strong weak. The second was Mao's talk with 'representatives of some Latin American Communist Parties'. To fully fledged revolutionaries such as these Mao related the salient aspects of China's party history considered to be of universal significance. At the same time he warned them against 'transplanting Chinese experience mechanically'. The two talks may be regarded as significant in discussion of China's role in the socialist camp because they constitute an authoritative attempt to universalise the lessons of China's revolution for the benefit of outsiders. These lessons were perceived to be relevant for anti-imperialists struggling for national independence as well as for Communist revolutionaries. The audiences involved were both from what is now called the Third World. As the timing of the talks followed well after Khrushchev's de-Stalinisation speech they denote an attempt to propagate the Chinese experience as peculiarly relevant to both nationalist and Communist revolutions. The Russian leadership by implication could not be trusted to propagate the lessons of the October Revolution. Significantly, people in the Third World were chosen as the appropriate audience.[54]

Sino-American Tension

In January 1957, however, Mao noted the expansion of the interests of the United States and, although typically Mao was able to detect an advantageous side to that from China's point of view, it was none the less true that according to his analysis America's influence was becoming more widespread. In the following analysis of the Suez crisis it is interesting to note in passing that Mao came close to introducing once again his 1946 concept of the intermediate zone, which was also moving towards his 1974 concept of the three worlds:

In the Middle East, there was that Suez Canal incident. A man called Nasser nationalized the canal, another called Eden sent in an invading army, and close on his heels came a third named Eisenhower who decided to drive the British out and have the place all to himself. The British bourgeoisie, past masters of machination and manoeuvre, are a class which knows best when to compromise. But this time they bungled and let the Middle East fall into the hands of the Americans. What a colossal mistake! Can one find many such mistakes in the history of the British bourgeoisie? How come that this time they lost their heads and made such a mistake? Because the pressure exerted by the United States was too much and they lost control of themselves in their anxiety to regain the Middle East and block the United States. Did Britain direct the spearhead chiefly at Egypt? No. Britain's moves were against the United States, much as the moves of the United States were against Britain.

From this incident we can pinpoint the focus of struggle in the world today. *The contradiction between the imperialist countries and the socialist countries is certainly most acute.* But the imperialist countries are now contending with each other for the control of different areas in the name of opposing communism. What areas are they contending for? Areas in Asia and Africa, inhabited by 1,000 million people. At present their contention converges on the Middle East, an area of great strategic significance . . . In the Middle East, *two kinds of contradictions and three kinds of forces are in conflict. The two kinds of contradictions are first those between different imperialist powers, that is, between the United States and Britain and between the United States and France and second, those between the imperialist powers and the oppressed nations. The three kinds of forces are: one the United States, the biggest imperialist power; two, Britain and France, second-rate imperialist powers; and three, the oppressed nations . . .* (emphasis added)[55]

Clearly for Mao, the Suez incident signalled an important change in the configuration of world forces. As the italicised passages indicate, Mao did not deny the contradiction between the two camps of imperialism and socialism, except that by describing it only as 'most acute' ('hen li-hai') it became possible to deduce that he did not necessarily regard it as the 'principal' one ('chu yao') to which all the others were subordinate. The focal points of his analysis, however, were clearly concentrated upon the contradictions among the imperialist powers, the emergence of the United States as the dominant expansive one and the resistance by the growing forces of nationalism. This concern of Mao with the nationalist forces in Africa, Asia and Latin America, the contradictions between the imperialist powers and the activities of the United States in the Third World, was to increase just as the links with the Soviet Union decreased. It would be misleading, however, to suggest that the increasing preoccupation with the former was a function of the reduced links with the latter. As we have seen, since 1951 China's leaders began to pay ever more serious attention to what is now called the Third World. Apart from the natural association between China and these countries, China's leaders were also responding to substantive changes which were occurring in world politics. The

Third World was indeed emerging on the world stage and indeed the United States was playing a more active role in its affairs. Moreover, at this stage Mao still placed China firmly within the socialist camp.

How then did Mao envisage the implications for China and the other socialist countries arising from his analysis of imperialist contention in Asia and Africa?

> Their embroilment is to our advantage. We, the socialist countries, should pursue the policy of consolidating ourselves and not yielding a single inch of our land. We will struggle against anyone who tries to make us do so. This is where we draw the line beyond which they can be left to quarrel among themselves. Then shall we speak up or not? Yes, we shall. We certainly will support the anti-imperialist struggles of the people in Asia, Africa and Latin America and the revolutionary struggles of the people of all countries.

Thus the socialist countries should get on with self-strengthening, guard themselves against imperialist encroachment, but not actually go out to seek direct conflict with the imperialist powers. Rather they should concentrate on supporting anti-imperialist and revolutionary struggles. He then went on to analyse the relations between the imperialists and the socialist countries on the basis that 'they are among us and we are among them'. In other words, the imperialist countries 'have our men in their midst' — i.e. Communists, revolutionary workers, progressives, etc.; while they 'have their men in our midst' — those of the bourgeois and landlord classes, etc. Therefore, 'we must absorb them and transform the landlords and capitalists into working people. This is also a strategic policy . . . '

Mao summed up:

> In short, our assessment of the international situation is still that the embroilment of the imperialist countries contending for colonies is the greater contradiction. They try to cover up the contradictions between themselves by playing up their contradictions with us. We can make use of their contradictions, a lot can be done in this connection. This is a matter of importance for our external policy.[56]

With regard to specifically Sino-American relations, Mao professed a degree of unconcern. Mao argued that Eisenhower had sought to restrain any impulsive tendencies of Chiang Kai-shek while at the same time assuring Chiang of his opposition to Communism, thus placing all hopes upon disturbances breaking out on the mainland of China. Mao then went on to argue that it was

> preferable to put off the establishment of diplomatic relations with the United States for some years . . . We adopt this policy to deprive the United States of as much political capital as possible and put it in the wrong and isolated position. You bar us from the United Nations and don't want to establish relations with us, all right, but the longer you stall, the more you will be in debt to us. The longer you stall, the more you will be in the wrong and the more isolated you will become in your own country and before world opinion.

This observation followed upon the rejection by the US Secretary of State Dulles of a Chou En-lai offer to have a group of respected journalists visit China, which doubtless accounts for its aggrieved moral tone. Nevertheless, it reflected a basic sense of moral rectitude and high principle which has characterised much of the Chinese style in foreign policy. As to the question of the possibility of war, Mao suggested that, while there was anxiety in all countries, 'the question is which side is more afraid of the other? I'm inclined to think that they are more afraid of us.' But to avoid complacency it was necessary to be prepared; after all, 'the imperialists may go beserk.' So irrational did Mao think any attack on China might be.[57]

Thus in January 1957 Mao perceived some important changes in international politics. While an attack on socialist countries was unlikely, the situation of a relaxation of tensions had come to an end because of imperialist rivalry for control of Afro-Asia. The United States had 'taken over' the Middle East from the British and French and was now seeking to press home its advantage elsewhere. Meanwhile the nationalist anti-imperialist struggles were becoming more active as a result. Lines were hardening and although Mao did not anticipate any major attack on China he no longer looked towards any diplomatic breakthrough with the Americans. This view of the sharpening of international tension focused particularly on Africa and Asia and, it should be noted, emerged well before the Hundred Flowers movement and not, as is often suggested, as a consequence of the domestic shifts in Chinese politics in the second half of 1957 and early 1958.

This sense of growing American activism was confirmed in the Chinese view by the Eisenhower Doctrine in the Middle East and by the decision in February and carried out in May to deploy nuclear Matador surface-to-surface missiles on Taiwan. On 5 March Chou En-lai reported on his visit to eleven countries in Asia and Europe, saying that 'the general trend of the world situation is towards the relaxation of tension and progress.' But he went on to observe that whenever a substantive move in this direction takes place, 'the United States will hastily create new tensions in a desperate effort to prevent a further relaxation', so that 'despite our willingness to coexist peacefully with all other countries the imperialists are threatening us with war. We must maintain constant vigilance and continue to reinforce our national defence along with the further development of our economy.'[58]

On 28 June Dulles made a major speech on US-China policy in San Francisco, in which he put an end to any remaining prospects for improved relations and committed the American administration to do all that it could to undermine the Chinese Communist government. At the same time the American military bases on China's periphery were being strengthened.

Thus China's overtures of 1955 and 1956 to the United States had come to naught. Any hopes entertained in Peking that the Nationalists on Taiwan might oppose the Americans and return to the embrace of the motherland had failed to materialise.[59] Moreover, Premier Kishi of Japan had endorsed publicly Chiang Kai-shek's goal of recovering the mainland, and at the end of May he had then proceeded to south-east Asia where he made highly critical remarks regarding the PRC. All this raised indignant protests from the Chinese Press, particularly as the Chinese had gone out of their way to cultivate Sino-Japanese relations.[60]

The End of the Close Alliance: The Moscow Conference, November 1957

Naturally, the Chinese were delighted by the demonstration of Soviet primacy in the most advanced sector of rocketry, the Inter-Continental Ballistic Missile (ICBM) later that summer. By the time that Mao had arrived in Moscow for the 40th anniversary of the October Revolution and for the twelve-power conference on the international Communist movement, the Russians had already successfully test fired their first ICBM and sent up the first Sputnik. The day after Mao's arrival the second Sputnik was sent up with a dog on board. The United States by this stage had not successfully tested even one ICBM. Mao asserted triumphantly that henceforth 'East Wind prevails over West Wind.' He now wanted a more cohesive bloc under Soviet leadership ready and able to meet the newly changed situation. The Chinese were now less tolerant of the manifestations of Polish independence and of the Yugoslav position.[61]

Accordingly, the Chinese emphasised the importance of Soviet leadership of the socialist camp to an extent that was embarrassing even for the Russians. By this stage Khrushchev (who was now far more secure in his leadership, having purged his rivals as an anti-party clique in the summer of 1957) wished to pursue more of a détente relationship with Yugoslavia and ultimately he looked forward to developing such a relationship with the United States. By stressing Soviet leadership, Mao was making it difficult for Khrushchev to pursue either goal. These tactical considerations were buttressed by the strategic calculation that American imperialist pressure upon China and the Third World could best be resisted by a united and determined camp under Soviet leadership. The reasons given by the Chinese for the need for Soviet leadership were not expressed in terms which suggested that they were preparing the ground for eventually claiming such leadership for themselves. The Chinese pointed out that the Soviet Union had forty years' experience behind it and that it was by far the most important member of the camp in terms of its economic and military capabilities. Indeed, the Chinese argued that as a result of the scientific and technological advances, especially in rocketry, by the Soviet Union, the camp had now established superiority over the West. As China could not hope to match the Soviet Union in these respects for a very long time to come, it could hardly be claimed that Mao was seeking to replace Khrushchev as camp leader. The Chinese would more likely have hoped to become the influential voice in determining the correct line which the Soviet leadership would be expected to follow – as had been applied, according to Chinese accounts, over the Polish and Hungarian uprisings.

At the Moscow conference Mao argued that 'international developments had reached a new turning point and that the forces of peace and socialism had already surpassed those of war and imperialism and were becoming more and more capable of preventing imperialism from unleashing a world war'. He listed ten events since the Second World War to show the failures of imperialist forces against those of socialism and nationalism. Thus, for example, the American nuclear monopoly and its economic and military strength had not prevented the incorporation of much of Eastern Europe into the socialist camp; nor had it been able to stop the revolutions in China and Indo-China. The number of people living under socialist systems had increased fivefold since the Second World War. Hundreds of millions of people had gained indepen-

dence from colonial rule and together with the countries of the socialist
camp these nationalist countries were firmly opposed to Western
imperialism. Mao found in Russia's technological advances confirma-
tion of his argument that the socialist system was superior to that of
imperialism. These triumphs had not been achieved by seeking compromises with the enemy. On the contrary, they had been won by
daring to confront him. This did not mean, however, that reckless confrontations should be sought.

Mao recalled his 1945 'paper tiger' image of imperialism and
reactionaries to illustrate his view that America should not be feared
from the strategic and long-term point of view, but at the same time
prudence was required in tackling the US in immediate tactical situations: 'In war, battles can only be fought one by one and the enemy
can only be annihilated bit by bit.' Mao did not think that the US
would dare to unleash a nuclear war, but the possibility had to be considered. He disagreed with Nehru and some of the Russian leaders who
argued that the whole of mankind would perish: 'In reality such talk
amounts to saying that there is no alternative to capitulation in the face
of imperialist nuclear blackmail.'[62] (It is as well to note here that Mao
was uniquely familiar with such threats, having been a recipient of them
from the Americans on at least seven separate occasions by the end of
1955, and an eighth in 1958.[63]) In Mao's view hundreds and perhaps
more than a thousand million people might be killed, but the end result
would be the total destruction of the imperialist system and the
triumph of socialism. In fact the Chinese leader did not expect a nuclear
war, nor did he call for an openly offensive strategy on behalf of the
camp. But he did expect a firmer position to be taken against imperialism, especially as personified by the United States. An article in the
Chinese journal *Shih Chieh Chih-shih* of 5 December 1957, citing
American publications, argued that the West, having been prevented
from launching a global war, would now concentrate upon local wars,
using perhaps tactical nuclear weapons. But here, too, the new international balance of forces would tell against the Americans. The Chinese
analysts did not specify whether the armed struggle in such a contingency would be waged primarily by the local progressives or by the
socialist camp in the guise of the Soviet Union.

The Soviet view differed in at least two critical respects; first, it
denied that the socialist camp was now superior to that of imperialism.
It confined itself to the important claim that a favourable change had
occurred in the balance between them. Second, the Soviet leadership
claimed that the growing deterrent situation between Russia and

America applied to local wars, too.

Thus, logically the Soviet position led to the desirability of establishing an American-Soviet detente based upon the situation of mutual deterrence, whereas the Chinese position ultimately meant that such an agreed arrangement would have to be considered a sell-out and that the correct Soviet strategy should be to take a firm stand against American imperialism in association with the burgeoning nationalist movements in Africa and Asia and as the leader of a socialist bloc.

Frequently in international relations ultimately logical positions give way before considerations of salience. In other words, although the consequences of these disagreements were to loom large later on in the Sino-Soviet dispute, the two great countries were able to agree in November 1957 on the main immediate task of consolidating the unity of the socialist camp, even though this meant for the present excluding the Yugoslavs. The Moscow Declaration was duly signed on 16 November 1957 after mutual compromises. The Russians had enough confidence and trust in their Chinese allies to offer them nuclear assistance (a sample atom bomb, according to later Chinese accounts) by an agreement 'on new technology for national defence', signed on 15 October. On 18 January 1958 a protocol was signed providing for a five-year programme of scientific co-operation. Immediate extra aid sufficient to finance the Second Five-Year Plan was not forthcoming because of the need to inject US$1,000 million into Eastern European reconstruction.[64] The Chinese could hardly have quarrelled with that objective and they have not done so subsequently.

Thus the basis for the later Sino-Soviet conflict was becoming evident, but by the end of 1957 the two countries had overcome their disagreement — at least to the extent that both sides felt their alliance was still mutually beneficial. China's role, meanwhile, had expanded. She was now a great actor on the world stage. Significant openings had been made to the nationalist forces of Afro-Asia and China had been highly influential in the international Communist movement, especially in Eastern Europe. More and more of Mao's concepts drawn from China's independent experience in revolution and foreign affairs were being reflected in China's international posture. Yet China was still very much circumscribed by the hostility of the more powerful United States and by the diverging interests of its powerful ally, the Soviet Union. Underlying this was China's evident lack of extensive economic and military capabilities. Yet there were already signs of an increasing independence of spirit and of vigorous creativity. Nevertheless this period marks the end of China's role as a close ally, for in the spring of 1958

China's leaders were to reject the Soviet offer of a joint naval fleet on the grounds that this was in fact a bid to try to control China.

Notes

1. Stuart Schram (ed.), *Mao Tse-tung Unrehearsed* (Penguin Books, 1974). See Introduction, p. 37, and the text on p. 114.
2. Roderick MacFarquhar, *Sino-American Relations 1949-71* (Praeger for Royal Institute of International Affairs, 1972), p. 141.
3. Political Report by Chou En-lai at the Second Session of the Second National Committee of the Chinese People's Political Consultative Conference, 30 January 1956, Supplement to *People's China*, No. 4 (1956), pp. 5-6.
4. *People's Daily* editorial, 22 July 1954. *People's China*, No. 15 (1974). p. 4.
5. See text of Sino-Korean Joint Statement of 19 February 1958 for the announcement of the intention to withdraw all troops by the end of the year in *Peking Review*, Vol. 1, No. 1 (4 March 1958), pp. 21-3. By 8 December 1958 both sides were able to declare that all China's forces had been withdrawn; *Peking Review*, No. 42 (1958), pp. 16-17.
6. Supplement to *People's China*, No. 20 (1954), pp. 4-5.
7. Ibid., p. 5.
8. Ho Cheng, 'Why Taiwan Must Be Liberated' in *People's China*, No. 21 (1954), pp. 10-12.
9. For analysis see J. Kalicki, *The Pattern of Sino-American Crises* (Cambridge University Press, 1975), pp. 120-55. See also Harold C. Hinton, *China on the World Stage* (Macmillan, 1966), pp. 258-63.
10. 'Chou En-lai's Report on Foreign Affairs' of early August 1954. Supplement to *People's China*, No. 17 (1954), pp. 3-12, where it is specifically mentioned on p. 10.
11. Speech at second session of the First National People's Congress, 'The Present International Situation and China's Foreign Policy', *People's China*, No. 16 (1955), pp. 3-8. The quotation is from p. 5.
12. In the talk of July 1964 to a visiting Japanese delegation. See text in John Gittings, *Survey of the Sino-Soviet Dispute* (Oxford University Press, 1968), p. 166.
13. *Pravda* editorial, 2 September 1967. Text in ibid., p. 166, footnote 2.
14. Nikita Khrushchev, *Khrushchev Remembers*, Vol. 2 (Penguin Books, 1974), p. 336.
15. JPRS 1, p. 28.
16. Ibid., p. 115.
17. Supplement to *People's China*, No. 20 (1954), pp. 6-14.
18. See 'On the Historical Experience of the Dictatorship of the Proletariat' of April and 'More On the Historical Experience of the Dictatorship of the Proletariat' of 28 December 1956 in R.R. Bowie and J.K. Fairbank, *Communist China 1955-59: Policy Documents With Analysis* (Harvard University Press, 1962), pp. 144-50 and pp. 257-72.
19. See Roderick MacFarquhar, *The Origins of the Cultural Revolution*, Vol. I (Oxford University Press, 1974), pp. 175-6. See also the discussion in Donald S. Zagoria, *The Sino-Soviet Conflict 1956-61* (Princeton University Press, 1962), Chapter 1 and esp. pp. 56-64.
20. See 'On the Draft Constitution of the People's Republic of China', *SW*,

Vol. V, p. 146 and 'In Commemoration of Dr. Sun Yat-sen', ibid., p. 351.

21. Harrison E. Salisbury, *To Peking and Beyond: A Report on the New Asia* (Quadrangle,1973), pp. 225-6.

22. For a contemporary enthusiastic account of this see George McT. Kahin, *The Asian-African Conference* (Cornell University Press, 1956). For a vivid and more considered account see G.H. Jansen, *Afro-Asia and Non-Alignment* (Faber, 1966).

23. For a Chinese account see Yeh Chi-chuang (Minister of Foreign Trade), 'China's Drive for Normal Trade Among Nations', *People's China*, No. 20 (1955), pp. 5-7. For a balanced and careful Western analysis see Alexander Eckstein, *Communist China's Economic Growth and Foreign Trade: Implications for US Policy* (McGraw-Hill, 1966), esp. Chapter 6, pp. 183-241.

24. Speech at the Conference, 19 April 1955, Supplement to *People's China*, No. 10 (1955), p. 10.

25. Ibid., pp. 11-13.

26. See the excellent study of China's relationships with three south-east Asian countries by M. Gurtov, *China and Southeast Asia: The Politics of Survival* (Heath Lexington Books, 1971). For Sino-Burmese relations in this regard see particularly pp. 90-4.

27. During the Bandung Conference Chou En-lai negotiated an agreement on the nationality of overseas Chinese with the Indonesian government. The agreement was not fully ratified until January 1960, but not before the overseas Chinese had been the subject of official discrimination and harassment during the previous year. The PRC had been unable to do much on behalf of these Chinese (see Harold C. Hinton, *Communist China in World Politics* (Macmillan, 1966), pp. 428-33). That this problem arose with the friendly government of President Sukarno illustrates the degree to which the problems posed by the overseas Chinese in south-east Asia extend beyond general strategic problems or indeed bilateral relations between the PRC and a local government. By 1959-60 Sukarno's government had better relations with China than any of the other non-neutralist and non-Communist governments in the area.

28. 'Chou En-lai's Statement on Relaxation of Tension', 23 April 1955. Supplement to *People's China*, No. 10 (1955), p. 13.

29. K.T. Young, *Negotiating With the Chinese Communists: The United States Experience* (McGraw-Hill, 1968). See esp. Chapters 4 and 5, pp. 91-134.

30. See for example Donald Klein, 'The Evolving Ministry of Foreign Affairs', *China Quarterly*, No. 3 (1960) and Bruce D. Larkin, *China and Africa 1949-1970: The Foreign Policy of the People's Republic of China* (University of California Press,1971).

31. For an interesting account by a British journalist who accompanied the Labour group see George Gale, *No Flies in China* (G. Allen, 1955).

32. For example, Chou En-lai's speeches at Geneva, in Supplement to *People's China*, Nos. 13 and 14 (1954).

33. Supplement to *People's China*, No. 22 (1956), p. 7.

34. Supplement to *People's China*, No. 14 (1956), pp. 5-6.

35. See John Gittings, *The World and China 1922-1972* (Eyre Methuen, 1974), pp. 200-1.

36. Salisbury, *To Peking and Beyond,* p. 9.

37. JPRS, 1, pp. 37-8.

38. Ibid., p. 29.

39. 'Summing-up Speech at the Sixth Expanded Plenum of the Seventh CPC Central Committee', ibid., pp. 14-26.

40. *Wan Sui*, p. 34.
41. Although it was not publicly criticised in 1956 and 1957, this public silence on the question and their affirmation of the correctness of Lenin's principles make credible their later claims to have criticised this in private. The Chinese side also submitted a special critique of peaceful transition to the 1957 Moscow Conference.
42. The first two sentences of the first paragraph were officially cited for the first time in *Peking Review*, No. 17 (1970), p. 6.
43. *SW*, Vol. V, pp. 341-2.
44. 'On the Historical Experience of the Dictatorship of the Proletariat' in Bowie and Fairbank, *Communist China 1955-59*.
45. 'More on the Historical Experience of the Dictatorship of the Proletariat', ibid.
46. Cited in Gittings, *Survey of the Sino-Soviet Dispute*, p. 69.
47. See MacFarquhar, *The Origins of the Cultural Revolution*, p. 170 and p. 364, note 4.
48. See Gittings, *Survey of the Sino-Soviet Dispute*, p. 70, especially note 3.
49. Schram (ed.), *Mao Tse-tung Unrehearsed*, p. 82.
50. MacFarquhar, *The Origins of the Sino-Soviet Dispute*, p. 170 and pp. 364-5, note 8.
51. Ibid., pp. 99-109.
52. *SW*, Vol. V, p. 365.
53. See 'Resolution of the Eighth Congress of the Central Committee's Political Report', Supplement to *People's China*, No. 22 (1956), p. 7.
54. 'US Imperialism is a Paper Tiger', *SW*, Vol. V, pp. 308-11 and 'Some Experiences in Our Party's History', ibid., pp. 324-9. As these talks were not published before 1977 the symbolic significance of the talks is applied retrospectively. Even so, the fact that Mao spoke in this way at that time is important, even though it was not made public then.
55. 'The Talk of January 27 1957', ibid., pp. 361-2.
56. Ibid., pp. 362-3.
57. Ibid., pp. 363-4.
58. Supplement to *People's China*, No. 7 (1957), pp. 3-19.
59. For an example of an article which sets out a rationale for the existence of local administrative, commercial and industrial opposition in Taiwan to increasing American penetration, see Lin Mu, 'US Economic Plunder of Taiwan', *People's China*, No. 22 (1957), pp. 34-7. See also 'Taiwan Under US Domination' by Ku Fan, *People's China*, No. 13 (1957), pp. 13-16.
60. See, for example, *People's China*, No. 17 (1957), p. 40.
61. See the analysis in Zagoria, *The Sino-Soviet Conflict 1956-61*, pp. 145-51 and pp. 160-8.
62. Mao's speech was reconstructed by John Gittings in his *Survey of the Sino-Soviet Dispute*, pp. 81-2. For what are unfortunately only extracts (and unremarkable ones at that) from a second speech by Mao in Moscow, see the last two articles in *SW*, Vol. V, pp. 514-18.
63. Listed and documented in Gittings, *The World and China*, p. 203.
64. See W. Klatt, 'Sino-Soviet Economic Relations' in G.F. Hudson, R. Lowenthal and R. MacFarquhar, *The Sino-Soviet Dispute* (Praeger, 1961).

4 THE BREAK WITH THE SOVIET UNION 1958-1963

The rift with the Soviet Union changed fundamentally the framework within which China's international role was cast. Since its inception the PRC, as we have seen, had been a member of the socialist camp and the major ally of the Soviet Union. The internationalist aspects of the Chinese Revolution, the development of socialism and economic construction within China as well as China's national security and its foreign policy were all based on the leaning to the side of the Soviet Union in a bipolar world. The break with the Soviet Union radically changed the entire paradigm on which all this was based. The new paradigm did not spring to life suddenly with the ending of the close Sino-Soviet relationship, but it rather unfolded in the process of the dispute with the Soviet Union and it also drew upon many of the distinctive characteristics of the Chinese revolutionary experience and indeed of the modern historical experience of the Chinese people.

The split with the Soviet Union was also intimately linked with the new directions in domestic Chinese affairs during this period. These brought about deep divisions in the leadership which led Mao especially to link the struggle against revisionism in the international sphere to the struggle against domestic revisionists. Thus in his speech to the Tenth Plenum of 24 September 1962 Mao added the following sentence to a new analysis of the contradictions 'between us and imperialism': 'I think that right wing opportunism in China should be renamed: it should be called Chinese revisionism.' The Sino-Soviet divide therefore led to a total re-evaluation of China's role in both its external and internal dimensions. The new directions which emerged in foreign affairs and alternative leadership preferences will be discussed in the next two chapters. This chapter will seek to outline the main features of the emergence of a new Chinese role in the course of the Sino-Soviet dispute.

The Chinese date the beginning of the Sino-Soviet dispute from the CPSU 20th Congress of February 1956. The Soviet leadership, however, has dated this from 1958. The Chinese maintain that the dispute was a highly principled one concerning the general line of the internationalist Communist movement and that as such Chinese principled objections to that congress were advanced at the time partly in public (on the Stalin question) and partly in private (e.g. on the question of peaceful transition) and that the issues raised then have been at the heart of the quarrel ever since. The Russians, however, argue that the Chinese polemic is based essentially upon long-standing nationalist perspectives which came to the fore under the leadership of Mao Tse-tung and his associates from 1958 onwards. The choice of the date here should not be regarded as an indication of support for the Soviet position.

Our concern here is with the identification of China's role in international affairs rather than with the Sino-Soviet dispute itself. And it is from that perspective that 1958 is a better turning-point than 1956. There is inevitably an element of artificiality in temporal divisions of this kind and certain continuities can be shown to carry on from the previous period to this. Nevertheless it is from 1958 onwards that the domestic break with the Soviet model becomes complete and it is also from 1958 onwards that the Chinese began to develop a view of the characteristics of the international environment that was totally at variance with that advanced by the Russians. At the same time it is also true that it was only in 1958 the Soviet leadership itself began to fully carry out the foreign policy features outlined at the CPSU 20th Congress. Furthermore, as was suggested in the previous chapter, however great the struggle and the division between the two sides at the time of the Moscow Conference at the end of 1957, unity was the predominant characteristic of the duality of division and unity which characterised their relationship.

What is of interest therefore is the process by which China's role changed from being a relatively independent and critical member of the socialist camp under some kind of Soviet leadership in early 1958 to the emergence of China as an entirely independent actor on the world stage challenging both superpowers by the summer of 1963.

The Soviet factor has been at the heart of Chinese politics from the establishment of the PRC, whether as a positive or a negative model. The move towards full independence was also a move away from the dominant Soviet influence. It also involved the positive affirmation of China's own revolutionary experiences and the development of a new view of international affairs in which the primary area of conflict with imperialism was once again located in the intermediate zone and in which China had become the international source of genuine Marxism-Leninism.

Self-Reliant Independence

The domestic basis for China's claim to have become self-reliant and fully independent was undoubtedly laid during 1958 with the abandonment of the Soviet model and the development of a Chinese way in the form of the Great Leap Forward and the establishment of communes, followed by retrenchment and survival through the three bitter years of 1959-61. In the course of these years China's leaders and especially Mao reacted against the new directions of Soviet foreign policy and its consequences for China and the international Communist movement to eventually accuse the Russian leadership of pursuing a revisionist, non-Marxist-Leninist line — which was but a short step from concluding that the Russian persistence in this revisionist line could only be due to the fact that the leadership itself was revisionist. Thus in January 1962, Mao declared in his 7,000 cadres speech that 'the Party and the state leadership of the Soviet Union has now been usurped by the revisionists.'[1] Although it may be considered to be only a small advance on his previous observations, Mao's assertion was momentous as it implied that for him at any rate the Soviet leaders were no longer Communists at all and that no compromises on ideological questions were possible from here on. This did not mean, however, that the positive aspects of the Sino-Soviet relationship were henceforth at an end. The final open foreign break did not come until the summer of 1963, and the ending of party-to-party relations between the two sides was not reached before the spring of 1966. We are thus dealing with a complex evolution which unfolded gradually and in a by no means linear fashion. Nevertheless in retrospect the trend is clear and we shall be concerned to identify the main turning points which shaped the emergence of China's new role.

The changing world situation which China's leaders had perceived in 1957 took an even clearer shape in the first half of 1958. We have already seen that Peking was alarmed by the introduction of nuclear missiles in Taiwan and South Korea. China's fears that the American administration was deliberately reversing the trend of the mid-1950s towards the relative relaxation of tensions were confirmed by American drives against the independence movements of what is now called the Third World and its involvement in a number of attempted *coups* against newly independent governments (for example, in Indonesia and elsewhere). Meanwhile, Chiang Kai-shek's armies were being put on an offensive footing.[2] The hard line of Dulles of June 1957 was now followed by the Kishi government of Japan, which under pressure from Washington and Taipei broke the terms of an official trade agreement and placed the Peking government in a situation in which it felt faced with the choice of humiliation or the cessation of trade. The Chinese chose the latter.[3] The importance which China attached to Japan can be seen from Mao's observation to a major conference on strategy and foreign policy in June 1958: 'In future wars in the East, America won't get anywhere without depending on Japan, so we must make a thorough study of Japanese conditions.'[4] Meanwhile the Soviet leadership, in the Chinese view, far from exploiting the new turning-point in the balance of forces between East and West consequent upon its ICBM successes, was in fact showing every intention of seeking to reach an accommodation with the Americans on terms which could only work against the interests of those currently subject to imperialist pressure.

Once again China was being circumscribed and pressurised by the two great powers, America and Russia. Mao then sought to encourage his associates at a time when the gloom of the international situation contrasted sharply with the heady enthusiasm of the Great Leap Forward in the domestic sphere. In a speech of 17 May 1958 at the Second Session of the 8th Party Congress, ten days before the convening of a long and stormy meeting on military affairs which was to take China away from military dependence on the Soviet Union, Mao directed his audience's attention to the troubles existing outside the socialist camp: 'All the troubles are in the capitalist world . . . Imperialism is squabbling within itself; it is suppressing Indonesia, Lebanon and Latin America and fighting over Algeria . . . ' But he then directed himself to the adverse circumstances facing China and in typical fashion drew deep on China's revolutionary experience as a source of inspiration:

> Generally speaking, sometimes the situation seems to be bad, dark clouds in the sky. At such times we must be far sighted. We must not be confused by temporary darkness and feel that things are wrong with us and with the world and that we have bad luck. There is no such thing! In the past, our worst period was the Long March, blocked in front and pursued from behind, and our troops, our land, and our party were reduced, with only one of our ten fingers left. Overcoming these difficulties tempered us. Later on, new opportunities appeared and we again developed ourselves. Our one finger grew into ten. We developed all the way to the founding of the PRC and gained a national victory . . . [5]

Interestingly, in the same speech when Mao addressed himself to the domestic situation he first returned to international perspectives since for the first time he was able to identify a new and special international role for China arising out of her domestic pattern of development.

China is an important component of the international scene. When we discuss the international situation we must discuss China. The Chinese example is proof that the labouring people and the oppressed have vigour. Currently, socialism has many allies. The national independence movement of Asia, Africa and Latin America is our ally. They are the near areas of imperialism and we have allies there. We shall circle round to the imperialist near area. Lenin said: 'Progressive Asia, backward Europe'.

Mao saw China not so much as a model for others to emulate but as a symbol of the vitality of the toilers and the oppressed and presumably as a source of inspiration for others. As his subsequent sentences made clear, the people he had in mind were those of what would now be called the Third World rather than those of Europe (which also included many of the members of the socialist camp).

The May-July enlarged meeting of the Military Affairs Commission after much debate evidently decided that henceforth China would chart an independent course in military and strategic matters.[6] During the course of the meeting Mao authoritatively confirmed the decision to develop an independent nuclear capability whose beginnings in China may be traced back to about 1956. Following the meeting the Great Leap Forward intensified with the universal establishment of people's communes in August. The militia, which had earlier been allowed to atrophy, was now revived and became an essential component of the communes. China was being reorganised to be better able to fight a people's war on which China's defences were increasingly to rely. It was also at this meeting that the decision was taken to activate the offshore islands crisis of August/September. A marked increase in the propaganda to liberate Taiwan followed upon the ending of the meeting on 23 July. It was too early, however, to speak of the Sino-Soviet alliance as being inoperative at this stage. Mao stressed the need for China to be independent of outlook while still continuing to learn from the Soviet Union:

We must not eat pre-cooked food. If we do we shall be defeated. We must clarify this point with our Soviet comrades. We have learned from the Soviet Union in the past, we are still learning today, and we shall still learn in the future. Nevertheless our study must be combined with our own concrete conditions. We must say to them: We learn from you, from whom did you learn? Why cannot we create something of our own?[7]

Meanwhile a crisis had broken out in the Middle East and the Chinese found Khrushchev's approach wanting. His appeal to the United Nations and his efforts to deal with the deployment of American and British troops to the Lebanon and Jordan by diplomatic means alone were scorned by the Chinese. As the pseudonymous writer in *Red Flag*, Yu Chao-li ('Strength of Millions') pointed out on the day of Khrushchev's arrival in Peking on 31 July,

> The peace-loving people certainly do not want war, but those who really treasure peace will never bow to threats of war. Peace cannot be got by begging from the imperialists. War can be stopped and peace won only through mass struggle.[8]

Apparently, the impending offshore islands crisis initiated by China was not discussed at the meeting between the Sino-Soviet leaders during Khrushchev's four-day stay in Peking. According to Mao, Khrushchev's purpose (perhaps because of the results of the recently concluded military meeting) was to persuade the Chinese leaders to establish a joint Sino-Soviet fleet for Far Eastern waters. His proposals were angrily rejected as being in effect designed to bring China under Soviet military control:

> From the second half of 1958 he wanted to blockade the Chinese coastline. He wanted to set up a joint fleet so as to have control over our coastline and blockade us. It was because of this question that Khrushchev came to our country.[9]

After Khrushchev's departure the PRC leadership engineered a major international crisis entirely on their own initiative. The implications regarding China's emerging new international role were great. The challenge was issued at a time when the Chinese had moved to self-reliance on defence questions and under conditions in which the ways of dealing with the Americans were in dispute with their major ally and strategic protector. China's leaders had to calculate the main risks and indeed undertake crisis management precisely in a situation when Soviet backing was at best uncertain. In fact, during the course of the crisis, the Chinese had to face a nuclear threat from the American side which was only answered — and even then with a degree of ambiguity — by the Russians after the Chinese had taken the first step to reduce tension and take the crisis off the boil by offering to resume ambassadorial talks with the Americans.[10]

Even though Mao had to back down in this crisis, his analysis of its significance and consequences both during and after the crisis are instructive of his understanding of the operation of forces in international politics which allowed China to play a more independent role despite its relative weakness and economic underdevelopment. Indeed on other occasions he argued that American recognition of China would only take place once China had become strong and economically advanced, but meanwhile no great harm would befall China through the lack of recognition.[11]

On 5 September (the day before the talks offer was made) Mao talked at the Supreme State Conference (which also included non-party members) about the crisis. Exuding confidence and reassurance, he invited his audience to take the long-term view and to consider 'who is more afraid of whom?', only to conclude that from the long-term perspective, 'Dulles is a little more afraid of us'. He went on to argue that China enjoyed popular support which meant strength and that China was close to the forces of nationalism of three continents. The Americans, however, were overstretched and by their expansion into the offshore islands and the Lebanon they had put their head into a noose. Moreover they were isolated on the Taiwan question, having the support of only Syngman Rhee of South Korea. The more they expanded, the more overstretched the Americans would become, while the people of the world would increasingly see that they were in the wrong.[12]

Mao may have had to back down on the immediate tactical aspects of the offshore islands crisis, but the general strategy of challenging American imperialism was seen to be correct in the long term. In a speech of 30 November he claimed various beneficial consequences from the crisis, including the rapid development of the militia in China and its influence on Khrushchev, who was praised for his handling of the Berlin crisis. But he concluded:

> We too have done a bit of crisis handling and we made the West ask us not to go on doing it. It's a good thing for us when the West gets afraid about making a crisis . . . All the evidence proves that imperialism has adopted a defensive position and it no longer has an ounce of offensiveness [i.e. towards China and the Soviet Union].[13]

Its offensiveness was said to be directed towards other countries in the capitalist camp and to the national independence movements.

Despite Mao's confidence that China was not under direct military threat, it was still necessary for him to develop a defensive framework and a strategic outlook which would enable China to deal with such contingencies as might arise. Mao's general view was that imperialism could only be held at bay by countervailing power allied to a proper appreciation of its internal contradictions at the tactical level, while at the same time having the long-term revolutionary optimistic perspective in which imperialism could be seen to be ultimately weak. Hence at this time there was the revival of Mao's paper tiger thesis, according to which imperialism was only superficially terrifying and needed to be despised from the strategic point of view, whilst respected at the tactical level. Presumably China's handling of the Taiwan crisis was a case in point.

Likewise Mao did not believe in the rationality of nuclear war. He saw it as fundamentally counter-productive, even for imperialists:

Exploitation means exploiting people; one has to exploit people before one can exploit the earth. There's no land without people, no wealth without land. If you kill all the people and seize the land, what can you do with it? I don't see any reason for using nuclear weapons, conventional weapons are better.[14]

Mao nevertheless conceded that, although unlikely, it was possible that because of 'war maniacs' or 'when imperialism wants to extricate itself from crisis' a nuclear war might break out. In such a contingency Mao warned his audience that

the best outcome may be that only half of the population is left, and the second best may be only a third. When 900 million are left out of 2.9 billion several Five Year Plans can be developed for the total elimination of capitalism and for permanent peace. It is not a bad thing.[15]

This rather chilling picture was advanced by a leader who had faced the threat of a nuclear attack several times in the previous five years, and who was about to be threatened again during the offshore islands crisis. Yet it was certainly not China's practice to go in for nuclear brinkmanship. Mao's analysis was in fact consistent with the paper tiger thesis, namely that one should not be cowed or blackmailed by imperialism, and if the worst should come it was necessary to face it. Interestingly, the two contingencies cited by Mao in which the outbreak of a nuclear war could occur were both beyond the control of the socialist camp — an act of a 'maniac' or a severe economic crisis in the capitalist world. There was no suggestion that a socialist country would provoke one.

The actual development of a Chinese defensive strategy to deal with a nuclear attack was best outlined by Marshal Yeh Chen-ying in a confidential military briefing in 1961, in which he argued that a nuclear attack on China would necessarily be followed by an invasion using conventional weapons. Then China would be able to defeat the invaders in a people's war.[16] Presumably, the reason why it was thought that a nuclear attack would have to be followed by a conventional attack was the same that Mao had given three years earlier in explaining why nuclear weapons were counter-productive. The significant point here, however, is that China's leaders believed that the defensive weapon of people's war allied to the balance of world forces meant that an actual American attack on China was considered extremely unlikely. Perhaps an unspoken assumption was that an entirely unprovoked attack would be deterred because of the Sino-Soviet alliance. Moreover, as we have seen, Mao believed that the target of American offensiveness was not China or the socialist camp: 'NATO is attacking its own nationalism and its own communism (the central attack is on the intermediate areas of Asia, Africa and Latin America), but towards the socialist camp it is on the defensive.'[17]

In 1958 and 1959 the strength of the Soviet Union was still a vital factor in Mao's calculations of the balance of world forces. Furthermore, even if Soviet economic aid was not as forthcoming for the Second Five-Year Plan which began in 1958 because of the Soviet need to direct resources to Eastern Europe,[18] the Soviet Union still undertook in August 1958 and in February 1959 to assist in the construction of an additional 125 industrial projects (aside from the 211 Soviet-aided projects in progress or already completed).[19]

In 1959-60 the Sino-Soviet dispute deepened. As the Chinese later complained, in June 1959, the Soviet government unilaterally tore up the agreement on new technology for national defence concluded between China and the Soviet Union in October 1957 and refused to supply China with a sample of an atomic bomb and technical data concerning its manufacture.

Then, on the eve of Khrushchev's visit to the United States, ignoring China's repeated objections, the leadership of the CPSU released the TASS statement of 9 September on the Sino-Indian border incident, siding with the Indian national bourgeois government, thereby revealing, as the Chinese claimed, Sino-Soviet differences before the outside world. (The Russians have claimed that this was done later by the open Chinese polemics of 1960.) These two moves were regarded by the Chinese as 'presentation gifts to Eisenhower so as to curry favour with the US imperialists and create the so-called "Spirit of Camp David".[20] Khrushchev's visit to the United States for the Camp David talks with Eisenhower and the accompanying suggestions by him that China should make concessions on the Taiwan issue culminated in his visit to Peking for the tenth anniversary of the PRC, when he publicly lectured the Chinese on the undesirability of testing by force the stability of the capitalist camp, and undoubtedly left the Chinese in a more isolated position. Moreover, what was seen by Mao as collusion between Khrushchev and Mao's domestic opponent Peng Teh-huai at the critical Politburo meeting was regarded as illegitimate interference in China's internal affairs.[21] As we have seen, in January 1962 Mao stated that the Soviet leadership had been 'usurped by revisionists'. At the Tenth Plenum in September that year Mao suggested that henceforth 'right-wing opportunism [the term hitherto used to characterise Peng's errors] in China should be renamed: it should be called Chinese revisionism.'[22] The suggestion was pregnant with meaning for the future struggles leading to the Cultural Revolution, but at the time it showed the line of congruence drawn between Mao's external and internal adversaries within the socialist framework.

In November 1960, however, both sides had been able to sign the Moscow Statement of the 81 parties, despite mutual open polemics and the withdrawal of all Soviet aid and technicians in August. The Soviet leadership doubtless sought to force Chinese concessions because of the magnitude of the disasters which had hit the Chinese economy and because of divisions in the Chinese leadership, some of whom were evidently unhappy with the rapid deterioration of Sino-Soviet relations at a time of such economic crisis.[23] From the latter half of 1960 China began to import wheat from Canada and later from Australia too in order to feed the big cities. The winter of 1960-1 was evidently a terrible one for the Chinese people, with much of the economy in disarray and agricultural production so low that near-famine conditions prevailed in many areas. The turn to Canada and Australia was born of necessity, but it was also a harbinger of things to come. If thwarted by the Russians of the socialist camp, the Chinese could begin to cultivate the medium capitalist countries. But for the time being the Chinese leaders had not entirely given up the prospects of a better Sino-Soviet relationship within the socialist camp. Accordingly, drawing back from the brink, Chinese criticisms of the Soviet Union abated somewhat. For example, the Khrushchev programme for the advance to Communism issued at the 22nd Congress of the CPSU in August 1961 hardly drew a rebuttal at the time, even though later it was to be bitterly derided as 'goulash communism'. A sign of Chinese pride and determination not to be bullied can be seen from the aid programme to Albania which Khrushchev had tried to pressurise by cutting off all economic ties. In February and August 1961 China's aid projects (at a time when famine conditions were reported from various parts of China) exceeded the total which had been sent there by the Russians in the previous five years.[24] This did not stop Peking being visited by a Soviet economic mission and the anniversary of the Sino-Soviet alliance being celebrated with particular aplomb in February 1961.[25]

The 22nd CPSU Congress of October 1961 and its aftermath was undoubtedly a turning-point in the relationship. Chou En-lai walked out of the Congress and was given a demonstrative welcome by Mao Tse-tung and other Chinese leaders on his arrival at Peking Airport. Subsequent attempts by the Soviet leaders to characterise the Khrushchev programme for 'goulash' Communism as the 'real Communist Manifesto of our time' and the 'common programme' of the Communist and Workers' Parties and 'of the people of countries of the socialist community'[26] must have been an important factor in Mao's observation in January 1962 that the Soviet leadership had been 'usurped by revisionists'.

In the event, 1962 can be regarded as the critical year for the impending break. The Chinese saw themselves challenged on three fronts, from the Russians in Sinkiang in the west, from Taiwan supported by the Americans in the east, and from the Indians in the Himalayas. The Chinese claimed that in Sinkiang in April and May 'several tens of thousands of Chinese citizens' were caused to cross the border to the Soviet Union as the result of 'large-scale subversive activities by Soviet personnel'.[27] In the summer of 1962 the Chinese leaders were described by a foreign ambassador in Peking as 'panicky' over the prospect of an attack from Taiwan. Ch'en Yi, the Foreign Minister, said in a public interview on 29 May that the harvest would 'not be favourable' and spoke of anti-Communist elements who in a population of 600 million 'may amount to several million' and together with specially trained concealed agents would come out of hiding 'in case Chiang Kai-shek drops paratroops and lands on the mainland with American support'. A NCNA despatch of 23 June claimed that the Chiang Kai-shek forces, 'with the support and encouragement of US imperialism, [are] preparing for a large-scale military adventure, and invasion of the coastal areas of the mainland'. Meanwhile over 100,000 troops had been moved to the littoral provinces of the Taiwan Strait, and at China's initiative a Sino-US ambassadorial meeting in Warsaw was hastily arranged at which the Chinese were assured that the Americans totally disassociated themselves from any Nationalist invasion — an assurance publicly confirmed four days later by President Kennedy himself. The crisis was diffused.[28]

The Sino-Indian border clashes of October-November 1962 may be seen to have been inevitable once the Indian side had begun to implement its 'forward policy' in the border areas from the autumn of 1961,[29] and in the spring of 1962 China began to issue protests and warnings regarding Indian troop incursions into areas hitherto held by the Chinese. Chinese latent fears of encirclement were doubtless stimulated by the knowledge of Soviet economic and military aid to India.[30]

An important blow in this regard was the Soviet formal notification to China in August 1962 that the Soviet Union would conclude an agreement with the United States on the prevention of nuclear proliferation. As the Chinese noted a year later, 'This was a joint Soviet-US plot to monopolise nuclear weapons and an attempt to deprive China of the right to possess nuclear weapons to resist the US nuclear threat. The Chinese government lodged repeated protests against this.'[31] The Chinese nuclear programme as a symbol of China's final drive to total independence and as an important source of Mao's power was in jeopardy.[32] Nor were the Chinese leaders reassured by the Soviet performance in the Cuba missile crisis, when Khrushchev was accused of compounding the initial error of adventurism with the final error of capitulationism. Both errors were said to have arisen from Khrushchev's departure from Marxism-Leninism. Moreover, it was a graphic example to Mao of the dangers of a weaker ally relying upon the Soviet nuclear deterrent. Sooner or later the ally would have to pay the price for Soviet great-power behaviour and its desire for *détente* with the United States.

Even at this late hour there were attempts to modify the Sino-Soviet dispute, and in 1962 there was an expansion in the exchanges of delegations and public messages between the two countries.[33] Nevertheless, the Sino-Soviet leadership delegations in Moscow in July were not seriously expected by either side to reach any significant agreement. On 15 July the Test-Ban Treaty talks between the USSR, the US and the UK opened in Moscow in a cordial atmosphere. On 20 July the Sino-Soviet talks were formally adjourned *sine die*, and on 25 July the Test-

Ban Treaty was initialled. Sino-Soviet relations had reached an open break. As a Chinese government spokesman explained on 15 August:

> First the Soviet Government tried to subdue and curry favour with the US imperialists by discontinuing assistance to China. Then it put forward all sorts of untenable arguments in an attempt to induce China to abandon its solemn stand. Failing in all this, it has brazenly ganged up with the imperialist bandits in exerting pressure on China.
>
> In view of all the above [a long catalogue of alleged Soviet misdeeds], China has long ceased to place any hope in the Soviet leaders in developing its own nuclear strength to resist the US nuclear threats.[34]

Thenceforth China saw itself not only as an independent major country, but it was also to cast itself in the role of the major opposition to both the superpowers. The above account, written from the context of Chinese perspectives, suggests a view of China emerging to independence primarily as a reaction to the actions of others. Other than the desire for dignity and independence, China's role would appear to be relatively passive. That this is a very one-sided view may be seen from China's burgeoning relationship with the Third World.

The Intermediate Zone

As has already been argued in the previous chapters, China's leaders since the turn-around in 1951 have consistently maintained that China shared two important characteristics with the countries of Asia, Africa and Latin America (AALA): a common history of colonial and semi-colonial oppression and economies which were relatively backward and non-industrialised. These two characteristics were not of course shared by the Soviet Union. (In the past the Soviet Union may have been relatively unindustrialised, but this must be qualified, since even in 1913 Russia ranked seventh in the world in terms of industrial production.)[35] But more important from this perspective is the fact that Imperial Russia was one of the great colonisers and imperialists rather than a target of such expansionism.

In the middle 1950s China's leaders tended to see the AALA as an ally and a supplementary wing of the socialist camp in what was still largely a bipolar world. By 1957, however, following the Egyptian experience in the Suez crisis Chou En-lai began to look at the AALA in a new light. The ability of newly independent countries led by the national bourgeoisie to defend their sovereignty from colonialist attack came as

> a great revelation to us, showing that although the Asian and African countries are not powerful in material strength, all aggression by the colonialists can be frustrated, as long as we maintain our solidarity and firmly unite with all peace-loving forces of the world and wage a resolute struggle.[36]

By 1958, however, the situation was seen to have sharpened. The more dangerous Americans were seen to have replaced the old-style imperialists, Britain and France, in much of AALA.[37] As has already been noted, in September 1958 Mao regarded the Americans as being on the defensive in relation to the socialist camp whereas they were on the offensive against AALA: 'NATO is attacking its own nationalism and its own communism (the central attack is on the intermediate areas of Asia, Africa and Latin America), but towards the Socialist camp it is on the defensive.' This theme was not only stated in private. The pseudonymous Yu Chao-li in *Red Flag* in August 1958 (after Khrushchev's visit to China from 31 July to 3 August) spelt out in vigorous terms Mao's view of the importance of AALA. The revolutionary victories since the First World War had led to a situation in which a weakened imperialism was finding its 'last bastions being shaken violently by irresistible popular revolutionary forces'. The billion-strong socialist camp was now joined in the anti-imperialist struggle by more than 700 million who had won national independence and the 600 million people still fighting for independence. As against this, 'the imperialist countries have a combined population of only 400 million, divided and at odds; everywhere beneath their feet are volcanoes of revolt ready to erupt at any moment.' Next followed examples to show that revolutionary forces which were often seemingly weaker than their foes to begin with, were nevertheless able to end up in total victory. The article then recalled Mao's talks with Anna Louise Strong of 1946 which described the American reactionaries as 'paper tigers'. But more than this was involved. In those talks Mao had sketched out a view of the world that has always been anathema to Moscow, with its concept of a two-camp world subsequently modified to include a neutral world in between, which could make progress only in so far as it was specifically linked to the socialist camp. Mao's 1946 views, long suppressed in the interests of Sino-Soviet solidarity, were now brought out again in the concluding paragraph, and repeated almost word for word:

The hue and cry against the Soviet Union and Communism raised by the US imperialists is in fact a smokescreen under cover of which they are invading and enslaving the countries in the intermediate regions between the Socialist camp and the USA. The United States is separated from the Socialist countries by whole oceans; almost the entire Capitalist world lies between them. To start a war against the Soviet Union, US imperialism must first bring this Capitalist world to its knees. In order to set up military bases in a country, the US imperialists must first invade that country. [Earlier, Yu Chao-li — who, as Gittings suggests, may have been Mao himself[38] — wrote: 'They have established over 250 bases in the vast intermediate areas around the Socialist countries; they have wooed the reactionaries in more than twenty countries . . . '] They want to build military bases everywhere, so they carry out aggression everywhere, so they are naturally everywhere encircled by the people.[39]

At this stage, since Mao saw 'nationalism as closer to Communism than to imperialism', an earlier Yu Chao-li article (published, incidentally, on the day of Khrushchev's arrival in Peking on 31 July) argued that, unlike other groups whose class interest may make them vacillate and temporise with imperialism,

Communists in every country are real patriots because they have no interests of their own apart from the interests of the people. It is understandable therefore that Communists in the oppressed nations are always in the forefront of the national struggle.[40]

This was not only a barb directed at Khrushchev, but also reflected a certain disillusionment with Nasser (the hero of 1956 and 1957) because of his behaviour during the Middle East crisis arising out of the 13 July *coup* in Iraq.[41]

China had thus expanded upon a dimension of its role as a member of AALA. China was seen by its leaders as the one country which truly understood the international problems of the current era and which had to do all it could within its limited powers to encourage the correct response in AALA to the new pressures from the Americans. Moreover, it followed that any anti-imperialist volcanic eruption automatically threatened the overstretched Americans and that it necessarily was an important asset to the struggle of the socialist camp. In fact they were mutually supportive. The important thing was to encourage unity in AALA and indeed to try and establish an internationalist united front.

But unlike later periods, the primary focus for China's loyalties in the 1950s was still the socialist camp. The Sino-Soviet alliance was still very much operative, and an alliance was a totally different phenomenon from a loose and potentially shifting internationalist united front.

A corollary of the Chinese insistence on the unsullied and disinterested patriotism of Communists in AALA was the notion that other forces might sell out to imperialism. Indeed, now that US imperialism was perceived as directing its aggression to AALA it was to be expected that the newly won independence in countries led by the national bourgeoisie would be put to the test. In this view either they would have to stand up to these threats to their independence and hence come more into conflict with imperialist forces (which would make them shift closer to the socialist camp) or they would temporise and serve imperialist interests. Something along these latter lines was perceived by the Chinese to have happened in the Middle East. But the clearest example was India in 1959 — and of course the Chinese were not surprised that the Yugoslavs, regarded as agents for American imperialism and as a disintegrative element for the socialist camp, should now with their theory of non-alignment side with the 'Indian reactionaries'. The Tibetan revolt in the spring of 1959, aided by CIA and Kuomintang airdrops, was rapidly put down by Chinese forces. The Chinese regarded Nehru's attitude, his reception of the Dalai Lama almost as head of a government in exile, and especially his statement of 21 April, as unwarranted interference in China's internal affairs. This was linked to the legacy of British imperialist attitudes towards Tibet and to the ties which many sections of the Indian bourgeoisie had with imperialism.[42] In the editorial on the question, the *People's Daily* also used the distinctive phrase 'anti Communist anti China' which was to figure so prominently during the Cultural Revolution. This suggested that the one was an inevitable consequence of the other.

Under conditions in which the Chinese believed that the main thrust of American offensive strategy was directed towards gaining dominance of the intermediate zone, it followed that the national bourgeois leaders of the newly independent countries were to be subject to new external pressures. The Sino-Indian border clashes in the autumn of 1959 coupled with the TASS statement of 9 September, which failed to support China and thereby in Chinese eyes exposed the Sino-Soviet dispute to the world for the first time, and perhaps the coincidental announcement of Soviet aid for India's new five-year plan, were important factors which led to the harshest statement made by a Chinese official on bourgeois nationalism since the very early days of the People's Republic. The Deputy Foreign Minister Wang Chia-hsiang wrote in *Red Flag* in October attacking (Soviet) theories of the transition to socialism in AALA in terms which also dealt with the comprador proclivities of certain national bourgeois leaders:

> The bourgeois class is, after all, a bourgeois class. As long as it controls political power it cannot adopt a resolute revolutionary line and it can only adopt a wavering conciliatory line. As a result, these states can never expect to effect the transition to socialism, nor indeed can they thoroughly fulfil the task of the nationalist democratic revolution. It should be added that even the national independence they have won is by no means secure . . . The capitalist classes that control the political power of certain Afro-Asian states prefer to develop their economy along the road of capitalism or state capitalism, and moreover call it by the beautiful name 'the road of democracy'. Actually, by following this road, they can hardly free themselves from the oppression and exploitation of imperialism and feudalism; indeed they may even pave the way for the emergence of bureaucratic capitalism, which is an ally of imperialism and feudalism . . . In the final analysis, they can never escape from the control and bondage of imperialism.[43]

This mode of class analysis for dealing with the countries of AALA did not last long — at least in overt discussions. Generally the key questions for China have tended to be not so much the class background and bases of the leaders of AALA as their attitudes towards what the Chinese regarded as the critical questions of the day. In fact even the article quoted above was directed probably more at the Russian leadership than towards the leaders of AALA. Khrushchev was then in Peking following his Camp David talks with Eisenhower. The Peking position was not one that led it to draw distinctions, for example, between workers and peasants in AALA. It continued to assert its belief in the revolutionary qualities of the 'people' of these countries. The problem concerned the orientation of the leadership and the influence of the bourgeoisie. Thus the Chinese Foreign Minister Ch'en Yi, in an article written for *Izvestia* of the Soviet Union, explained the situation as follows: 'The imperialists have always made use of the right-wing forces in the nationalist countries to sow discord between these countries and China, to undermine the friendship cherished by the peoples of these countries for the Chinese people.'[44] Ch'en Yi also claimed a special kind of leadership role with regard to the people of AALA: 'In the Chinese people they see their own tomorrow and the Chinese people see in all oppressed nations their yesterday.'[45] The leadership role should be seen as more a didactic one befitting a people with experiences which others were due to undergo themselves soon.

In this period, in fact, the Chinese leaders were very distrustful of any independence which was not hard-won. They were thus very hostile to de Gaulle's proposals of September 1959 to negotiate with the Provincial Revolutionary Government of Algeria, and they were highly critical of Khrushchev's acceptance of the French offer at the end of October.[46] In this period of the rapid expansion of the gaining of independence by African countries which was soon to characterise the early 1960s, the Chinese were active in promoting their own viewpoints and in supporting a variety of groups and leaders within these countries. China began to be a supplier of aid.[47] They had less compunction than in later periods in dividing these leaders into more or less progressive and more or less revolutionary. But class analysis was not the paradigm guiding Chinese actions, it was rather analogies with Chinese historical experience. The general analogy was that Africa was more like the period of Warring States (403-221 BC) in China, and that what was needed was for the Chinese to familiarise Africans with China's experiences from the Taiping Uprising through to 1949.[48]

In the summer of 1960 Mao received delegations from AALA (including Japan) on five separate occasions, and his talks with them were widely publicised. Symbolically these meetings were greatly significant. The Chairman of the Chinese Communist Party was visibly identifying himself and China with the peoples of the world — the broad message was that they were mutually supportive in their struggles and that 'The people are the decisive factor.' They faced a common enemy in US imperialism, 'we all stand on the same front and need to unite with and support each other' and therefore 'it is necessary to form a broad united front and unite with all forces, excluding the enemy, that can be united with and continue to wage arduous struggles.' He argued that 'what imperialism fears most is the awakening of the Asian, African and Latin American peoples.' As for the Russians, Mao praised the Soviet people for having shot down the U-2 plane (which had been the occasion for the collapse of the four-power summit before it began) and 'hoped' that those people (Khrushchev), who had described Eisenhower as a great lover of peace, 'will be awakened by these facts'.[49] Thus for Mao the centre of the struggle against imperialism was among the people of AALA rather than in the socialist camp. With regard to the Asian countries on China's borders, the Chinese objective was to encourage them towards neutrality and not to fall in with American military plans in Asia.[50] From 1960 to March 1963 China signed border agreements with Afghanistan, Burma, Mongolia, Nepal and Pakistan on the basis of mutual concessions. The land borders with North Korea, North Vietnam and Laos were not then in dispute. Thus only the borders with India and the Soviet Union were still in contention.

As the Sino-Soviet dispute intensified, so did the emphasis on the significance of AALA gain in importance. Thus in his speech at the Tenth Plenum on 24 September Mao surveyed the international scene by noting the victories in AALA. Interestingly, with regard to our previous discussion of Chinese attitudes towards right and left in AALA, Mao observed that what was really critical was the question of opposition to imperialism: 'The United Arab Republic is inclined towards the right, but then Iraq emerged. Both are to the right of centre, but both oppose imperialism.'

Perhaps the most important aspect of the speech, as we shall see further below, was Mao's analysis of the contradiction with imperialism which showed a new order of priority in which the one with socialism was relegated to last (see p p. 123-4).[51] Thus a theoretical framework was emerging for the special focus on AALA. This was the true centre where the conflict with imperialism was located. China's historical experience and its struggle for economic construction from poverty and blankness provided the CPR with a new and significant role. In some ways it paralleled the Soviet relationship to China in the 1950s. China was to be a teacher by example to AALA, a giver of aid and the leading country in the struggle against imperialism. The parallel is, of course, suggestive rather than exact. Their social systems, ideologies, patterns of interactions, etc. were totally different. But the didactic role was to be an important dimension of China's policies to AALA (and as I shall argue in a later chapter, has become a general feature of China's foreign policy). The Chinese also seem to have applied the lessons of their experience of Russian aid. Chinese aid from the outset was free of dependency building patterns, their experts were paid according to local rates and the methods of repayment were designed not to become burdensome to the recipients.

As the Sino-Soviet alliance was decaying, so a new framework for China's foreign policy was simultaneously taking shape. China was to be in the forefront of the people of the world in their struggle with imperialism.

China as the True Source of Marxism-Leninism

> I think there are two 'swords': one is Lenin and the other Stalin.
> The sword of Stalin has now been discarded by the Russians. The
> sword of Lenin [was] by and large . . . thrown out by them. (15
> November 1956)[52]
> The Party and State leadership of the Soviet Union has now been
> usurped by the revisionists.(January 1962)[53]

It is clear from these citations of inner party speeches that Mao was
implicitly claiming well before 1963 that the centre of Marxist-Leninist
orthodoxy was in Peking and not in Moscow. In that sense, as we have
seen, the Chinese leadership had already embraced a new role for China
as an independent centre for correct ideology for the socialist camp as
early as 1956. But what distinguishes the 1958-63 period from the latter
years of the previous one is that China's leaders were no longer seeking
to act as, perhaps, the teachers of their greater ally seeking to push the
Soviet leaders back on to the 'correct' path. In this period the Chinese
leadership took on the role first of a critic, then as an ideological rival
and finally as the sole true source of Marxism-Leninism in the international Communist movement. By 1962 the Chinese were openly
encouraging and supporting breakaway groups from the established
Communist parties throughout the world. Henceforth China's international role as the true upholder and source of Marxism-Leninism was to
go well beyond the question of Sino-Soviet relations themselves. Up
until this point China's leaders did not claim to be doing more than
applying the universal principles of Marxism-Leninism to the concrete
conditions of China. This was the meaning of the Sinification of
Marxism. But once China had become the sole source of Marxism-
Leninism itself in the contemporary world, the relationship between the
application of general principles to the specific situation in China and
the actual generation of these principles themselves from revolutionary
practice in China itself became much more complex. From now on,
universalist Marxist-Leninist theory and its further development would
be expounded in Mao Tse-tung Thought which in turn emanated from
the practice of revolution within China. Many of the major themes of
the continuation of revolution in China were undoubtedly of universal
significance, but at the same time many were of local relevance only.
The problem of distinguishing between the universal and the local significance of the Chinese revolutionary experience has been formulated
differently at different times. Thus a resolution of the Central Committee's Military Affairs Committee of 20 October 1960, which had

been revised personally by Mao and which marked the beginning of the campaigns to elevate and glorify Mao Tse-tung Thought as the supreme source of authority in China, stated it as follows for an exclusively domestic audience:

> Comrade Mao Tse-tung is a great Marxist-Leninist. Through the application of the universal truth of Marxism-Leninism in an era when imperialism is heading for annihilation, and socialism is approaching victory, Mao Tse-tung's thought developed and improved Marxism-Leninism through concrete practice in the Chinese revolution and the collective struggle of the Party and the people.[54]

This is still a far cry from the position adopted in the Cultural Revolution when it was stated that Mao was 'the greatest Marxist-Leninist of our era' and that he had brought Marxism-Leninism 'to a higher and completely new stage'. In fact in 1966 the 'people of the world' were required to carry out 'Mao Tse-tung Thought' rather than even 'apply it to the concrete conditions' of their particular countries. The fact that some Chinese leaders like Ch'en Yi complained that this Thought was 'too Chinese for foreigners to understand' is illustrative of the kind of problem which could arise from universalising too freely the Chinese experience.

The Military Affairs Committee Resolution is noteworthy neverthe-less for at least three reasons. First, as Stuart Schram has pointed out, it is the direct harbinger of the Cultural Revolution and it served as the draft for a much stronger statement in the introduction for the 'Little Red Book' a few years later.[55] Second, although the claims on Mao's behalf are modest in comparison with the extravagant eulogisation of the Cultural Revolution, they nevertheless went beyond any public statements at the time. But it accurately spelt out the premise on which China's attitude at the 81 Communist Parties' Conference in Moscow the following month was based and about which the Italian Communist Luigi Lonzo complained: 'No one may consider himself, by order of his own decision, the sole depository of Marxism-Leninism.'[56] For that was what the Chinese position amounted to. Third, a new era in world affairs had been identified — 'an era when imperialism is heading for annihilation, and socialism is approaching'. The public announcement of the coming of this new era had to wait until the Cultural Revolution. The reasons for the delay have not been given in Chinese sources. It can only be surmised that there were tactical constraints which militated against saying this before party-to-party relations with the CPSU had been broken in the spring of 1966, which also coincided with the end of an attempt to establish a like-minded coalition of Asian Communist parties. Moreover, other party leaders may have disapproved.

If the full implications of China's new ideological role were not to become clear until the Cultural Revolution, many of the essential positions which were to characterise that role were spelt out in the course of the Sino-Soviet dispute. All the same, much of the Chinese analysis until 1962 and 1963 was still based on the assumption that the socialist camp as such was still a very important factor in world affairs. Thus a confidential and authoritative analysis of the international situation issued in April 1961 (well after the withdrawal of all Soviet aid and technicians in the summer of 1960 and after the divisive Moscow meeting) started with an affirmation of the great strength of the camp and spoke of the need to maintain 'friendly relations with the Soviet Union' because that would be 'advantageous to the peoples of China, the Soviet Union and the world'. The analysis went on to explain:

> As there is no exact identification between the circumstances of China and the Soviet Union, it is impossible for the two countries to have an exactly identical point of view on every problem. The policy of our country towards the United States must also be different from that of the Soviet Union. But this difference will not hinder the transition from Socialism to Communism or the overall opposition to imperialism.

The analysis then went on to note remarkably: 'At present both China and the Soviet Union are fundamentally unanimous in their attitude toward problems like Kennedy, disarmament, Laos, Cuba and the Congo.'[57] Within a year the Laos and Congo issues had been more or less settled, but the other three questions became central to Sino-Soviet differences.

Mao's observation of January 1962 that the Soviet leadership had been usurped by revisionists was followed by a speech in September in which, after surveying many examples of the vigorous assertion of national independence struggles in AALA, he went on to make the interesting analysis in theoretical terms of the kinds of basic conflicts which characterised the contemporary world:

> The contradiction between the people of the whole world and

> imperialism is the primary one. There is the opposition of the
> people of all countries to the reactionary bourgeoisie and to reac-
> tionary nationalism. There are also the contradictions between the
> people of all countries and revisionism, the contradictions among
> imperialist countries, the contradiction between nationalist coun-
> tries and imperialism, internal contradictions within imperialist
> countries, and the contradiction between socialism and imperial-
> ism.[58]

The word 'primary' in the first sentence should have been translated as
'principal' ('chu yao'). In this context it has a specific technical meaning
in ideological terms. Once a contradiction has been identified as
'principal' all the other contradictions become automatically secondary
and subordinate to it. By placing the contradiction between socialism
and imperialism last on the list, especially after having extolled the
significance of AALA developments, Mao was arguing in effect that the
immediate destiny of world history was to be settled in AALA without
reference to the socialist camp headed by the Soviet Union. Indeed Mao
went even further, because he listed the contradiction between 'the
people of all countries and revisionism' before the standard four basic
contradictions habitually listed by all Communists beginning with
Lenin.

This analysis was directed to an inner party audience, but it was to
form the underlying basis for the ensuing phases of China's foreign
policy and it was to find expression in the bitter Sino-Soviet exchanges
of 1963. It also implicitly identified an altogether new role for China.
China, of course, was a socialist country in AALA. It was also the sole
repository of genuine Marxism-Leninism in the world as a whole. It fell
then to socialist China therefore to direct the struggle against imperialism. China too was the best qualified to identify 'the reactionary
bourgeoisie', and China had long been at the forefront of the conflict
with revisionism. China's new role was indeed a global and all-embracing
one. The consistent opposition to the theory of peaceful transition to
socialism or the parliamentary road meant that China's task was to
support such Communist parties or dissident groups in the industrialised
as well as the less developed countries which also opposed the view that
it was possible to arrive at socialism without armed struggle. A corollary
to this of course was that there were no immediate expectations of a
revolutionary situation emerging in Europe or elsewhere in the developed countries. By 1963 the Russians were accusing the Chinese of
having fomented party dissidents in countries as diverse as the US,

Brazil, Italy, Belgium, Australia and India. This was more than an Asian coalition. And indeed in addition to the mixed support of several Asian Communist parties, the Chinese had the support of the parties from New Zealand and Albania.

The Chinese leaders clearly felt that modern Chinese history and their own revolutionary experience provided them with all the necessary understanding to deal with the problems thrown up by the outside world. The analogy with the different kinds of bourgeoisie in China in the first half of this century was the key with which the Chinese leaders sought to make the relevant distinction between the progressive and reactionary bourgeoisie in AALA. In fact China's leaders sought to go further. Far from being content to use Chinese history as a means by analogy to understand the problems of other people, China's leaders at one stage actually proposed to teach Africans Chinese history so that they might better understand African conditions:

> Africa itself looks like the seven powers of [China's] Warring States [403 BC to 221 BC] with its Nasser, Nkrumah, Hussein [sic], Sekou Touré, Bourguiba and Abbas [sic], each with his own way of leading others. In general everyone is trying to sell his own goods. Africa is now like a huge political exhibition, where a hundred flowers are truly blooming, waiting there for anybody to pick. But everything must go through the experience of facts. History and realistic life can help the Africans to take the road of healthy development. We must tell them about the Chinese revolutionary experience in order to reveal the true nature of both new and old colonialism. In Africa we do no harm to anyone, we introduce no illusions, for all we say is true.[59]

Whether or not China's historical experience is a useful framework within which African problems can be best understood, there can be few if any Africans who have sought to use it and certainly there is not a single leader of an African independent country who is known to have done so. However much the Chinese model may be admired in Africa, Chinese attempts to universalise their experience on the basis of the late Foreign Minister Ch'en Yi's remark that 'our yesterday is their today and our today is their tomorrow' are conducive to producing mutual incomprehension rather than co-operative understanding. Thus Chou En-lai's famous statement of 1964 that 'an excellent revolutionary situation exists in Africa' (which clearly meant the national democratic and not the socialist-proletarian revolution) alarmed rather than encouraged many African leaders.[60]

At the same time it is critically important to note that China's didactic intentions did not call upon the Chinese to direct and instruct the Africans. Even though Peking was perceived as the true source of Marxism-Leninism and as the centre of principled opposition to imperialism, there was no sign that China's leaders sought to establish a latter day Third International which would direct its member constituents as to how to act at every given strategic and tactical turning-point. The Chinese position was still country-centred. It was up to the people of every country to apply to their specific conditions the universal principles of Marxism-Leninism (in the case of genuine Communists) or of proper opposition to American imperialism as increasingly articulated in Peking.

Mao had never practised the export of revolution. The historical experience of the Chinese Revolution under his leadership confirmed the importance of being free of external controls, and that any external interference was likely to be counter-productive. Moreover Sino-Soviet relations since 1949 doubtless sensitised Mao to the dangers of great-power chauvinism. The Chinese leaders could hardly begin to carry out practices of which they had so bitterly and effectively criticised the Russians without undermining totally their credibility at the outset. We have already seen that with regard to Korea the Chinese had forsworn the accepted pattern of great-power behaviour. Thus China's revolutionary experience, principles and actual mode of operations all militated against an activist interventionist role. Another powerful constraint against taking up such a role was China's military and economic weakness relative to its principal adversaries. Even if it be conceded that China could successfully defend itself from an American attack by resorting to a people's war, it was simply impossible for China to challenge militarily such a powerful antagonist beyond its own borders.

Notes

1. Stuart Schram (ed.), *Mao Tse-tung Unrehearsed* (Penguin Books, 1974), p. 181.
2. Joyce Kallgren, 'Nationalist China's Armed Forces', *The China Quarterly*, No. 15 (July-September 1963).
3. See the account of the Nagasaki flag episode by Gene T. Hsiao in Jerome Cohen (ed.), *The Dynamics of China's Foreign Relations* (Harvard University Press, 1971).
4. Schram, *Mao Tse-tung Unrehearsed*, p. 128.

5. JPRS I, pp. 99-101; *Wan Sui*, pp. 197-8.
6. For analyses of the military aspects see John Gittings, *The Role of the Chinese Army* (Oxford University Press, 1967), p. 285 ff; and Harold P. Ford, 'The Eruption of Sino-Soviet Politico-Military Problems 1957-1960' in Raymond L. Garthoff (ed.), *Sino-Soviet Military Relations* (Praeger, 1966), pp. 100-13.
7. Schram, *Mao Tse-tung Unrehearsed*, p. 129.
8. Yu Chao-li, 'A New Upsurge in National Revolution' in *Peking Review*, No. 26 (1958), pp. 8-9.
9. Speech at the Tenth Plenum, 24 September 1962 in Schram, *Mao Tse-tung Unrehearsed*, p. 90.
10. For detailed analyses of the crisis see J. Kalicki, *The Pattern of Sino-American Crises* (Cambridge University Press, 1975), pp. 168-208; Harold C. Hinton, *Communist China in World Politics* (Macmillan, 1966), pp. 265-70; and D.S. Zagoria, *The Sino-Soviet Conflict 1956-61* (Princeton University Press, 1962), pp. 206-17.
11. John Gittings, *The World and China 1922-72* (Eyre Methuen, 1974), pp. 229-30.
12. Ibid., p. 225 and *Wan Sui*, pp. 231-2.
13. JPRS I, pp. 108-9.
14. Used in Gittings, *The World and China*, p. 231.
15. JPRS I, pp. 108-9. For an interesting analysis see Allen S. Whiting, 'Mao, China and the Cold War', in Yōnosuke Nagai and Akira Iriye (eds.), *The Origins of the Cold War in Asia* (Columbia University Press 1977).
16. 'Speech of Comrade Yeh Chien-ying at the Training Meeting of the Military Affairs Commission' in J. Chester Cheng, *The Politics of the Chinese Red Army* (Hoover, Stanford University Press, 1966), pp. 249-55.
17. Speech of September 1958 in *Wan Sui*, p. 254. See also Gittings, *The World and China*, p. 226.
18. See unsigned article (by Dr W. Klatt), 'Sino-Soviet Economic Relations' in G.F. Hudson, Richard Lowenthal and Roderick MacFarquhar, *The Sino-Soviet Dispute* (Praeger, 1961), pp. 35-8.
19. John Gittings, *Survey of the Sino-Soviet Dispute* (Oxford University Press, 1968), p. 181.
20. In the first comment on the open letter of the CC of the CPSU, 6 September 1963. See *The Polemic on the General Line of the International Communist Movement* (FLP, 1965).
21. For full documentation see *The Case of Peng Teh-huai* (Union Research Institute, Hong Kong, 1968); see also Nikita Khrushchev, *Khrushchev Remembers*, esp. Vol. 2 (Penguin Books, 1974).
22. Schram (ed.), *Mao Tse-tung Unrehearsed*, p. 192.
23. See, for example, the speech by T'ao Chu of 30 March 1960 in SCMP, No. 2287, p. 16, cited by Zagoria, *The Sino-Soviet Conflict*, p. 371.
24. Ibid., p. 377.
25. See *Peking Review*, No. 7 (1961), pp. 5-9.
26. See the sarcastic references in *The Polemic on the General Line*, p. 94.
27. For analysis of this see Allen S. Whiting, *The Chinese Calculus of Deterrence* (University of Michigan Press, 1975), pp. 32-3.
28. Ibid., pp. 67-9, from which this account is taken.
29. For the authoritative account see N. Maxwell, *India's China War* (Pelican Books, 1970).
30. See Gittings, *Survey of the Sino-Soviet Dispute*, pp. 110-11; Arthur Stein, *India and the Soviet Union: The Nehru Era* (University of Chicago Press, 1969), p. 125; and the discussion in Whiting, *The Chinese Calculus*,

pp. 72-5.

31.   *The Polemic on the General Line*, p. 96.

32.   See the stimulating discussion on the importance of nuclear weapons as a dimension of the political power of national leaders within their domestic political systems in F. Schurmann, *The Logic of World Power* (Pantheon, 1974), pp. 83-107 and 384-98.

33.   See the account in W.E. Griffith, *The Sino-Soviet Rift* (M.I.T. Press, 1966). Also see Gittings, *Survey of the Sino-Soviet Dispute*, p. 155 and pp. 184-5; and A. Dallin, *Diversity in International Communism* (Columbia University Press, 1963), p. 652.

34.   *Peking Review*, No. 33 (1963), pp. 7-15. The quotation is on p. 15.

35.   See M. Fainsod, *How Russia is Ruled* (Harvard University Press, 1963), Chapter I, esp. on pre-revolutionary Russia's industrial development, pp. 20-4.

36.   Chou En-lai, 'Report on a Visit to Eleven Countries in Asia and Europe', 5 March 1957, supplement to *People's China*, 1 April 1957.

37.   For an account as to how this was perceived to have operated in the Middle East see Yitzhak Shichor, 'The Middle East in China's Foreign Policy, 1949-1974', London University Ph.D. thesis (1976), Chapter 3, in particular pp. 167-74.

38.   Gittings, *The World and China*, p. 219.

39.   Yu Chao-li, 'The Forces of the New are bound to Defeat the Forces of Decay', *Peking Review*, No. 25 (1958), pp. 8-9.

40.   See note 8 above.

41.   For details see Schichor, 'The Middle East in China's Foreign Policy', pp. 179-200.

42.   See 'The Revolution in Tibet and Nehru's Philosophy' by the Editorial Department of the *People's Daily*, 6 May 1959 in *Peking Review*, No. 19 (1959), pp. 6-15. For evidence cited by the Chinese of American-KMT material aid to the Tibetan rebels see Anna Louise Strong, *Tibetan Interviews* (FLP,1959), pp.94-5. For evidence culled from American and other sources see M. Peissel, *The Secret War in Tibet* (Little Brown and Co., 1972). See also the careful discussion in Whiting, *The Chinese Calculus*, pp. 12-21.

43.   Wang Chia-hsiang, 'International Significance of the Victory of the Chinese People', *Red Flag*, 1 October 1959; JPRS 1013-D, 16 November 1959. Also cited in Gittings, *The World and China*, p. 214.

44.   Chen Yi, 'Ten Years of Struggle for World Peace and Human Progress', *Peking Review*, No. 40 (1959), p. 22.

45.   Ibid., p. 21.

46.   See Alaba Ogunsanwo, *China's Policy in Africa 1958-71* (Cambridge University Press, 1974), p. 58. See also B. Larkin, *China and Africa 1949-1970* (University of California Press, 1971).

47.   For figures see Carol H. Fogarty, 'China's Economic Relations with the Third World' in US Congress Joint Economic Committee, *China: A Reassessment of the Economy* (Washington, 10 July 1975).

48.   See statement to this effect in reference material on the current international situation (April 1961) in Cheng, *The Politics of the Chinese Red Army*, p. 484.

49.   See Chairman Mao Tse-tung's *Important Talks with Guests from Asia, Africa and Latin America* (FLP, 1960).

50.   For a useful analysis of several important case studies see M. Gurtov, *China and Southeast Asia: The Politics of Survival* (Heath Lexington Books, 1971).

51.   Schram (ed.), *Mao Tse-tung Unrehearsed*, p. 192.

52. *SW*, Vol. V, p. 341.
53. See note 1 above.
54. In Cheng, *The Politics of the Chinese Red Army*, p. 33.
55. Stuart R. Schram (ed.), *Authority, Participation and Cultural Change in China* (Cambridge University Press, 1973), pp. 66-7.
56. Cited in H. Carrere d'Encausse and Stuart R. Schram, *Marxism and Asia* (Allen Lane, 1969), p. 79.
57. Cheng, *The Politics of the Chinese Red Army*, pp. 480-7.
58. Schram (ed.), *Mao Tse-tung Unrehearsed*, p. 192.
59. Cheng, *The Politics of the Chinese Red Army*, p. 484.
60. See Larkin, *China and Africa*, p. 70 and Alan Hutchison, *China's Africa Revolution* (Hutchinson, 1976), pp. 68-9.

PART TWO

CHINA AS A SELF-RELIANT AUTONOMOUS INTERNATIONAL ACTOR: 1963 ONWARDS

INTRODUCTION

The public breach of Sino-Soviet relations in the summer of 1963 meant that the period in which China's international role was predicated on the Sino-Soviet alliance had come to an end. To be sure, the breach was not total − party-to-party relations continued until the spring of 1966, the St Valentine's Day anniversary of the signing of the alliance treaty continued to be marked in both capitals in 1964 and 1965, and there were occasional references to the extension of mutual support in the event of aggression against either. It was not until 1966 that the possibility of some kind of concerted action over the issues arising from the Vietnam War was finally dismissed in Peking. Nevertheless whatever residual aspects of the alliance remained, from July 1963 China had become very much an independent actor and indeed a major autonomous force in international affairs. The charge of revisionism hurled at Khrushchev had now been joined by the accusation that he was colluding with the United States against China. The Test-Ban Treaty of 25 July was seen as an attempt by the existing nuclear powers to snuff out China's nuclear programme. An editorial in the *People's Daily* observed:

> It is most obvious that the tripartite treaty is aimed at tying China's hands. The U.S. representative to the Moscow talks has said publicly that the United States, Britain and the Soviet Union were able to arrive at an agreement, because 'we could work together to prevent China getting a nuclear capability' . . . This is a US-Soviet alliance against China pure and simple.[1]

Other Chinese statements argued that the treaty facilitated in particular American offensive designs against AALA and that it could lead through the strategy of flexible response of the Kennedy administration to limited tactical nuclear strikes in local wars against national liberation movements.

China now found itself pitted against both the great global powers of the nuclear age, the United States and the Soviet Union, before having acquired even the most elementary nuclear deterrent against either. We have already seen that Mao in particular was confident that the thrust of America's offensiveness was directed against AALA rather than directly against the socialist countries. Moreover, the Chinese leadership had just survived the three bitter years after the Great Leap Forward and had triumphed over their adversaries in 1962. While there was internal leadership conflict leading up to the Cultural Revolution, it was not until 1965-6, when the flames of the Vietnam War threatened a Sino-American war that the underlying strategic seriousness of China's position became a critical issue in Peking. Thus available Chinese sources for the period do not reflect the awesomeness of the task taken up by Peking in confronting both the great powers.

New concepts and a new framework within which to conduct foreign policy were required. Since there were already grave ideological differences in the Chinese leadership over domestic issues it is hardly surprising that there should also have emerged differences on international affairs, particularly on questions of such fundamental importance as the international orientation of China and its revolution, and on the attitude to take towards the Soviet Union. These differences, partly of tactics and partly of general strategy and basic orientation, did not begin with 1963. In a sense they have always been present in one form or another since the establishment of the CPC in 1921, if not before.[2] But from our perspective the questions regarding the turning-point of China's role in world affairs consequent upon the Sino-Soviet split, the differences in the Chinese leadership are best seen within a temporal framework of 1960-6. Since the concern here is with the identification of China's changing role on the world stage it will facilitate analysis to examine first the main policies and outlook evident in the course charted by the Chinese ship of state as a coherent unit in the period 1963-6 before turning to investigate possible counter-currents among the leadership. Furthermore, it is clear in retrospect that the main driving force behind the direction of China's foreign policy came from Mao Tse-tung and that he and his line prevailed over the others at the critical moment of decision in the spring of 1966, just as it was to prevail in 1971 when the opening was made to the United States.

The Nuclear Factor[3]

Before seeking to analyse the different phases and the different ways in which China's role as an independent force in world affairs was articulated, it seems relevant to pause first to consider the implications of China's nuclear programme and policy for the entire period after 1963. This has been a relatively constant factor in China's international relations in the sense that not only has China's nuclear capability been overwhelmingly inferior to that of either of the superpowers, but also it has always been vulnerable to a first-strike attack which would totally destroy any retaliatory capacity at one blow. There is a case for arguing that as China's nuclear delivery systems have increased in number and have been variously deployed in the 1970s, so has the prospect increased of the possible survival of a limited portion of its systems in the event of a first strike by one of the superpowers. In that sense China may have the beginnings of a second-strike capability. But some caveats are in order here: first, China has still not demonstrated the capacity to fire an Inter-Continental Ballistic Missile (ICBM) – which means that the United States is still out of range and that the only superpower within range is the Soviet Union; second, China's nuclear missiles are still liquid-fuelled, which means that they take a relatively long time to be fired and that potentially any surviving missiles could be destroyed after a putative first strike by the rapid-firing solid-fuel rockets available to China's principal adversary; and third, that because of the strategic asymmetry with, say, the Soviet Union, China's very limited possible second-strike capability even in the latter half of the 1970s rests on what has been called the 'bee-sting' strategy. In other words, the super-powers have the capacity to inflict massive destruction on China whilst in return China's retaliatory force could only hope to inflict marginal but painful damage, rather like that of a bee sting on a human being. Nevertheless that limited retaliatory capability (which is increasing and being diversified with the passage of time) may be sufficient to deter a nuclear attack upon China. If the nuclear strategic deterrence between the Soviet Union and the United States rests upon the certainty of knowledge that both adversaries would be destroyed by a nuclear exchange (the doctrine of Mutual Assured Destruction), China's nuclear deterrence rests very much on the uncertainties of the strategic asymmetries between it and either of the superpowers. But so inferior is the Chinese nuclear capability compared to that arrayed against it by the Soviet Union that much of the ensuing discussion based on the situation of the 1960s still applies in the 1970s, though subject to the qualification of the 'bee-sting' strategy outlined above.

In many ways the breach with the Soviet Union heralded the most dangerous phase of China's foreign policy. One of the most important reasons given by Mao from the late 1950s onwards that the thrust of America's imperialist offensive was directed towards AALA necessarily lost cogency. Previously Mao had argued that the socialist camp had obtained a decisive advantage in the balance of forces against the imperialist camp headed by the United States and that partly because of this the socialist countries were not in danger of direct attack. This argument could no longer be advanced as a convincing basis for suggesting that China would not be an immediate target for aggression by America. On the contrary, once China had acquired a limited nuclear capability the country became possibly a more inviting object for attack. It would obviously take a considerable time for China to acquire a second-strike capability. Under such conditions the only possible strategy for the weaker country when faced with a crisis situation in which nuclear weapons might be used would be to strike first. Otherwise it would be condemned supinely to wait until its limited nuclear arsenal was totally destroyed. A potential nuclear adversary therefore would be perforce tempted to strike first in a crisis situation. The weaker power could not carry out a pre-emptive strike. If it were to strike first it could only be with the aim of inflicting some damage in the sure expectation of a totally devastating reply. The alternative, however, would be to face a pre-emptive strike.

These necessarily abstract considerations were none the less the strategic factors which have provided the backcloth against which China's nuclear programme developed. During the 1960s the theory of the surgical strike in which China's nuclear capability could be destroyed (or 'taken out') in one fell swoop was current in American strategic thinking and in 1969 the Russians seriously considered a pre-emptive strike against the Chinese installations. But despite the uncertainties or rather perhaps because of them and the possible ramifications of such action no such strikes were made and what could have been a destabilising factor regarding China's security has emerged in retrospect as one which has enhanced China's defences.

Having discussed some of the military strategic aspects affecting China's nuclear programme about which Chinese sources (both official and unofficial) have been reticent, it is appropriate to consider Chinese analyses and statements about the role of nuclear weapons and the purpose of their nuclear programme.

Mao's views as expounded in his various comments and discussions of the subject in the late 1950s and early 1960s reflect the position stated in the slogan first advanced in 1946: 'the atomic bomb is a paper tiger.' Namely that, powerful as it was, it could not be decisive in determining the long-term outcome of the prospects for revolution. A revolutionary should not be intimidated by it into capitulating. At the same time it was a powerful weapon. Thus it should be despised from the long-term point of view while respected in any immediate tactical sense. As we have seen, in the 1950s Mao argued that the Americans were unlikely to attack China, but the possibility existed on a 'worst case' basis. At the same time he consistently rebutted the view both to domestic and foreign audiences that an atomic war would totally destroy the socialist camp. However destructive it would be, at least a third of the socialist camp would survive to build a better world. To have conceded otherwise would necessarily have meant succumbing to American nuclear blackmail.

Writing in 1960-1 on a Soviet book on economics, at one point Mao discussed the question of war in which he argued that war could not be abolished while classes continued to exist, and he then went on:

> whether there is going to be a world war or not does not hinge upon us. Even if a no-war agreement is signed, the possibility of war still exists. When the imperialists want war, no agreement can be taken seriously. As to whether atomic bombs and hydrogen bombs are used when war begins, that is another question. Although there were chemical weapons, conventional arms were used in the wars instead of the former.

He then analysed what wars were possible in the contemporary world and returned to the philosophical theme of the class basis of war and observed:

> It is just not possible to destroy the weapons of war without eliminating classes. In the history of class society of mankind, all classes and all nations have paid attention to positions of strength. To set up positions of strength is in fact an inevitable trend of history. Forces are the concrete manifestations of class strength.

Mao then proceeded to endorse efforts to establish conditions of peace obviously tempered by his previous dialectical analysis: 'We are in favour of making great efforts to prohibit atomic warfare and striving for the signing of a non-aggression pact between the two camps.'[4]

What is noteworthy here is that Mao considered it possible that, even if war did occur, nuclear weapons might not be used just as chemical weapons were not used in the Second World War or the Korean War. Likewise, for Mao the source of war lay in the contradictions of capitalism and imperialism. The question of a new world war 'does not hinge upon us'.

In the 1960s, as the Chinese contemplated the 'worst case' of having to defend China without external assistance against a major attack, they considered that the principal type of attack which was likely was a sudden and deliberate one by long-range nuclear strikes combined with massive physical invasion of Chinese territory, using both nuclear and conventional weapons. The enemy would seek to destroy at one stroke the military strength, economic centres and hubs of communication in China. The objective would be in the tradition of Clausewitz to destroy China's 'will to resist'. The war would be fought on 'an extensive front and in great depth'. 'Rear areas might be attacked first.' However, the Chinese argued that in the end the infantry would still be decisive. Nuclear weapons could not replace 'a decisive battle by ground forces'.[5] Because of its vast territorial size and its huge population China could not be destroyed by a nuclear strike. Thus in the final analysis China's ground forces and the surviving population would resort to the strategy and tactics of a people's war.

Implicit in this doctrine of defence is the assumption that the Chinese forces would be faced with an adversary superior to them in the air, at sea and in terms of conventional fire-power on the ground. These considerations still apply in the 1970s, but because of a possible Soviet threat to detach certain border regions, the situation has become more complicated than allowed for in the above doctrine. Nevertheless the essential aspects of the doctrine are still valid in the 1970s: it is a doctrine of ultimate invincibility which is of immense psychological value to a country under the threat of more powerful adversaries; it is a doctrine in keeping with Maoist military and political theories; and it is inherently defensive rather than offensive, in that it emphasises the annihilation of the enemy forces in the field in China as the basic military objective, rather than aiming at the destruction of the enemy's economic resources to wage war.

Obviously, China's military strategy had to take into account a variety of contingencies other than the one outlined above. However, that was the Chinese view of the 'worst case' for which they had to prepare. Moreover, as China's nuclear capability improved and the conventional forces strengthened, this picture of the 'worst case' was undoubtedly modified.

China's official statements accompanying each of its nuclear tests, beginning with the first, have always stressed that its nuclear weapons are for defensive purposes only and they have always stated that 'China will never at any time and under any circumstances be the first to use nuclear weapons.' Not only has this meant that China has abjured the concept of the first strike or the limited pre-emptive strike (discussed earlier as the only, but counter-productive option, for a country without second-strike capability) and thus perhaps reduced the risk of China being attacked now that it has become a more attractive target, but it also reaffirmed the principled Maoist view that in the final analysis nuclear weapons are of secondary importance. China's world role would not be deflected by giving primacy to considerations of the need to avoid at all costs a nuclear war. (In the Chinese view that was one of the first manifestations of the Soviet betrayal of revolution and Marxism-Leninism.) As the first such official statement put it:

> The atom bomb is a paper tiger. This famous saying by Chairman Mao Tse-tung is known to all. This was our view in the past and this is still our view at present. China is developing nuclear weapons not because we believe in the omnipotence of nuclear weapons and that China plans to use nuclear weapons. The truth is exactly to the contrary. In developing nuclear weapons, China's aim is to break the monopoly of the nuclear powers and to eliminate nuclear weapons.[6]

The statement went on to observe: 'On the question of nuclear weapons, China will neither commit the error of adventurism nor the error of capitulationism. The Chinese people can be trusted.' The deliberate references to the Chinese charges against Soviet behaviour over the Cuban missile crisis were presumably meant to be read both by revolutionaries as an assurance that China would not gamble with their fate for nuclear advantage and by American decision-makers as an assurance that China would behave with greater responsibility.

China's leaders have drawn attention to what might be regarded as three other important political implications of this nuclear programme: first, it symbolised China's quest for autonomy in world affairs and for recognition as a great power. Thus in 1961 Chou En-lai explained China's position to Lord Montgomery as follows: 'Other great nations had such weapons and smaller ones would have them in due course . . . China must have these too . . . China will not be dependent on any other nation.'[7] Foreign Minister Ch'en Yi explained a year later: 'We are likewise working to develop an atomic bomb of our own for the sole reason that the capitalists consider us underdeveloped and defenceless as long as we lack the ultimate weapons.'[8] Second, China's nuclear programme was also a blow against the Soviet Union and its pretensions to provide a nuclear umbrella to the socialist countries, thereby subordinating them to it in an important sense in the nuclear age. Thus, when asked in December 1963 why China wished to develop its own atomic weapons in view of Soviet assurances to defend it, Ch'en Yi replied:

what is this Soviet assurance worth? . . . This sort of promise is easy
to make, but worthless. Soviet protection is worth nothing to us . . .
No outsiders can give us protection in fact because they always
attach conditions and want to control us.[9]

It should be noted that Khrushchev's ouster occurred on the same
day as the detonation of China's first nuclear test on 16 October 1964
and that there is some evidence to suggest that China's leaders hoped
that the new leadership might change course.[10] Third, China was the
first AALA country to acquire a nuclear capability. Given China's role
as the true source of Marxism-Leninism, as a country with a semi-
colonial history and a relatively unmodernised economy practising self-
reliance, and as the centre of opposition to American imperialism, the
Chinese expected their nuclear programme and their nuclear testing to
be a source of inspiration to all nationalist and revolutionary forces. As
the Chinese government statement on the first test declared: 'The
mastering of the nuclear weapon by China is a great encouragement to
the revolutionary peoples of the world in'their struggles and a great
contribution to the cause of world peace.'

This brief analysis would not be complete without attempting to
illustrate the significance of China's nuclear programme in the context
of the Chinese sense of dignity and independence as a nation as displayed in the following lengthy extract from an official reply in September 1963 to a Soviet government statement:

> The real point is that the Soviet leaders hold that China should not,
> and must not, manufacture nuclear weapons . . .
>
> The Soviet statement asserts that China can rely on the nuclear
> weapons of the Soviet Union and need not manufacture them itself;
> that if it tries to manufacture them it will result in a great strain on
> China's economy.
>
> Should or should not China itself master the means of resisting
> US nuclear blackmail?
>
> True, if the Soviet leaders really practised proletarian interna-
> tionalism, China might consider it unnecessary to manufacture its
> own nuclear weapons.
>
> But it is equally true that if the Soviet Union really practised
> proletarian internationalism, they would have no reason whatsoever
> for obstructing China from manufacturing nuclear weapons.
>
> Is not China very poor and backward? Yes, it is. The Soviet
> leaders say, how can the Chinese be qualified to manufacture nuclear

weapons when they eat watery soup out of a common bowl and do not even have pants to wear?

The Soviet leaders are perhaps too hasty in deriding China for its backwardness. They may or may not have judged right. But in any case, even if we Chinese people are unable to produce an atomic bomb for a hundred years, we will neither crawl to the baton of the Soviet leaders nor kneel before the nuclear blackmail of the U.S. imperialists.

The Soviet statement says that if China were to produce two or three atom bombs, the imperialists would aim many more atom bombs at China. This is in effect instigating the imperialists to threaten China with atom bombs.

Of course the fact that the U.S. imperialists may wish to aim more atom and hydrogen bombs at China merits attention and vigilance. But there is nothing terrifying about it. At this very moment the United States has many such bombs poised against China. It will not make much difference if the United States listens to the Soviet leaders and adds a few more. The Chinese people will not tremble before U.S. nuclear threats. But one must ask: where do the Soviet leaders place themselves in making such an instigation?

In the eyes of the Soviet leaders, the whole world and the destiny of all mankind revolve around nuclear weapons. Therefore they hold on tightly to their nuclear weapons, afraid that someone might take them away or come to possess them, and so break up their monopoly. They are very nervous. They attribute China's principal criticism of the tripartite treaty to its failure to obtain the atom bombs it desires.

We feel that this attitude of the Soviet leaders is ludicrous. It calls to mind the following ancient Chinese fable:

Hui Tzu was Prime Minister of the State of Liang. Chuang Tzu was on his way to call on him.

Somebody said to Hui Tzu, 'Chuang is coming with the intention of taking over your place as Prime Minister.'

Hui Tzu became afraid and hunted for Chuang Tzu high and low for three days and three nights.

Chuang Tzu appeared before Hui Tzu and said, 'Have you heard about the southern bird, the phoenix? It set out from the South Sea to fly to the North Sea. It would not alight except on the Wutung tree. It would eat nothing except the fruit of the bamboo. It would drink nothing except the purest spring water. An owl, which had got hold of a dead rat, looked up as the phoenix flew over and screeched

to warn it off. Are you, too, not screeching at me, over your Kingdom of Liang?'

The moral of this fable is that different people have different
aspirations, and it is improper to measure the stature of great men by
the yardstick of small men.[11]

The above text brings out fully the Chinese sense of outrage and their
refusal to be humiliated by richer and more powerful adversaries. There
is also a powerful moral passion running through this passage culminating in the devastating last sentence. The resurgence of national
dignity, moral rectitude and ideological correctness which have been
important concomitants in the revolutionary tide in China both before
and since the establishment of the PRC find their reflection too in the
way in which China's leaders have thought about their nuclear programme. At the same time it is important to note that even the passionate passage quoted above included the very practical observation that
indeed further nuclear weapons may be targeted upon China as a result
of the nuclear programme and that this 'merits attention and vigilance'.
And it is important to note that China, unlike the other nuclear powers,
has not exported any aspect of its nuclear technology or contributed to
nuclear proliferation (other than indirectly by its own example of
having acquired an independent nuclear capability). Indeed the only
known case of a direct request for the supply of a nuclear weapon from
China was refused point-blank.[12] Moreover, the Chinese are not known
to have issued any nuclear threats to any third country or to have
offered any country the protection of their nuclear umbrella. They have
steadfastly held on to their view that nuclear weapons cannot determine the outcome of the revolutionary struggle or the anti-imperialist
struggle. In proof of this proposition they have repeatedly cited the
numerous examples of successful revolutionary wars and the anti-
colonialist movement since the Second World War.

To summarise briefly and finally the impact of China's nuclear programme on China's evolving role in world affairs, it should be regarded
as a supportive rather than a determining factor. In this sense it has contributed to the doctrine of ultimate invincibility and it has not affected
China's defensive posture, which is crucial for a proper appreciation of
the Chinese view of their role in world affairs. It has enhanced China's
great-power status, its sense of national dignity and pride in the
achievements of self-reliance by a 'poor and backward' country. It has
not of itself brought China into the realm of *realpolitik* nor has China's
nuclear capability of itself caused China's leaders to modify their view

of China's revolutionary responsibilities. Writing in 1969, I suggested in an article that in time China would adopt a deterrence posture which would involve it in 'a process of interaction with the adversary, which necessitates minimally a two-way communication of intentions, capabilities, and, beyond that, policies and strategies'.[13] It was strongly implied that China would necessarily be drawn into the language, framework and processes of the nuclear strategic framework of the Soviet-American relationship. This has not happened nor is there any sign that it is about to happen. Should China be inducted into such processes in the future that would then mark a fundamental change in its perceived role in world affairs.

Notes

1. Editorial, 3 August 1963, 'This is Betrayal of the Soviet People' in *People of the World, Unite for the Complete, Thorough, Total and Resolute Prohibition and Destruction of Nuclear Weapons* (FLP, 1963), p. 95.

2. For an excellent discussion of some of these see S.R. Schram's introductory essay in the book edited by him, *Authority, Participation and Cultural Change in China* (Cambridge University Press, 1973), pp. 1-108.

3. For extended analyses of China and nuclear questions see Alice Langley Hsieh, *Communist China's Strategy in the Nuclear Era* (Prentice-Hall, 1962); Morton H. Halperin, *China and the Bomb* (Praeger, 1965); and H. Gelber, *Nuclear Weapons and Chinese Policy*, Adelphi Paper No. 99 (International Institute for Strategic Studies, London, 1973).

4. JPRS II, p. 265.

5. Yeh Chien-ying in J. Chester Cheng, *The Politics of the Chinese Red Army* (Hoover, Stanford University Press, 1966).

6. Chinese government statement, 16 October 1964, 'China Successfully Explodes its First Atom Bomb', special supplement to *Peking Review*, No. 42 (1964).

7. Viscount Montgomery, 'China on the Move', *Sunday Times*, 15 November 1961.

8. *Frankfurter Rundschau*, 6 August 1962.

9. Interview with John Dixon, an Australian television producer, cited in A.L. Hsieh, 'The Sino-Soviet Nuclear Dialogue 1963', *The Journal of Conflict Resolution*, No. 2 (1964).

10. See *Red Flag* editorial, 'Why Khrushchev Fell', 21 November 1964 in *The Polemic on the General Line of the International Communist Movement* (FLP, 1965), pp. 483-92. For Soviet corroboration see O. Ivanov, *Soviet-Chinese Relations Surveyed* (Novosti Press Agency, Moscow, 1975), pp. 45-8.

11. 'Statement by the Spokesman of the Chinese Government: A Comment on the Soviet Government's Statement of August 21', 1 September 1963, *Peking Review*, No. 36 (1963). The quotation is from p. 9.

12. According to Mohammed Heikal (*Nasser, The Cairo Documents* (New English Library, 1972), p. 283) President Nasser had written to Premier Chou En-lai after the 1967 war to ask for nuclear assistance. Chou refused

and emphasised the importance of self-reliance: 'If the Egyptians wanted to step into the atomic field they would have to do it themselves. This was the way the Chinese did it and it was best.'

13. See 'China's Nuclear Option' in the *Bulletin of the Atomic Scientists* (February 1969), p. 77.

5 THE LEADER OF AN INTERNATIONALIST UNITED FRONT AGAINST AMERICAN IMPERIALISM 1963-1966

'To defeat the reactionary rule of imperialism,' Comrade Mao Tse-tung said, 'it is necessary to form a broad front and unite with all forces, except the enemy, and continue to wage arduous struggles . . . We should unite and drive US imperialism from Asia, Africa and Latin America back to where it came from' (Mao Tse-tung, May 1960).[1]

The concept of an internationalist united front against American imperialism by this time was not new in Chinese formulations. But what is important to note is that this period marked the first stage in the development of a Chinese foreign policy which was truly independent and self-reliant and that the framework within which foreign policy was to be conducted was that of a united front rather than that of an alliance or membership of a bloc.

The critical distinction in the Chinese revolutionary experience under Mao's leadership between the two frameworks is that the united front is a more fluid and less formal relationship between divergent classes, forces and interests who are agreed upon the necessity of linking together to confront a common enemy; whereas a formal alliance implies a common fundamental class-based identity which calls for long-term, strategically shared goals which transcend immediate tactical considerations of the tolerable degrees of diversity. The experience of the Sino-Soviet alliance showed how difficult it was to translate these principles into actual practice. And it could be argued that the alliance structure itself contributed to the Sino-Soviet rupture. The very fact that they were supposed to be close allies made it difficult to prevent significant disagreements from leading to a split. A looser association might have been able to contain within it a wider margin for diversity and disagreement. A united front structure, by contrast, is characterised by both unity and struggle between its various components who maintain their particular separate identities and freedom to pursue their particular long-term objectives subject to the overall goal of tactically uniting to oppose the common enemy.[2]

Another important characteristic of the united front approach in Maoist usage is that it is based upon a careful analysis of contradictions. The world is seen less in terms of bipolar blocs in which it is essential to belong to one or the other. It is seen rather in terms of a complex pattern of conflicts or contradictions, some of which are enduring and some temporary. In Schurmann's graphic terms, the world is depicted as a volcanic terrain in which eruptions are bound to occur.[3] Thus, operating within a united front framework, the task is not to try and control or direct conflicts; rather it is to determine which incipient conflicts or contradictions are basic and then which of these is the principal one to which the others should be subordinated until the underlying structure of world affairs undergoes a significant (or qualitative) change. At the very least, the location where these contradictions are concentrated should be made clear. As we have seen, already by 1962 Mao in an unpublished speech identified the contradictions between US imperialism and the people of the world as the primary one. It was not to be until 1965 that the Chinese were pre-pared to declare in public that the contradiction between the oppressed nations and imperialism had become the principal contradiction on which the whole cause of world revolution hinged.[4]

The united front approach is also significant since it enabled Chinese leaders to try to bring together a wide range of diverse and competing, if not antagonistic, forces bound in their relative hostility to the United States. Notionally this stretched from genuine Marxist-Leninists through to the national liberation movements and nationalist govern-ments in AALA and to include finally even small and medium capitalist powers. In the language of contradictions this meant that advantage was being taken of the fundamental irreconcilable contradictions between socialism and imperialism, the oppressed nations and imperialism and between the imperialist countries themselves. It is interesting to note that in the first of a series of major statements supporting those engaged in active opposition to American imperialism, Mao Tsé-tung directed his attention to internal struggles within the United States, thus using the last of the four basic contradictions (since Lenin's day these were accepted by all Communists as characterising the underlying structure of world politics and as explaining why imperialism would eventually be replaced by socialism), namely that between the proletariat and the bourgeoisie (or rather the people and monopoly capitalists) in the imperialist heartland. Significantly Mao's statement was concerned with the struggle of the blacks. Although this was described as at root a class struggle rather than a racial one, it was certainly the issue which would make the most impact in AALA and which provided a linkage with the other contradictions with which Mao was concerned.[5]

From the beginning it was axiomatic in Chinese calculations that the Soviet Union, 'bourgeois reactionaries' like Nehru, and 'revisionist agents of US imperialism' like Tito would have no place in the united front. As the Chinese developed their foreign policy during this period, some of their sharpest barbs were directed against the principles of non-alignment. One reason for this was that Nehru and Tito were the main flag-carriers of the movement. (Of course, once China's leaders had drawn the conclusion that the socialist camp had ceased to exist and that the Soviet Union was an out-and-out imperialist state as shown by its invasion of Czechoslovakia in 1968, so the Chinese view of Tito changed. Instead of being regarded as a Trojan horse inside the socialist camp Tito came to symbolise heroic national resistance to Russian expansionism.) But up until the Soviet invasion of Czechoslovakia the non-alignment movement was depicted as something which deflected AALA from the main task of opposing American imperialism on the basis of mass struggle. Instead, AALA allegedly would have been led down the road towards compromise, temporising and, indeed, a sell-out. Nevertheless the primary Chinese concern was the insistence on the necessity of excluding the Soviet Union from the front.

The Soviet Union was no longer regarded as a country which simply followed an erroneous revisionist line in world affairs; it was now seen to be in league with the United States on a number of important questions. As the commentator in *Red Flag* put it, the Soviet leaders had entered into a 'holy alliance' parallel to that established after the Congress of Vienna of 1815.[6] By December 1963 the Chinese leadership declared flatly: 'The heart and soul of the general line of peaceful co-existence pursued by the leaders of the CPSU is Soviet-US collaboration for the domination of the world.'[7] Other Chinese statements described the Soviet-American relationship as one of both collusion and contention. But whichever aspect of that double-edged relationship was regarded as dominant, the essential characteristic of the united front as operated from Peking during this period was the insistence on the exclusion of the Soviet Union. When the Chinese leadership returned to the internationalist united front framework after the early stages of the Cultural Revolution, the Soviet Union was to be regarded alongside the United States as the *target* against which the people of the world should unite. In fact this period of 1963-6 ends with the failure of the united front and the affirmation that the Soviet Union had gone beyond the stage of revisionism to that of a counter-revolutionary power so that China was prepared to stand alone as a 'revolutionary bastion' with the 'people of the world' against 'imperialism, revisionism and all reactionaries'.

China's role in this pre-Cultural Revolution period was to be the leader of the internationalist united front. China alone embraced all three dimensions of the front. China now claimed to be the true source of Marxism-Leninism and thus both in theory and in terms of practical politics it linked the genuine Marxist-Leninists throughout the world and especially the Communist parties of Asia. As we have seen, China's leaders had long since established a common identity with the peoples, nations and anti-imperialist governments (which also did not oppose China) in AALA. They were bound together by a common history of colonialism or semi-colonialism and by their economic backwardness. A new dimension of China's perceived identity was to emerge under the aegis of the united front strategy and that was its common cause with the small and medium capitalist powers supposedly standing up to American domination.

The concept of leadership which can be deduced from the implementation of the united front is a complex one which is very much removed from the realm of power politics, even though the front itself was very much concerned with questions of power in both its military and political aspects. The underlying strategic conception of the front was that the United States was engaged in an ambitious offensive to gain control over the vast intermediate zone of AALA and also the smaller capitalist powers. In the first instance, however, the US offensive was seen to be directed against AALA. Because the people were awakening, the United States would be faced with more and more instances of opposition, some of which would necessarily take the form of armed struggle. Since American resources for domination were not limitless they would be bound to become overstretched. Therefore all struggles against American imperialism were mutually supportive. Since much of the opposition was based on national feeling and class interests within nations, continued opposition was inevitable in the Chinese view. China's role therefore was to supply a sense of collective purpose and direction. Where possible, the Chinese could and did offer limited military assistance to guerrilla movements – but never to the extent in which direct control of the movement passed to their hands. Established governments and states of special importance to China like Albania, Pakistan, Tanzania and a few others received more substantial aid – but again never to the extent that it resulted in Chinese control over the countries concerned.[8] This has also meant that China was largely free of encumbrances and dependencies. China's leaders maintained their own freedom of manoeuvre and independence.

If there is a distinctive style to the Chinese pattern of leadership in this period it is its didactic quality according to which, in 1964, the Chinese leaders lectured their European counterparts on the nature of their true interests and urged African leaders, partly by example and partly by exhortation, to follow the Chinese line. It meant that on questions regarding the principles of the purpose of the united front the Chinese were relentless and unyielding. Chinese diplomats were later accused of unscrupulous behaviour over the convening of the 'Second Bandung' at Algiers in the latter half of 1965.[9] Perhaps because of inexperience, but more likely because of the position on principled revolutionary struggles which had been taken in the Sino-Soviet dispute, the Chinese in this period displayed for them an uncharacteristic tendency to interfere, particularly in the affairs of African countries.[10] Since in this period of the united front (unlike that adopted after the Cultural Revolution) the Chinese distinguished very sharply between 'progressives' and 'revolutionaries' among the national bourgeoisie in AALA, it was a constant temptation to them to help the progressives when the opportunity arose. This was also a period in which the Chinese encouraged genuine Marxist-Leninists to split away from orthodox pro-Moscow Communist parties. They thus manifested a tendency which on the whole has not been characteristic of the Chinese style of leadership in world affairs. More typical has been the didactic quality of their approach. This is a theme to which I shall have occasion to return in later chapters.

The Second Intermediate Zone

On 21 January 1964 a *People's Daily* editorial, significantly entitled 'All the World's Forces Opposing U.S. Imperialism, Unite!', presented for the first time the concept of there being two intermediate zones. Having quoted the political leaders of Britain, France, Germany and Japan voicing nationalistic aspirations of not wishing to be totally dominated by their superior ally, or desiring independence and, in the case of de Gaulle, of seeking an authentic national identity, the editorial concluded that 'The U.S. position as leader of its allies has been shaken to its very foundations.' It then went on to make the following analysis:

It can thus be seen that the U.S. imperialist attempt to seize the intermediate zone is bound to run up against the opposition of all the peoples and countries in that region. This vast intermediate zone is composed of two parts. One part consists of the independent countries and those striving for independence in Asia, Africa and Latin America; it may be called the first intermediate zone.

The second part consists of the whole of Western Europe, Oceania, Canada, and other capitalist countries; it may be called the second intermediate zone. Countries in this second intermediate zone have a dual character. While their ruling classes are exploiters and oppressors, these countries themselves are subjected to U.S. control, interference and bullying. They therefore try their best to free themselves from U.S. control. In this regard they have something in common with the socialist countries and the peoples of various countries. By making itself antagonistic to the whole world, U.S. imperialism inevitably finds itself tightly encircled.[11]

In accordance with this conceptualisation China was thus proposing to make common cause not simply with the proletariat and people of Western Europe but rather with the ruling classes of these countries. In a very real sense the bourgeoisie of Western Europe was seen as analogous to the national bourgeoisie in China before 1949 or to the national bourgeoisie in AALA.

The context in which this editorial appeared is of considerable importance. The establishment of diplomatic relations with France was about to be announced (28 January 1964) and a broad-based French parliamentary delegation was about to arrive in China the following day (21 January). The first steps towards recognition were made in the autumn of 1963. It was possible to argue that the 'mavericks' of East and West were thereby acknowledging a certain common identity. But as the editorial makes clear, the Chinese did not see de Gaulle as a 'maverick'. He was seen as part of a common response of the medium capitalist powers.

The themes of the editorial, however, were not entirely new. They were rather a further development of concepts which had always been central to Mao's views of world affairs. The first use of the intermediate zone theory (which in the introduction was seen as traceable to Mao's analysis as to why red bases could exist in the China of the 1920s) was in 1946. At that time he depicted it as a huge entity comprising all the regions and countries lying between America and the Soviet Union. He specifically included the colonies and former colonies together with Western Europe. In 1958, when it was revived again, the region clearly specified was AALA. Common to both periods was the notion that the socialist countries were not the immediate target of American imperialism. Anti-Communism was regarded as a convenient American smokescreen to disguise the fact that the real objective was the intermediate zone. To this must be added Mao's view of 1957 on the lessons of Suez in which he sharply distinguished between France and Britain on the one side and the United States which was replacing them as the dominant active imperialist power in the Middle East on the other. He then regarded them as two separate forces, to which the third, the oppressed nations, was added.

Now, however, Mao was to go much further. In reported interviews with the aforementioned French delegation Mao was quoted as saying, 'France herself, Germany, England on the condition that she ceases to be the courier of America, Japan and *we ourselves* — there is your Third World' (emphasis added).[12] Soviet sources have included Italy and Canada and 'other countries' in this list.[13] The statement is remarkable for having included China as one of the second intermediate zone (or as he then put it, 'Third World' — before it acquired an altogether different meaning) countries. Mao did not specify the basis for this common identity. It may not have been meant to be taken seriously as a literal statement, but rather its purpose may have been deliberately to exaggerate the point that they could co-operate to mutual advantage because they shared certain common interests. However, there are other indications that China's position as a great power was indeed an important aspect of Mao's conception of China's international role. To be sure, that would not hold good over a long-term fundamental ideological analysis, but in terms of the exigencies of the current era of world affairs Mao did perceive China as a great country. For example, the *People's Daily* editorial on the establishment of relations with France specifically focused on this theme: 'China and France are great nations and play important roles in international affairs.'[14] In his statement of 27 January in support of the 'Japanese People's Great Patriotic Struggle', using similar language Mao declared: 'Japan is a great nation. It will never allow U.S. imperialism to ride roughshod over it for long.'[15] In his talks with Japanese guests Mao also reportedly made the following observations:

> Japan . . . may help us in many respects . . . In the political respect we must also support each other . . . Japanese monopoly capital belongs to the second intermediate zone. Even this capital is displeased with the United States and some of its representatives openly come out against the U.S. Although the monopoly capital of Japan is now dependent on the U.S.A., time will pass and it will throw off the American yoke.[16]

A more comprehensive account of Mao's thinking on international issues at this time, which also gives a rationale for the shift in China's trade patterns from the Soviet-dominated camp to the countries of the second intermediate zone, is in his remarks to both party and non-party senior colleagues on 13 February:

> It is no fun being a running dog. Nehru is in bad shape, imperialism and revisionism have robbed him blind. Revisionism is being rebuffed everywhere. It was rebuffed in Romania, it is not listened to in Poland. In Cuba they listen to half and reject half; they listen to half because they cannot do otherwise, since they don't produce oil or weapons. Imperialism is having a hard time too. Japan is opposing the United States, and it's not only the Japanese Communist Party and the Japanese people that are opposing the United States — the big capitalists are doing so too. Not long ago, Hu Kita ironworks rejected an American inspection. De Gaulle's opposition to the United States is also in response to the demands of the capitalists. They are also behind his establishment of diplomatic relations with China. China opposes the United States; formerly in Peking there was Shen Ch'ung[17], the whole country opposed U.S. imperialism. The Khrushchevite revisionists abuse us as dogmatists, pseudo-revolutionaries — they really curse us. Not long ago, a letter from the Central Committee of the CPSU to the Central Committee of the CPC put forward four points: 1) An end to open polemics; 2) The return of the [Soviet] experts [to China]; 3) Talks on the Sino-Soviet border; 4) The expansion of commerce. We can have talks about the border; they will begin on 25th February. We can do a little business but we can't do too much, for Soviet products are heavy, crude, high-priced and they always keep something back . . .
> They are first crude, second expensive, third inferior and fourth they keep something back, so it's not so good to deal with them as with the French bourgeoisie, who still have some notion of business ethics.[18]

Once again it is the attitude of the big capitalists which is regarded by Mao as decisive. There is also the suggestion that in their relationship with the Soviet Union the socialist countries share the same problem as the smaller capitalist countries have with regard to their relationship with the United States. This point was to be developed further once the Soviet Union came to be seen as the socialist-imperialist country from late 1968. Likewise the explanation as to why it was better to trade with the French bourgeoisie than with the Russians was to feature

greatly in the critique of Soviet social imperialism after 1968. Of
interest at this juncture is the remark that Sino-Soviet border talks were
due to begin on 25 February 1964.[19] By July Mao was quoted in
Japanese newspapers as claiming, 'There are too many places occupied
by the Soviet Union.' He went on to list Mongolia, a part of Romania, a
portion of Poland (which was compensated by a section of East
Germany after the eviction of the population) and a bit of Finland. 'The
Russians took everything they could.' He accused them of wanting
Sinkiang. Mao then suggested that it was time 'to put an end to this
allotment'. China had not yet 'presented our account' for the vast
tracts seized by the Tsars. Meanwhile China fully supported Japan's
claims to the Kurile Islands: 'they must be returned to Japan.'[20]

The two intermediate zones approach thus involved not only opposition to the United States but, where relevant, the Soviet Union too
was opposed. In fact right from its origins through to the current
formulation, the intermediate zone(s) theory has differed fundamentally from Soviet concepts and views of international affairs. These latter
have always accorded the Soviet Union and 'bloc thinking' a more
central role in the critical struggles determining the future of the world
revolution. By contrast, hostility to the Soviet Union as a collaborator
with US imperialism is implicit in the 21 January *People's Daily* editorial and it is explicit in Mao's reported statements. The question of
whom to support or oppose according to united front thinking was
decided in the first instance by one's attitude on the issue of the principal contradiction at the relevant stage of the historical process. It was
not decided on the basis of greater or lesser class affinity or according
to 'bloc thinking'. It was conceivable, therefore, that out-and-out
monopoly capitalists might be preferred even to Communists, especially
of the revisionist type. Indeed, beginning with the 1960s the Chinese
openly preferred the French big capitalists to the Communist Party of
France, as the *Polemic* of 22 October 1963 explained:

> Over a long period of time, the leaders of the CPF have abandoned
> the struggle against US imperialism, refusing to put up a firm fight
> against US imperialist control over and restrictions on France in the
> political, economic and military fields and surrendering this banner
> of French national struggle against the United States to people like
> de Gaulle.[21]

The second intermediate zone concept may be seen as the first fruit
of China's fully independent foreign policy as a state. It was one that

was particularly associated with Mao personally and it surfaced again in the early 1970s but in a different form. In this pre-Cultural Revolution period the second intermediate zone was designed to complement China's first intermediate zone diplomacy. As we have seen, like the AALA policy, it carried with it a profound challenge to the Russians. The concept, however, lapsed in practice towards the end of 1964, probably because the countries concerned did not respond so vigorously as Mao may have wished to the sharpening of the struggle with the United States, particularly in Vietnam. It is also possible that some of the other leaders in Peking were less than enthusiastic about the concept and its current applicability and that, in the absence of much evidence of the zone as an effective restraining influence on the Americans, Mao may not have wished to pursue the matter further at that stage. By 1965 the disputes on strategic and foreign affairs turned on other issues. Nevertheless the concept considerably expanded the dimensions of China's role. It is an issue to which we shall return in later chapters.

The (First) Revolutionary Intermediate Zone

The overwhelming bulk of China's diplomatic and foreign affairs effort in this period was directed to this zone of the 'vast areas of AALA' in which all of the world's contradictions were 'concentrated' and which was 'the storm centre of world revolution'. In the view from Peking 'the whole cause of the international proletarian revolution hinge[d] on the outcome of the revolutionary struggles of the people of these areas.'[22]

The Chinese diplomatic effort concentrated on the attempt to reconvene 'a second Bandung Conference' in Algiers in the second half of 1965. Two conditions were regarded as absolutely essential by the Chinese, namely that this conference, which was to give a kind of organisational focus to the internationalist front desired by Peking, should take a strong anti-American imperialism line and simultaneously exclude the Soviet Union from membership of the conference. An early example of this latter point was the joint statement of Chinese and Tanganyikan trade unions in November 1963 which stated succinctly that 'in order to fight imperialism and colonialism effectively, it was necessary for the people of the various countries to oppose modern revisionism.'[23]

China's leaders, like Premier Chou En-lai, Foreign Minister Ch'en Yi and the then Chairman of the PRC, Liu Shao-ch'i, travelled more frequently and more extensively in Africa and Asia in the few years of this period than in all the other years since 1949 put together. Chou En-lai,

for example, in the period between early 1964 and mid-1965 made
three trips to Africa. No Chinese leader of comparable significance has
visited Africa before or since.[24] These visits were designed not so much
as to improve and extend China's diplomatic relations (even though
relations were established with Tunisia and several other former French
colonies in the wake of the French recognition) as to cajole and
persuade leaders and groups in Africa and Asia to adopt the Chinese
view.[25] China's leaders were prepared to go to extraordinary lengths
to secure adherence to their point of view. For example, as a means
of trying to dissuade the Indian government (for so long the butt
of Chinese criticism) from insisting on the admission of the Soviet
Union to the Afro-Asian Conference, the Chinese said that they would
not raise the Sino-Indian dispute and told the Pakistanis not to raise the
question of Kashmir. When Indonesia indicated that it might not be
able to oppose Soviet participation, China hinted that in such an eventuality it would be unable to support Indonesia with regard to Malaysia.
(Hitherto China had enthusiastically supported Indonesia's campaign
to 'crush Malaysia'.) Chou En-lai, while persisting in upholding China's
basic principles, even found it possible to incorporate some aspects of
the hitherto objectionable non-alignment framework into the Afro-
Asian solidarity movement:

> The solidarity has thoroughly crushed the imperialists' vicious
> scheme of making Asians fight Asians and Africans fight Africans.
> The non-alignment policy of peace and neutrality pursued by Asian
> and African countries is in fact pointed at U.S. imperialism ... It is
> very clear that though there are different peculiarities between the
> endeavour of Afro-Asian solidarity and the genuine non-alignment
> policy, however, they have common aims and both of them have
> been developed in the struggle against imperialism and old and new
> colonialism headed by the United States. This can be seen clearly
> from the main resolutions of the first Afro-Asian Conference and the
> two summit conferences of the non-aligned states.[26]

Another important dimension of China's Afro-Asian policy in this
period was the revolutionary one. In part this must be seen within the
context of the Sino-Soviet dispute, as the Chinese sought to demonstrate that the Russians were indeed (as they had charged) attempting
to emasculate the anti-imperialist and nationalist struggles in AALA. At
the same time, it is important to note that other factors were involved,
including both strategic ideological calculations and emotional visceral

reactions. To take the latter first, an important element in the Sino-Soviet rupture was the assertion of China's dignity, independence and the authentic universal significance of the Chinese revolutionary experience. From the beginning this was identified as peculiarly relevant to the colonial and former colonial areas of the world. Although the precise way in which this relevance has been asserted has varied over time, China's leaders have always placed China within this political geographical world. The peoples in this area were seen as sharing a common history of oppression by and resistance to colonial powers and they also shared a relatively backward economy. They therefore had common aspirations and common needs. As Helene Correre d'Encausse and Stuart Schram have pointed out, there are important psychological and cultural dimensions to the Chinese position which may go even deeper than careful political calculations and which underlie the Maoist development of Marxism-Leninism.[27] But the overt Chinese analysis is important in its own right, regardless of the psychological and cultural factors which inform it. It is therefore appropriate at this point to consider AALA in Chinese Marxist-Leninist perspective as applied to this period.

Like all Marxists, the Chinese distinguish sharply between the socialist and nationalist democratic revolutions. The former is necessarily guided by Marxist-Leninist ideology; it is led by a Communist Party and it involves the establishment of the dictatorship of the proletariat. When Chou En-lai made his celebrated remark early in 1964 that Africa was 'ripe for revolution' (his actual words were 'revolutionary prospects are excellent throughout the African continent'[28]), it was not the socialist variety that he had in mind. Nowhere in Africa at that time did the Chinese either publicly or privately perceive a socialist revolutionary situation. In Asia, however, such incipient situations could be identified. But here it is necessary to draw attention to a critical distinction in Chinese theory regarding nationalist democratic revolutions. Extrapolating from their own revolutionary experience, Chinese leaders and theorists maintained that under the conditions of imperialist oppression a new kind of nationalist democratic revolution was possible which they called 'new democracy'.[29] This revolution was against imperialism, feudalism and bureaucratic capitalism waged by the 'people' under the leadership of the proletariat, or more precisely, the Communist Party. The 'people' should consist typically of the workers, peasants, urban petit bourgeoisie and the national bourgeoisie — indeed all patriotic and anti-imperialist democrats. They should be organised along the pattern of a united front under proletarian hegemony. Finally

it should be noted that in theory and in Chinese practice the new democratic revolution leads to socialism, and not to capitalism.

   Although there were a few movements in Asia (or more accurately,
south-east Asia) which were either actually or incipiently of the new
democratic type led by Communist parties and guided by 'genuine'
Marxism-Leninism, this was far from true of the rest of AALA. With
regard to the vast majority of AALA the Chinese also drew distinctions
in their terminology between 'independence', 'national liberation
struggles' and 'liberation'. 'Independence' in Chinese usage was used to
describe the achievements of countries which had won this from their
colonial masters without having undergone a prolonged armed struggle.
In such countries power was in the hands of national bourgeois governments which under certain conditions, as we saw in Wang Chia-hsiang's
1959 analysis, could shift to the right. In the fourth reply to the CPSU
in October 1963, the Chinese analysed the circumstances of such
countries as follows:

> Consider first, the situation in Asia and Africa. There a whole group
> of countries have declared their independence. But many of these
> countries have not completely shaken off imperialist and colonial
> control and enslavement and remain objects of imperialist plunder
> and aggression as well as arenas of contention between old and new
> colonialists. In some the old colonialists have changed into neo-
> colonialists and retain their colonial rule through their trained agents.
> In others the wolf has left by the front door, but the tiger has
> entered through the back door, the old colonialism being replaced
> by the new, more powerful and more dangerous U.S. imperialism.
> The peoples of Asia and Africa are seriously menaced by the ten-
> tacles of neo-colonialism, represented by U.S. imperialism.[30]

A country which won its independence on the basis of a war of
national liberation, like that of Algeria, rather than on the basis of a
'declaration', obviously in the Chinese view had its independence built
on more solid foundations. But even in this regard the Chinese consistently used the term 'independence' rather than 'liberation'.[31] 'Liberation' was reserved for countries like China itself or North Vietnam,
which had achieved full independence on the basis of a united front and
armed struggle under the leadership of a Marxist-Leninist party.

   The Chinese leadership thus demonstrated an awareness both in
theory and in practice that the predominant patterns of the anti-
imperialist struggles in AALA did not follow the Chinese model. But

they nevertheless felt that knowledge of the Chinese experience would be useful in AALA and that it would help nationalist leaders to stand up to Soviet blandishments regarding 'national democracy' and the 'non-capitalist road of development'.[32] The Chinese argued that the critical question was not what kind of paternalist aid and advice Europeans (even of the revolutionary variety) could give to the movements in AALA; rather it was what were the consequences of realising that the anti-imperialist struggles of AALA constituted the 'storm centre' of world revolution. Marx and Lenin in their day had maintained that as imperialism was weakened here, so its rule at home was also weakened. But if this were now the world's 'storm centre', then not only were the anti-imperialist struggles here and the revolutionary struggles in Europe and America mutually supportive, but the former had priority over the latter.

The Chinese analysis of the anti-imperialist struggle in AALA also helps to explain the rationale for the concentration of their diplomatic efforts in Africa on the so-called 'radical' states such as Nyerere's Tanzania, Nkrumah's Ghana, Sekou Touré's Guinea and so on. If the danger was neo-colonialism, then the issue turned on the character of the national bourgeois leadership of the countries concerned. Thus in Africa in particular, Chinese diplomatic behaviour in this period was characterised by active support for opposition groups and leaders within certain countries where the official leadership itself was regarded as more or less reactionary. This sometimes led to the expulsion of Chinese diplomats and it contributed to a certain suspicion and misunderstanding of China and its role in Africa.[33] Apart from irritation and bewilderment with the Chinese for having brought the Sino-Soviet dispute into Afro-Asian forums, many African and Asian leaders felt that China was another great power with special interests to promote, analogous to but different from the previous great powers which had intervened in Africa. There was little appreciation that China's capabilities, outlook and intentions were fundamentally different. As Bruce Larkin observed with reference to Africa (but which is also true with regard to other parts of the world), there is not a single government or revolutionary movement which has gained power primarily because of Chinese aid and support. China's aid has never been such as to be the primary factor in determining the decisive outcome of the struggles of others.

The Chinese conceptualised their role as a kind of 'base area' which would support the front line struggles of others: 'The Socialist countries must become the base areas for supporting and developing the revolution of the oppressed nations and peoples throughout the world, form the closest alliance with them and carry the proletarian world revolution through to completion.'[34] The linking theme between the various struggles in AALA and indeed in the world as a whole was anti-imperialism. There was, however, a natural tendency by the Chinese to perceive a linkage between their opponents. During the Cultural Revolution their pronouncements often used the phrase 'anti Communist anti China' as if the one was equivalent to the other. In this period the connection was not made in so stark a fashion, but this way of thinking did surface occasionally. For example, Russian aid to India was depicted as 'obviously intended to encourage the Nehru government in its policies directed against communism, against the people and against socialist countries'.[35] (The latter was an obvious reference to China.) In a systematic study of China's support for wars of national liberation for the year 1965, Peter Van Ness went even further to suggest that this was subordinated to the needs of the Chinese state. By listing three elements important to state policy (whether or not the relevant state had (1) diplomatic relations with Peking; (2) voted in favour of the admission of Peking to the UN in 1965; and (3) had trade relations with Peking in excess of $75 million in 1964 and 1965), Van Ness was able to test whether the nature of state-to-state relations correlated better than officially articulated revolutionary theory. He concluded that 'whether a foreign non-communist country was seen to be "peace-loving" or ruled by "reactionaries", or whether a Communist Party state was viewed in Peking as "socialist" or denounced as "revisionist" largely depended on the extent to which that country's foreign policy coincided with China's own.'[36] This perhaps is to go too far. After all, in 1963 as part of the decision to try to mobilise AALA support for China's position there was a deliberate attempt to increase trade with AALA countries generally and with those like Egypt regarded as key countries in particular.[37] Moreover, Mao Tse-tung's statement of support for the people of Panama in their conflict with the United States, the enormous rallies in China and the official government message to the President of Panama in January 1964 were all directed towards a country which at that time had diplomatic relations with Taipei and not Peking.[38] China's foreign policy concerns went beyond those of narrow state interests. China's self-image regarding its role in AALA was different from those of other great powers and it would be misleading to ignore the impact of that on the actual conduct of foreign policy. China's criticism of Soviet aid in 1963 was followed up in early 1964 by Chou En-lai's enunciation of 'China's Eight Principles of Providing Economic Aid':

> (1) The Chinese Government always bases itself on the principle of equality and mutual benefit in providing aid to other countries. It never regards such aid as a kind of unilateral alms but as something mutual and helpful to economic co-operation.
> (2) In providing aid to other countries, the Chinese Government strictly respects the sovereignty and independence of the recipient countries, and never attaches any conditions or asks for any privileges.
> (3) China provides economic aid in the form of interest-free or low-interest loans and extends the time limit for the repayment when necessary so as to lighten, as far as possible, the burden of the recipient countries.
> (4) In providing aid to other countries, the purpose of the Chinese Government is not to make the recipient countries dependent on China but to help them embark step by step on the road of self-reliance and independent economic development.
> (5) The Chinese Government tries its best to help the recipient countries build projects which require less investment while yielding quick results so that the recipient governments may increase their income and accumulate capital.
> (6) The Chinese Government provides the best quality equipment and material of its own manufacture at international market prices. If the equipment and material provided by the Chinese Government are not up to the agreed specifications and quality, the Chinese Government undertakes to replace them.
> (7) In giving any particular technical assistance, the Chinese Government will see to it that the personnel of the recipient country fully master such techniques.
> (8) The experts and technical personnel dispatched by China to help in construction in the recipient countries will have the same standard of living as the experts and technical personnel of the recipient country. The Chinese experts and technical personnel are not allowed to make any special demands or enjoy any special amenities.[39]

These aid principles should not be seen as simply a by-product of the Sino-Soviet dispute in the sense that they imply that Soviet aid is not so disinterested. They reflect China's own unfruitful experience of aid in the first half of this century. They also illustrate in a practical way some interesting aspects of China's view of its role in AALA. China's own perception of self-reliance and independence was projected on to these countries as being necessary and desired by their people. The countries of AALA, including China, were seen as independent entities whose struggles and achievements were mutually supportive. The aid was seen in terms of China's internationalist duty. Although equality, reciprocity and mutual benefit underlay much of the thinking developed by Chou En-lai, at no point has it ever occurred to China's leaders that China in turn might also receive aid from any AALA countries in the same way. Thus China is implicitly regarded as a great power with a leadership role and a donor of aid, but as a great power of a special kind which does not follow the chauvinist and imperialist patterns of others.

As the American intervention in Vietnam deepened in 1965, beginning with the bombing of the North in February and extending to the despatch of combat forces to the South from April onwards, so the tempo of Chinese diplomatic activities in Afro-Asia increased. The convening of the second Afro-Asian conference in Algiers in accordance with their terms assumed overwhelming importance in the priorities of China's foreign policy. Chou En-lai, Foreign Minister Ch'en Yi and other Chinese leaders visited no less than fifteen Afro-Asian countries in the period April-June 1965. Chou En-lai himself visited eight (some on two or three separate occasions); in this three-month period he made four separate trips, spending in all 33 days outside China. Not a few Afro-Asian states, some of which like Tanzania were well disposed towards China, were becoming decidedly unenthusiastic about holding the conference at all. Just as the conference was due to be held in June, the Algerian host, Ben Bella, was overthrown in a *coup*. In what seemed to many to be indecent haste, the Chinese recognised the new leader, Boumedienne, and pressed ahead. But the conference was postponed until November. In the intervening period China's attitude cooled. For one thing, many states said that they would not attend. The abortive *coup* in Indonesia destroyed a vital pillar in China's Afro-Asian policy, and finally, there was a growing possibility that the Soviet Union might be invited to participate after all. Thus in the end China decided against the conference. An unsympathetic source described the Chinese shifting stand with considerable accuracy:

On June 25 the Chinese were arguing the conference would be a blow to imperialism; on 29 June they defined its postponement as a victory over imperialist attempts to sabotage it; in July they were looking forward to the new November opening as another victory over imperialism; by October they equated convening the conference with an imperialist plot; and in November the perhaps permanent postponement was again hailed as a triumph over imperialism.[40]

With the failure of the projected conference and the *coup* in Indonesia much of China's AALA united front policy lay in ruins. There is a certain irony in that the most explicit and fully developed theoretical analysis of the importance of China's revolutionary experiment for AALA ('Long Live the Victory of People's War' by Lin Piao) should appear just before the denouement of China's AALA strategy. The article analysed at length Mao's theory of people's war which was regarded as peculiarly appropriate to the conditions of AALA. Indeed it asserted, 'Comrade Mao Tse-tung's theory of establishing revolutionary base areas in the rural districts and encircling cities from the countryside is attracting more and more attention among the people in these regions.'

It was at this point that Lin Piao made the famous pronouncement:

> Taking the entire globe, if North America and Western Europe can be called 'the cities of the world', then Asia, Africa and Latin America constitute 'the rural areas of the world'. Since World War II, the proletarian revolutionary movement has for various reasons been temporarily held back in the North American and West European capitalist countries, while the people's revolutionary movement in Asia, Africa and Latin America has been growing vigorously. In a sense the contemporary world revolution also presents a picture of the encirclement of cities by the rural areas.

The essay as a whole, as a paean to people's war, has remarkably little to contribute to China's role at the state level in AALA. Rather it is concerned with promoting the applicability of the Chinese model of revolutionary armed struggle. In some ways it may be regarded as the harbinger of the Cultural Revolution because of its rather undifferentiated attempt to universalise the Chinese revolutionary experience. Interestingly, the essay also characterised the current epoch in terms which were to become very familiar during the Cultural Revolution but which were subsequently dropped: 'Ours is the epoch in which world capitalism and imperialism are heading for their doom and socialism and communism are marching to victory.' Basically, China is not characterised as having a particularly active role in world affairs: as the pioneer of people's war and as the country which produced Mao Tse-tung's Thought ('a common asset of the revolutionary people of the whole world') China's role is simply to offer its example to others and to be prepared to fight a people's war in the unlikely event of an American attack. In so far as this article had a special message beyond providing a synthesis and theoretical analysis of Mao's theory of people's war (which in the context of a possible war with America gave it a timely significance) it was directed to the domestic strategic debate and to the Vietnamese revolutionaries suggesting that China was not going to intervene in the war or significantly upgrade its aid.[41] (These are considerations to which we shall return shortly).

Lin Piao's emphasis upon the importance of holding back American imperialism through the revolutionary armed struggle of people's war rather than through the diplomacy of an internationalist united front was given a theoretical justification, or at least it was backed by a new analysis of world affairs, in the November 1965 article, 'Refutation of the New Leaders of the CPSU on United Action':

> The characteristic of the present world situation is that, with the daily deepening of the international class struggle, a process of great upheaval, great division and great reorganisation is taking place . . . Drastic divisions and realignments of political forces are taking place on a world scale.[42]

China's response to the end of its AALA united front policy and its foreign policy setbacks[43] was to see the world as undergoing a fundamental realignment. The extent of this would be shown in the Cultural Revolution. Meanwhile, in early 1966, the Chinese published editorials in the *People's Daily* which explained that temporary setbacks are inevitable in the ebb and swell of revolutionary tides. Thus an editorial on 1 March explained:

> Under certain circumstances a counter attack mounted by the imperialists and reactionaries may gain the upper hand for the time being, but this will only raise still higher the political consciousness of the people and mobilise still greater numbers, thereby helping the revolutionary movement to grow in depth and in scope on its onward march.[44]

Just as the policy of uniting with the second intermediate zone lapsed by the end of 1964 so the policy of uniting with the first intermediate zone as a major organising principle of China's foreign relations came to an end in the late autumn of 1965. To be sure, bilateral relations with a few select countries like Tanzania with which China's relations were especially close continued. But an important phase in China's foreign policy and in its definition of its place in world affairs had passed.

Vietnam and the Internationalist Communist Movement

An important development of China's perceived role in world affairs was the extension from being the self-proclaimed source and centre of genuine Marxism-Leninism to actually leading some Communist parties and breakaway (Marxist-Leninist) parties in the context of the Sino-Soviet dispute.[45] Of the 81 Communist and Workers' parties which attended the 1960 Moscow Conference, only two (Albania and New Zealand) supported China without wavering in this period. The Vietnamese party tried not to become too committed to either side of the Sino-Soviet debate, but on the whole it was regarded by the Chinese in this period as belonging to their side. The Chinese regarded the Communist parties of Korea, Japan and Indonesia (until its virtual destruction in late 1965) as more or less on their side, too.

Whether or not there were those in Peking who would have liked to have used these as a pressure group within the international Communist movement, the problem of the proper response to the Vietnam War came to dominate Sino-Soviet relations from late 1964 onwards. For the Chinese, of course, American escalation posed a grave strategic threat of an attack upon China itself.[46] Thus a number of Chinese global and national security concerns converged upon the Vietnam issue. Moreover, the question of revisionism provided a linkage for Mao between domestic and external foreign policy concerns. To have compromised with the Soviet Union would have meant compromising with revisionism. Yet at the same time, throughout 1965, Mao was preoccupied with opposing revisionism in the Chinese Communist Party at home. Much of the support for united action from within China came precisely from those sources which Mao suspected of revisionism. In 1965, after an internal debate, the Chinese leaders rejected the Soviet proposals for a programme of united action to deal with American intervention in the Vietnam War. But in early 1966 the situation became critical once again.

By the end of 1965 the strategem of uniting the Afro-Asian world against American imperialism had not been crowned with success. There was a current danger that further escalation by the Americans at this stage might lead to a Sino-American war. It was against this background that matters came to a head in the early spring of 1966. In February and March a Japanese party delegation visited China, North Korea and North Vietnam to promote a new kind of united action programme to embrace all the socialist countries (the Soviet Union included). Communiqués agreeing to this were signed in Vietnam and Korea and one was on the point of being signed in China when Mao personally intervened and stopped it. In his view the Russian leadership was to be regarded not just as revisionist but as counter-revolutionary. According to later Japanese reports, he envisaged that an American attack on China would lead to a Soviet intervention in pursuit of its own chauvinistic objectives. That would eventually lead to armed confrontation between the Soviet and Chinese armies at the Yangtse river.[47]

In March the Chinese Central Committee, at the instigation of Mao, turned down the invitation to attend the 23rd Congress of the CPSU. Mao explained to an enlarged meeting of the Political Bureau:

> We shall rely on self-reliance. We shall not depend on the Soviet Union. We shall not become befuddled. If we wish people to stand firm, we ourselves must first be unwavering . . . Our banners must be fresh, they must not be soiled in mud.[48]

Henceforth Mao said any congratulatory telegrams for future Congresses should be sent only to the Soviet people.

This meant that China was in effect severing party-to-party relations with the Soviet Union. The rejection of the Japanese proposal led to the break in party relations with them too, and it signified that the attempt to maintain a coalition of Asian parties within the Communist movement had also come to an end.

Henceforth China was to stand with an unsoiled banner prepared to face all enemies on the basis of self-reliance. In fact in April 1966 the Americans and the Chinese signalled to each other their intentions not to attack unless attacked first.[49]

China's world role had changed yet again. The attempts to lead an internationalist united front of the smaller capitalist powers, the Afro-Asian countries and a coalition of Asian Communist parties had ended in failure. Mao was driven to accepting the challenge of actually confronting the two superpowers simultaneously. That had always been a possible consequence of the Sino-Soviet rupture.

On the basis of lengthy discussions with Mao and Chou, Edgar Snow described Mao's reasoning as follows:

> Mao resolutely refused to be drawn into a position of dependence, as

in Korea, and a possible double cross. Instead he insisted upon a posture of complete self-reliance on a people's war of defence — while continuing to build the bomb — and heavy support for, but not intervention in, Vietnam.

Mao's line seemed madly unorthodox when viewed against the background of traditional Chinese strategy in handling threats of foreign aggression. *Yi yi chih yi* — use barbarians to fight barbarians — was an age-old cardinal principle in China, comparable to the *divide et impera* principle sacred to Rome and her successors. Among tradition-bound Chinese as well as Western Peking elegists versed in Chinese history, it was said that Mao had lost his mind. A weaker power following a policy which seemed to unite its enemies and invite a 'war on two fronts'? An international propaganda offensive calling for 'a plague on both their houses'? But Mao knew what he was doing. The greater threat was internal, not external. Compromising with either of the superpowers could then only lead to a split on the home front. A resolutely independent and united China could weather any storm. A China torn apart internally by factions seeking to exploit alliance with Russia could not stand.[50]

Notes

1.   *Chairman Mao Tse-tung's Important Talks with Guests from Asia, Africa and Latin America* (FLP, 1970), pp. 5-6.
2.   For an analysis of the Maoist theory and experience of united fronts see S. Van Slyke, *Enemies and Friends* (Stanford University Press, 1967).
3.   F. Shurmann, *The Logic of World Power* (Pantheon, 1974) p. 358.
4.   See, for example, a speech by P'eng Chen, *Peking Review*, No. 24 (1965) and an article by Lin Piao, *Peking Review,* No. 36 (1965).
5.   'Chairman Mao Tse-tung's statement calling upon the people of the world to unite to oppose racial discrimination by US imperialism and support the American negroes in their struggle against racial discrimination', 8 August 1963. *Peking Review*, No. 33 (1963), p. 8.
6.   See *Red Flag*, No. 17; Commentator in *Peking Review*, No. 41 (1963): 'The New "Holy Alliance" Will End Up No Better Than the Old'.
7.   The Editorial Departments of the *People's Daily* and *Red Flag*, 'Peaceful Coexistence — two diametrically opposed views'. Sixth Comment on the Open Letter of the CC of the CPSU, 12 December 1963, *Peking Review*, No. 51 (1963), p. 16.
8.   See for example on Tanzania, George Yu, *China and Tanzania: A Study in Cooperative Interaction* (University of California, Centre for Chinese Studies, 1970).
9.   See Alaba Ogunsanwo, *China's Policy in Africa 1958-1971* (Cambridge University Press for International Studies, London School of Economics and Political Science, 1974), pp. 126-34.
10. See the discussion in Alan Hutchison, *China's African Revolution*

(Hutchinson, 1975), Chapter 9, pp. 103-32.
11. See *Peking Review*, No. 4 (1964), p. 7.
12. *New York Times*,21 February 1964.
13. *Soviet News,* London, 2 September 1964, quoting *Pravda.*
14. *Peking Review,* No. 5 (1964), p. 10.
15. Ibid., p. 5.
16. *Sunday Times,* 22 January 1964.
17. A girl student who was raped by an American marine in 1946. The incident led to widespread demonstrations against the American presence in China.
18. 'Remarks at the Spring Festival' in S.R. Schram (ed.), *Mao Tse-tung Unrehearsed* (Penguin Books, 1974), pp. 198-9. See also JPRS II, p. 327.
19. For a good brief account of the border dispute in 1962-4 see John Gittings, *Survey of the Sino-Soviet Dispute* (Oxford University Press, 1968), pp. 158-216 and accompanying select documentation, pp. 161-8. For a fuller documentation see Dennis J. Doolin, *Territorial Claims in the Sino-Soviet Conflict* (Hoover, Stanford University Press, 1965).
20. Doolin, *Territorial Claims,* pp. 42-4.
21. *People's Daily* and *Red Flag* Editorial Departments, Fourth Comment on the Open Letter of the CC of the CPSU, 22 October 1963, in *The Polemic on the General Line of the International Communist Movement* (FLP, 1965), p. 210.
22. 'A Proposal Concerning the General Line of the International Communist Movement', 14 June 1963, in *The Polemic,* p. 13.
23. Cited in Hutchison, *China's African Revolution*, p. 79.
24. For a contemporary analysis of the first of these see W.A.C. Adie, 'Chou En-lai on Safari', *China Quarterly* (April-June 1964). For analyses which place the visits within the context of China's African policy as a whole see B. Larkin, *China and Africa, 1949-1970* (University of California Press, 1971); C. Ogunsanwo, *China's Policy in Africa* and Hutchison, *China's African Revolution.*
25. This point is made with regard to Africa by C. Neuhauser in *Third World Politics,* Harvard East Asian Monographs, No. 27 (East Asian Research Centre, Harvard, 1968), p. 54 and with regard to the Middle East by Y. Shichor in 'The Middle East in China's Foreign Policy', London University Ph.D. thesis (1976), p. 246.
26. NCNA, 2 April 1965, cited in Neuhauser, *Third World Politics*, p. 56.
27. See their *Marxism and Asia* (Allen Lane, 1969), esp. pp. 76-87.
28. *Peking Review*, No. 7 (1964), p. 6.
29. For the first and authoritative outline, see Mao's essay of that title in *Selected Works*, Vol. II.
30. *The Polemic,* p. 189.
31. See, for example, the way in which the Algerian struggle is discussed in ibid., pp. 198-9.
32. For analysis of these Soviet theories see d'Encausse and Schram,*Marxism in Asia.*
33. For analyses of these events and the general lack of understanding of China's position in Africa and the Middle East see Hutchison, *China's African Revolution*, Chapter 9, pp. 103-32 and Shichor, 'The Middle East in China's Foreign Policy', pp. 291-303 and 310-11 respectively.
34. *The Polemic*, p. 207.
35. Ibid., p. 195.
36. Peter Van Ness, *Revolution and Chinese Foreign Policy* (University of California Press, 1970), p. 190.
37. See Shichor, 'The Middle East in China's Foreign Policy', pp. 260-3.

According to Shichor's figures, after four years of balanced trade figures with the Arab countries as a result of agreements made in 1963, China more than doubled its imports and again had a negative balance. A similar pattern of expansion occurred in aid: of the $786.5 million offered to countries outside the socialist camp by the end of 1964, $337.8 million or 43 per cent was offered in 1964. Moreover, 85 per cent of China's aid offered to the Middle East in the years 1956-64 was offered in the two years 1963 and 1964.

38.   See *Peking Review*, No. 3 (1964), pp. 5-10.
39.   'Premier Chou En-lai, Revolutionary Prospects in Africa Excellent!', speech in Mogadishu, Somalia, 3 February 1964, in *Peking Review*, No. 7 (1964), p. 8.
40.   *Current Scene*, 31 March 1966, cited in Neuhauser, *Third World Politics*, p. 62, to which reference may be made for further details.
41.   See *Peking Review*, No. 36 (1965), pp. 9-30, esp. 24-5.
42.   *Peking Review*, No. 46 (1965), p. 20. For an interesting and somewhat different analysis of this phase of China's foreign policy see A.M. Halpern, 'China's Foreign Policy Since the Cultural Revolution' in R. MacFarquhar (ed.), *Sino-American Relations 1949-71* (Praeger, 1972), pp. 21-4.
43.   These included the decimation of the PKI in Indonesia, diplomatic breaks by a few African countries, the ouster of Nkrumah as he arrived in China, Castro's denunciation of China, etc.
44.   Cited in *China Quarterly*, No. 26 (April-June 1966), Chronicle and Documentation, p. 215.
45.   For analysis of this development within the context of the Sino-Soviet conflict in this period, see W.E. Griffith, *Sino-Soviet Relations 1964-1965* (MIT Press, 1967).
46.   For an analysis of China's strategic response see A.S. Whiting, *The Chinese Calculus of Deterrence* (University of Michigan Press, 1975), Chapter 6, pp. 170-95.
47.   See my own analysis, 'Kremlinology and the Chinese Strategic Debate 1965-1966' in *China Quarterly* (March 1972), pp. 32-75. For an analysis which links the external and internal dimensions of opposition to revisionism, see Byung-joon Ahn, *Chinese Politics and the Cultural Revolution* (University of Washington Press, 1976), pp. 186-94.
48.   *Wan Sui*, p. 634; JPRS II, p. 375.
49.   See statements by American Secretary of State, Dean Rusk, on US-China Policy and by Chou En-lai on China's policy towards the US, cited in R. MacFarquhar, *Sino-American Relations*, pp. 222-6.
50.   Edgar Snow, *The Long Revolution* (Random House, 1972), pp. 19-20.

6 THE ALTERNATIVE ROLE OF A MODIFIED LINK WITH THE SOVIET UNION 1959-1966

So far China's changing foreign policy has been discussed on the basis of Mao's writings and the official delineations emanating from Peking so as to suggest that at any given time there was a coherent and generally agreed line on foreign affairs by the leadership in Peking. This has been done primarily for the purposes of analytical clarity. It should be obvious, however, that decision-making processes never exhibit the kind of monolithic unity which may have been implied by the analysis in the previous chapters. Beginning with the Cultural Revolution, the Chinese have analysed the history of the PRC in terms of a two-line struggle between the socialist road as defined by Mao and the capitalist road followed by his opponents. The Russians have analysed this history in terms of a struggle between nationalists (the 'Mao Tse-tung clique') and internationalists (unnamed, apart from Wang Ming, who are claimed to exist in the CPC).[1] A considerable body of literature has been built up in the West on political cleavages in China. A summary of recent approaches in Western scholarly writing maintained that China's political system can be regarded usefully as divided along 'six axes': 'cliques based on personal loyalties, interest groups based on organizational affiliation, factions based on shared ideological positions, classes, regional groups and age, gender and ethnic groupings'.[2] Since the concern of this book is less with the details of China's foreign relations than with the concepts and approaches underlying them, there is much of interest with regard to the impact of these cleavages and disagreements upon foreign policy and its decision-making process which necessarily lies outside the scope of this book. Thus analysis will focus on the question as to whether it is possible to identify alternative frameworks for the conduct of China's foreign policy as having emerged among the leadership in Peking. In other words, is there evidence to suggest that some of China's leaders held views about foreign policy which would have led to China adopting a different role in the international arena?

The previous chapters have shown how far decision turning-points in China's foreign policy have been shaped very much by Mao himself. It may be argued that this Mao-centred view is misleading because first, as the victor in the leadership struggles, his would be the dominant voice that we should hear and, second, that the voices of his opponents on the questions of interest to us here are known to the outside world primarily through the retrospective criticisms levelled against them. The first objection need not detain us long since it does not deny the importance of Mao's role, it merely provides a different explanation for it. As for the second objection, it should be noted that some contemporary evidence does exist. Thus, some of the speeches and writings of other leaders which were published officially at the time certainly provide clues as to their thinking and opinions even on foreign policy questions, so that we are not entirely dependent upon hostile critics for access to the views of those who opposed Mao. The reason as to the dominance of Mao's voice has been well described by John Gittings:

> No-one else has struck the spark or defined the turning-point or summed up the state of the world to the same decisive effect upon the course of Chinese foreign policy. For it is above all in the strategy and style of Chinese diplomacy that Mao's influence has been crucial . . . The very phrases which he has coined to rally the doubters, with his invocation of 'a single spark', 'paper tigers', the 'spiritual atom bomb' and the triumph of 'revolution over war', have a theatrical quality absent in the pronouncements of any other Chinese leaders, matching the drama of China's position on the world stage which throughout his lifetime Mao has always stressed.[3]

Indeed it could be argued that Mao's foreign policy opponents did not really propose carefully considered alternative model roles for China. They rather sought to hold on to established patterns which Mao was seeking to break or, alternatively, at times of great emergency they tended to be more cautious and lacked the bold dramatic vision of the Chairman. It is, nevertheless, a fact that alternative foreign policy suggestions and alternative modes of analysing international affairs were advanced from time to time in Peking. These will be considered to see whether implicit in them were different visions of China's place in the world and of the significance of China's revolutionary experience.

There is no evidence to suggest that Communist Party leaders objected to the broad framework of the 'lean to one side' policy of the 1950s. To be sure, there were non-party people who, according to Mao, entertained in 1949 the notion that China could pursue a neutralist third road, cleaving neither to the Soviet Union nor to the United States.[4] In 1956 Mao again had occasion to dispel the suggestion from non-Communist sources that China could act as a bridge between Russia and America.[5] There was evidence, however, of a certain dissatisfaction with Soviet behaviour towards China – as when the *People's Daily* during the Hundred Flowers period published criticism of the Soviet demands for payment for the military aid given during the Korean War.[6]

The domestic disagreements on power policy questions, including to a certain extent attitudes to be taken towards the applicability of the Soviet model to China,[7] did not on the whole spill over into foreign policy questions. Only once Sino-Soviet ties began to weaken and a total schism had become a distinct prospect did fundamental differences emerge in Peking. The Military Affairs Commission meeting between May and July 1958 (which decided that China should be more self-reliant militarily, develop its own nuclear weapons, prepare more for people's war and generally depend upon its own military experience rather than on Russian experts and manuals) was the scene of a debate at the end of which the then Chief of the General Staff was replaced. What linked the relevant military and domestic issues involved directly with foreign policy was that this was the meeting at which Khrushchev's proposal for a joint Pacific fleet was rejected.[8] The linkage between political conflict on domestic issues and the Sino-Soviet dispute was drawn even more sharply at the Lu Shan Plenum of August 1959 in the wake of the problems brought about by the Great Leap Forward. The Minister of Defence, Peng Teh-huai, was accused of having established 'illicit relations' with Khrushchev prior to launching his critique of the Great Leap. But it was not suggested that Peng had developed a different foreign policy direction for China – although it can be argued that this would have been regarded as implicit in his position.

The Three Reconciliations and the One Reduction (San Ho Yi shao)

During the 'three bitter years' of 1959-62 in the aftermath of the Great Leap Forward, there emerged among some of the leaders in Peking a current of opinion which was alarmed by the drift of China's foreign policy towards a more hostile relationship with its adversaries at a time of domestic weakness and insecurity. The abrupt withdrawal of Soviet aid and technicians in the summer of 1960 hit the already hard-pressed economy very severely indeed.[9] It was hardly surprising that in such circumstances the view should have emerged that it would be better for China to tone down its militancy in foreign affairs, adopt a policy of conflict avoidance and cut back on the aid given abroad. The three difficult years culminated in the crunch year of 1962, when Peking saw itself faced with major national security crises on nearly all fronts: in the east there was a scare of invasion from Taiwan forces backed by American air and sea cover; in the south-west an actual border war was fought with India; trouble occurred on the far western border as tens of thousands of Kazakhs crossed into the Soviet Union; and on the strategic level the Chinese were informed of the Soviet intention to sign a non-proliferation agreement with the United States (interpreted in China as a measure designed to prevent it from acquiring a nuclear capability).

In 1961 there were moves in high political circles to have Peng Teh-huai rehabilitated. Mao himself was lampooned in local Peking news-papers as a stubborn figure out of touch with reality. In the period 1960-1 Mao's influence in shaping and running domestic affairs had declined considerably relative to 1958 and earlier years. Yet by 1962 Mao was beginning to come off the shelf to which he felt he had been assigned, so that by the Tenth Plenum of the Central Committee in September his was the dominant voice in the communiqué which ringingly declared: 'Never forget the class struggle!' As we have seen in his speech to the session he made the seemingly casual remark, 'I think right-wing opportunism [the fault of which Peng Teh-huai had been accused] should be called revisionism.' The full significance of this was not to become clear until the Cultural Revolution. But for Mao, at least, henceforth revisionism was no longer a phenomenon to be observed outside China. Yet there is evidence that despite the resurgence of Mao, more than one senior Chinese leader took the view that it would be better to assume a much lower profile.[10]

After the crisis had passed, subsequent Chinese comments upon this mood dubbed it as the policy of 'the three reconciliations and the one reduction', i.e. reconciliation with imperialism (the US), revisionism (the USSR), and reactionaries (India); and the reduction of aid to foreign revolutionaries and to Asian countries. Much was made of this in the Cultural Revolution criticisms of Liu Shao-ch'i and his alleged associates. It was seen as the corollary of a revisionist viewpoint on domestic issues. It is important to note that this criticism predates the Cultural Revolution itself. Thus, in his Report on the Work of the Government in December 1954, Chou En-lai stated:

From 1959 to 1962, when China's economy experienced temporary difficulties and when the imperialists, the reactionaries and the modern revisionists launched repeated campaigns against China, the class enemies at home launched renewed attacks on socialism, and consequently once again fierce class struggles ensued. In the domestic field, quite a few people actively advocated the extension of plots for private use and of free markets, the increase of small enterprises with sole responsibility for their own profits and losses, the fixing of output quotas based on the household, going it alone [i.e. the restoration of individual economy] liberalization; reversing previous correct decisions; and capitulationism in united front work. In the international field they advocated the liquidation of struggle in our relations with imperialism, the reactionaries and modern revisionism, and reduction of assistance and support to the revolutionary struggle of other peoples. They used their bourgeois and revisionist viewpoints to oppose our general line of socialist construction and the general line of our foreign policy.[11]

In his self-criticism of 23 October 1966, Liu Shao-ch'i maintained that it was Teng Hsiao-p'ing (then Secretary-General of the CPC) who 'advocated' at the Ninth Plenum of the Central Committee (14-18 January 1961) 'the contracting of farm production to each household and proposed the so-called "three reconciliations and one reduction"'.[12] More than six months later Liu put it a little differently:

The Three Reconciliations and One Reduction was put forward by an individual comrade in a rough draft and was not brought up at a Central Committee meeting. At the time I still did not know that this point of view had appeared. Afterwards, it was removed from that comrade's safe.[13]

Since these texts are drawn from Red Guard sources neither may be totally reliable so perhaps it would be wrong to infer too much from the textual differences, except to note that Liu Shao-ch'i confirmed that the viewpoint had appeared at a very high level in the party at this time of economic crisis.

In his only comment on this episode that I have seen, Mao linked this period with previous divisions in the party's history and he certainly saw the international line as part and parcel of the outlook that also produced the soft domestic line. Thus in March 1964 he observed:

In 1962 they again made a fuss of not talking about classes and class struggle. How unstable each department is alas! Teng Tzu-hui wanted to 'contract production to the households'. In the past Wang Chia-hsiang had always been ill. For that half-year he had no illness and really pursued the 'three reconciliations and one reduction'. How active he was! What all must now do is 'three struggles and one increase'. The United Front Department wanted the political parties of the bourgeoisie [Mao was referring here to the rump of so-called democratic parties still surviving since 1949] to become socialist political parties and drew up a five year plan. They became flabby and weakened; it was a surrender to the bourgeoisie. At that time they wanted to carry out internationally the 'three reconciliations and one reduction' and domestically 'the three freedoms and one contract'. Peng Teh-huai's letter of attack [his long plan for reinstatement] also came out at that time.[14]

A clearer indication of the perspectives and analyses upon which this alternative foreign policy proposal was based can be seen from some of the extracts of satirical articles in Peking's local newspapers published between the Ninth and Tenth Plenums (January 1961-September 1962) and then reissued with critical comments during the Cultural Revolution. Three principal writers, holding senior positions in the party's propaganda apparatus and in the Peking municipal party organisation, wrote in this period under the general heading of 'Three Family Village'.[15] These articles were generally satirical and allegorical pieces which criticised and ridiculed cherished policies and attitudes of China's leaders, especially Mao himself. By implication, Mao was accused of being like an autocratic monarch out of touch with reality, deluded by his own rhetoric and unable to accept just criticism. Thus an article criticising 'empty talk' evoked a supposedly child's poem ending with the lines, 'The east wind is our benefactor/and the west wind is our enemy' (referring to Mao's famous statement of November 1957, 'East Wind prevails over West Wind') as a typical example of a 'mere cliché'. The writer adds, 'the more such clichés are uttered the worse the situation will become', and advises people given to 'such empty talk' to 'read more, think more, say less and take a rest when the time comes for talking'. Another article called for special treatment for those with a kind of amnesia which makes one capricious, mad and idiotic. One way to treat such a patient is to hit him on the head 'with a specially made club to induce a state of "shock" and thus restore him to consciousness'. Elsewhere the moral is drawn that a man 'who poses as Chu ke Liang' (a fabled ever-resourceful and successful strategist) 'will never scare people, and the day is bound to come when he will be revealed in his true colours and laughed at by the whole world'. Other articles criticised the Great Leap Forward as deriving from empty boasting and

over-emphasis on the psychological factor and went on to warn that
'those who were deceived by charlatans will certainly not let them off
lightly after calling their bluff.'[16] The goals of the Great Leap Forward
were deemed to be 'beyond your capacity' and self-reliance could only be
obtained, if at all, as the result of being 'excessively forced'. What was
required (as explained in an article entitled, 'The Way to Make Friends
and Entertain Guests') was the 'learning from' and 'uniting with'
countries 'stronger than our own'. 'We should be pleased if a friend is
stronger than we are'. In another essay, presumably Mao's attitude on
this question was lampooned as follows: 'If a man with a swelled head
thinks he can learn a subject with ease and kicks his teacher out, he will
never learn anything.' Yet another article warned: 'One will eventually
suffer heavy reverses' if 'one makes all decisions oneself in the hope of
achieving success with original ideas,' without accepting 'good advice
from below'.[17]

The general foreign policy conclusion to be drawn from the analyses
of these writers is that China should revert to the close Sino-Soviet
alliance, renounce the policies of the Great Leap Forward and the
strategy of self-reliance so as to pursue a more modest but realistic
world role. The starting-point of the critique of Maoist policy was
domestic. The foreign-policy pretensions of Mao were seen as following
from the domestic manifestations of an arrogant autocracy divorced
from socio-economic realities and unable to accept loyal honest advice
from below.

There is very little evidence to suggest that the proposal of 'Three
Reconciliations and One Reduction' had any impact on China's actual
conduct of foreign affairs. To be sure, Sino-Soviet relations in 1961-2
did not plummet downwards without reverse. As has already been
noted, a trade agreement was signed in 1961 and mutual criticism did
go through periods of relative restraint at this time. But the tactics of
Sino-Soviet relations depended upon many factors and not just upon
the will of the Peking leadership. The policy area where decisions made
in Peking could immediately decisively reflect this current was foreign
aid. After all, if a decision had been made to cut back on foreign aid it
would be automatically reflected in the figures regarding new economic
aid commitments. But in fact, far from being cut back, foreign aid
commitments were increased: the figures for 1960 and 1961 combined
are more than double those for the total of the previous three years.[18]
Thus whatever influence this current may have had, it was not so significant as to substantially shift China's priorities or deflect China from its
emerging role at that time as an independent self-reliant revolutionary

country challenging both the superpowers.

The Renewal of the Sino-Soviet Link 1963-1966

Liu [Shao-ch'i] wanted to send a Chinese delegation to the Soviet
Twenty-third Party Congress to reactivate the Sino-Soviet alliance
(Mao Tse-tung).[19]

In the spring of 1966 the long-standing issue reached a climax as to
whether to join with the other Asian socialist states to form a united
programme with the Soviet Union against the United States or to break
once and for all with the Soviet Union and face whatever dangers the
outside world presented. As we have seen, Mao preferred China to stand
alone and not drag China's Marxist-Leninist banner through Soviet
revisionist mud. Liu Shao-ch'i, according to Mao, thought otherwise.
According to Red Guard sources, so did the high-ranking P'eng Chen,
who was later accused of

insisting on sending [a delegation], saying that even if a large delegation were not sent, a smaller should be sent. In actual fact, he
wanted the Centre to despatch a delegation under his leadership.
When others refused to draft for him a report on participation in the
23rd Congress of the Soviet revisionists, he did it himself, and had the
report released in the name of others. Subsequently, he was sharply
criticised by the Centre for this.[20]

Although this account has not been fully confirmed by official
sources in Peking, there is no reason to doubt its substance. No account
of Liu Shao-ch'i or P'eng Chen explaining their position is available in
the West. Their perspective has to be constructed largely on circumstantial evidence and in the light of their known positions throughout
the period of the unfolding of the Sino-Soviet schism.

It is clear, in retrospect especially, that Mao Tse-tung was the main
driving force on the Chinese side directing not only the Sino-Soviet
schism but also in identifying the sources of the emergence of
revisionism in China itself. As has already been argued, Mao personally
can be seen to have initiated the main turning-points in China's
responses to the Soviet Union. Likewise, it was he who in 1961 identified right-wing opportunism in China as being in fact revisionism. It
was he who during the ensuing four years, culminating in the Cultural
Revolution, regarded the domestic political struggles as a polarised
affair between what was later called two headquarters. So little did Liu

Shao-ch'i think in these terms that in Edgar Snow's words: 'it did not seem that [he] made any planned serious attempt to meet Mao's challenge in all-out warfare, or even fully realized, before August, that he himself was the No. 1 Target.'[21] Indeed Lowell Dittmer's careful study of Liu Shao-ch'i concludes that for Liu the problem of revisionism was something which belonged to the international Communist movement and that it was not an evident domestic threat within China.[22] For Liu, as indeed for the large majority of China's leaders, the international situation and China's tasks therein were things to which responses were made on an *ad hoc* basis rather than in Mao's distinctive manner of alertness for significant turning-points. The main question that arises therefore is whether or not Liu, together with the others, operated on a more or less pragmatic basis, or whether there was a coherent intellectual and political framework within which he and the others operated which predisposed them to accept certain kinds of options and reject others. In other words, can a distinctive view of the putative role for China be identified here?

Neither the Chinese nor the Soviet explanations are totally convincing. The Chinese, beginning with the Cultural Revolution, have depicted Liu Shao-ch'i as having headed a bourgeois headquarters in the party which consciously and deliberately pursued revisionist policies at home and capitulationism to Soviet revisionism and American imperialism abroad. Certainly Liu can be shown to have consistently had a higher regard than Mao for the importance of organisation, party dominance and institutionalised patterns of control both inside and outside the party. Associated with this was opposition to the elevation of Mao above the party.[23] But this hardly shows that Liu was revisionist in the Soviet sense or that he and those associated with him pursued the role of which they were later accused. P'eng Chen, who has frequently been linked with Liu's supposed headquarters, was in fact the first Chinese leader to state in public that AALA was not only the focal point of the basic contradictions in the world but that its contradiction with imperialism was the principal one in the current era.[24] This statement at the time in 1965 took the Sino-Soviet dispute to a new and sharper phase. The Soviet explanation based on the division of the Chinese leadership into nationalists and internationalists is even less satisfactory, since many of the leaders in the spring of 1966 who were supposedly prepared to 'reactivate' the Sino-Soviet alliance were precisely those who had long been identified by the Russians as not only 'nationalists', but as long-standing anti-Soviet elements. P'eng Chen, for instance, had been so classified as early as 1946 and again in 1965.[25]

Yet the Soviet explanation for China's open 'anti-Sovietism', beginning with the Cultural Revolution, is that the alleged long struggle between the 'internationalist Marxist-Leninist and the nationalist petty bourgeois' lines in the CPC culminated in the late 1960s when those who 'seized power' because of the Cultural Revolution 'foisted on the PRC an anti-Soviet course, which they have long favoured, but had previously found impossible to implement'.[26] By implication, Liu, P'eng and the others have suddenly in retrospect (contrary to what was said at the time) become what the Soviets regarded as 'internationalists'.

The views of those leaders with whom Mao clashed in the spring of 1966 on the issues of continuing party relations with the Soviet Union and of endorsing some kind of united action with the socialist countries (including the Russians) should be seen within the context of the time and within the framework of their known policies and attitudes in the previous six years. It seems appropriate first to consider the development of their thinking in the intervening period before examining in detail the decisive events of spring 1966. Since Liu Shao-ch'i was the most prominent of these leaders and more is known of his position, analysis will focus primarily upon him.

Like the other leaders subsequently accused in the Cultural Revolution of pursuing an erroneous line regarding Soviet revisionism, such as Teng Hsiao-p'ing and P'eng Chen, Liu Shao-ch'i had played a prominent role in the Sino-Soviet dispute. However, as befits a man who took a more orthodox Leninist view than Mao to questions of party organisation and in administering the economy, Liu tended to pay higher regard to keeping China within the orthodox internationalist Communist movement. While critical of the Soviet Union on the grounds of revisionism, he was more prepared than Mao to entertain the notion of an accommodation with the Russians and to keep the dispute within certain limits. It seems that as the leader of the Chinese delegation to the 1960 Moscow Conference of the 81 Parties, he was prepared to accept certain objectionable clauses in the draft statement, but that it was only on Mao's insistence from Peking that Liu was forced to dig in his heels until the Russians agreed to back down. Moreover, Liu was said to have proposed to Khrushchev that the Soviet leader should withdraw to the second rank in polemics and that the two sets of leaders should consult in advance of conferences so that in the event of disagreements the disputed clauses would be withdrawn so as to avoid attempts to impose one side's will on the other.[27]

Perhaps the most extensive available text outlining Liu's views after the Sino-Soviet breach in July 1963 is his report to an Academy of

Sciences Conference on 30 November 1963.[28] The first half of the
report is concerned with the need to improve and deepen theoretical
awareness and study both to meet the challenge of Soviet revisionism
and to develop Marxism-Leninism. Although he notes the importance
of guarding against the emergence of development of revisionism in
China, he nowhere develops Mao's more urgent theme that class
struggle is vital in China and that the struggle against revisionism was
already being waged in China. Indeed Liu states that 'the current
principal task is to oppose foreign revisionism'. After that had been
done well it would be possible to write up 'our own history, political
economy, international relations, literary theory, legal studies and
world history'. That would be of international and domestic significance, 'especially with regard to our modern history from the Opium
War to the completion of land reform [because] all the countries
which have not yet succeeded in revolution want to learn from us'. It is
interesting to note that like Mao and the other Chinese leaders Liu too
thought that China's distinctive modern history was of direct relevance
to other countries whose people were depicted as anxious to learn from
it. But where Liu differs from Mao at this stage is that he does not
develop the theme of there being a two-line struggle which was still
continuing and taking shape within China. For him revisionism was
something that could possibly appear in the future, rather than a
phenomenon which had already made its appearance in China.

The second half of the report is taken up with an idiosyncratic
analysis of the international situation. To be sure, Liu was critical of
the Soviet Union and he reports having debated with the Vietnamese
the cost of the emergence of revisionism in Russia:

> When I went to Vietnam some comrades said regarding the develop-
> ment of the international communist movement that the cost arising
> out of the emergence of revisionism in the Soviet Union was not very
> high. I replied that the cost was high, but if we just summarised the
> experience well we shall avoid the later emergence of revisionism in
> ours and other socialist countries.

Otherwise more countries 'would also become revisionist'. However,
Liu went on to analyse the relations between the three great powers in
ways that differed from Mao and indeed from the Sixth Reply to the
Soviet Central Committee published less than a fortnight after Liu's
report. Thus Liu explained Soviet-American relations as follows:

Since even the contradictions among imperialists are irreconcilable, can it be said that imperialism is so fond of revisionism? The US and the USSR may make some compromises on a few unimportant questions affecting their current interests – for example, not to land on the moon. On important questions no compromise is impossible ... The principal enemy of the United States and its principal rival is the Soviet Union. That is the country they fear most; it is not China.

Now this can be compared with the stark view of the Sixth Reply: 'The heart and soul of the general line of peaceful coexistence pursued by the leaders of the CPSU is Soviet-US collaboration for the domination of the world.'[29] It will be recalled the official governmental response of China to the Test-Ban Treaty four months earlier had specifically condemned it as an agreement between the Soviet and American leaders 'to manacle China'. To be sure, these and other documents pointed out 'the imperialist United States' could not 'live in harmony with the socialist Soviet Union', indeed they reflected the later Maoist analysis that the two both colluded and contended. What was significant about Liu's observation at this time was his view that the two powers could only agree on matters without substance. Presumably not even Liu would think that 'manacling' China was insubstantial and thus it suggests that he did not altogether agree with the view that the two powers were in league together against China.

Liu even went to the extent of outlining scenarios in which China might have a war with either power. Interestingly, he revealed that 'many people fear the breakout of a Sino-Soviet war.' He thought that was impossible because the Soviet people were unprepared ideologically and psychologically, being still imbued with the spirit of Sino-Soviet friendship – as were the Chinese people. As for a Sino-American war, Liu argued that the Chinese could match the Americans in a war on Chinese soil. Since the Chinese would not go to fight in Washington the balance of forces would be on their side.

Another case in which Liu's analysis differed from Mao's is in his account of China's friends. Both leaders at this time were concerned to show that China was not isolated and that the enemy camp was weakened by its contradictions. Those mentioned by Liu as friends and allies were typically the select Marxist-Leninist countries (Korea, Vietnam and Albania), non-governing parties (Indonesia, Japan, Malaya, New Zealand, Thailand, Burma and Laos) and various Marxist-Leninist breakaway parties. He also noted the improvement of relations with Pakistan and with unnamed countries in south-east Asia. Liu drew attention to what was regarded as the rejection of US imperialist controls in Western Europe and in Japan as indicative of American problems rather than (like Mao) as opening up potential new allies. Likewise, although Liu paid attention to AALA, it was less to the nationalist aspirations, which at this time were being so assiduously acclaimed by Mao as engaged in a common struggle with China. Liu's observation was that 'imperialism could not suppress or revisionism obstruct the revolution of the people of the world'. Towards the end of his report Liu made the remarkable observation that there were still good and correct Soviet achievements and experiences (as well as the bad and mistaken ones) from which the Chinese should learn.

It is interesting to note that while Mao made striking statements in support of AALA anti-American struggles, met delegations from Western countries and Japan, gave interviews to be published in Western newspapers and advanced new ideas and concepts for China's foreign policy, Liu Shao-ch'i contributed very little to foreign affairs. He travelled on the Asian periphery of China on two or three occasions and as Chairman of the PRC he received various visiting Presidents to China. Although his visit to Indonesia in April 1963 became a *cause célébre* in the Cultural Revolution, his public statements at the time were unexceptional in terms of the then prevailing foreign policy line.

If there was a consistent theme characterising his statements and actions in foreign affairs, it was that he rarely strayed into the realm of the complex theories of contradictions which were such a distinctive feature of Mao's approach. His main efforts seem to have been directed towards encouraging the emergence of an Asian constituency against the United States and of the Asian Communist parties to act as a kind of pressure group within the internationalist Communist movement. Thus it is not surprising that this man who above all had always promoted a certain view of the central role of the Communist Party should at the last moment hesitate to make the final break in party relations with the Soviet Union. His last public statement was that of 22 July 1966, on the Vietnam issue.

He committed China more vigorously, with less qualification and without condemnation of the Soviet Union, to the support of the Vietnamese struggle against the Americans than did similar statements earlier in the month by Premier Chou En-lai and Foreign Minister Ch'en Yi.[30]

The case of P'eng Chen was rather different. As has been noted earlier, it was he who in the summer of 1965 had first advanced the view in public that the principal contradiction in the world was between imperialism and AALA. Right through 1965 he had been prominent in the criticism of Soviet revisionism. He clearly went further than Liu Shao-ch'i in this regard. Indeed his approach to foreign affairs in 1965 more closely corresponded to that of Lin Piao's famous 'Long live the Victory of People's War'. Even the image of the world countryside surrounding the cities of the world appeared in his writing before that of Lin Piao.[31] Following the crushing of the PKI in Indonesia and the various setbacks for China's policy in AALA P'eng became associated with the initiative of the Japanese Communist Party in the spring of 1966 (supported by the North Vietnamese and North Koreans) to establish a new kind of united action. Liu Shao-ch'i, however, was little involved. The available record, therefore, does not show the two men acting in concert on foreign affairs in this period, even though they ended up on the eve of the Cultural Revolution by supporting a similar initiative to send a delegation to the 23rd Congress of the CPSU.

Before analysing in more detail the events of that spring it seems appropriate to indicate briefly that on the available public evidence there is little to suggest that in 1965-6 there was a group either of military professionals or economic modernisers in the Peking leadership which was anxious to intervene directly in the Vietnam War on the basis of the united action proposals of the Soviet Union in the expectation of obtaining highly modern equipment from the Soviet side. To be sure, there was a strategic debate in Peking during these years as to how best to deal with the problems arising from the Americanisation of the Vietnam War and as to whether or not it would escalate into a Sino-American war and finally as to how best to deal with that possibility. But as I have argued at length elsewhere, there is no tangible evidence showing that a group argued in favour of a particular strategy so as to obtain Soviet equipment.[32]

The step of formally breaking off party relations with the Soviet Union and of turning China's back on the expressed demands for some kind of unity by the Asian Communist parties in the context of the Vietnam War was clearly an immense step to take. The available evidence suggests that rather than Liu Shao-Ch'i, P'eng Chen and their associates suddenly stepping out of line, it was Mao who at this decisive point in China's history developed the new and startling direction in foreign policy.

Mao Shifts to Joint Opposition to America and Russia

The failure of the united front strategy with AALA towards the end of 1965, coupled with the menace of US military escalation in Vietnam and the possibility even of a Sino-Soviet war, made the winter of 1965-6 particularly tense and anxious in China. Chinese publications noted that the United States had shifted its strategic global focus from Europe to Asia. Preparations were undertaken in south China for defence against possible American attack. According to Allen S. Whiting, who was then Director of the Office of Research and Analysis, Far East, of the Bureau of Intelligence and Research in the State Department, between September and December 1965 approximately 35,000 Chinese military personnel (mainly of the railway and construction corps) crossed into North Vietnam. By early spring the number reached 50,000.[33] Whiting also notes that Communist publications in Hong Kong in January 1966 discussed in great detail the inevitability of an early Sino-American war.[34] Foreign Minister Ch'en Yi, in his well known press conference of 29 September, and Chou En-lai on 20 December 1965, both spoke as if war were a real possibility.[35] China was relatively isolated and vulnerable but it was determined not to be intimidated by American threats from giving assistance to Vietnam. As Whiting has shown, the despatch of 50,000 regular troops to North Vietnam was meant to be detected by the Americans, and although their presence was not publicly admitted by either the Chinese or the Vietnamese, it was a very tangible indication of China's commitment.

Chinese criticisms of the Soviet Union also took on a sharper note at this time. Hitherto the main charge levied against the Russians was that they were seeking to emasculate the revolutionary war in Vietnam by bringing it into the sphere of Soviet-American *détente*. By the turn of the year, when there were already 200,000 US soldiers in Vietnam, and when it was evident that more were on the way, Chinese commentaries became especially bitter about Soviet policies which facilitated the shift of American forces from the European theatre to the Far East. During this period, much to the alarm of the Chinese, Russo-Japanese inter-state relations were also becoming more cordial.

It was in this context of a gathering storm and crisis that a delegation of the Japanese Communist Party (JCP) came to China on 10 February 1966 to argue that some limited co-operation with all the socialist countries including the Soviet Union was necessary for victory in Vietnam.[36] The delegation did not finally leave China for Japan until two months later, on 4 April. In the intervening period it visited North Vietnam (17-27 February) and North Korea (11-21 March), where joint communiqués were issued calling for united action with *all* the socialist countries. The issue came to a head after the JCP returned from Korea. A communiqué was about to be issued when Mao intervened and insisted that *Soviet* modern revisionism was to be specifically condemned, otherwise it would be better not to have a communiqué at all.

The JCP position can be inferred from Miyamoto's speech to a Peking rally of 26 March 1966. Although he condemned 'modern revisionists headed by Khrushchev' in many respects, Miyamoto repeated the following phrase more than once: 'To ensure victory in the struggle against US imperialist policies of war and aggression, it is essential to oppose modern revisionism, the main danger in the present internationalist communist movement, *while guarding against dogmatism and sectarianism*' (emphasis added).[37] The qualification at the end of the sentence (which was a veiled criticism of the Chinese position) of course was entirely absent from any equivalent Chinese statement. Miyamoto also outlined a variant of the peaceful transition theme by calling for a national democratic united front in Japan to establish a democratic coalition government. Particularly after the Indonesian experience, in which the Communist Party opposed the revisionist road externally, while domestically it followed a line of peaceful transition which ended in disaster, it was unlikely that this would have been endorsed in Peking.

By the end of March, however, the Japanese and Chinese representatives (who included Chou En-lai, Teng Hsiao-p'ing, P'eng Chen, Liao Ch'eng-chih and Liu Ning-yi – K'ang Sheng and T'ao Chu travelled with them to see Mao in Canton and they too had been involved in the negotiations) were prepared to release a joint communiqué which did not specifically condemn Soviet modern revisionism. Liu Shao-ch'i may have been involved at an earlier stage in the negotiations, but he had left with Ch'en Yi on a visit to Pakistan and Afghanistan on 26 March and he therefore missed the confrontation with Mao. The JCP and CPC were received by Mao at a hot-springs resort outside Canton on 29 March. He was very angry and shouted at his colleagues in front of the Japanese: 'You weak-kneed people in Peking!'

As has been already noted, the arraigned people included practically the whole of the Peking leadership and not just the associates of Liu Shao-ch'i. As was indicated in the previous chapter, Mao's calculations included domestic considerations. As he put it to Edgar Snow a few years later, 'compromising with either of the super-powers could then only lead to a split on the home front.' He rejected any notion of once again becoming dependent on the Soviet Union, as that could lead to a double-cross. In Mao's view the Soviets were no longer just revisionists, they were now to be considered as counter-revolutionaries. A JCP argument that the dividing line in the world was between warmongers (principally the US) and peace-lovers (by definition the socialist coun-tries, including the Soviet Union) was, in Mao's view, misconceived.

Mao is reported to have outlined his views to the Japanese as follows:

> A war between China and America is inevitable. This year at the earliest, or within two years at the latest, such a war will occur. America will attack us from four points, namely the Vietnam frontier, the Korean frontier, and through Japan by way of Taiwan and Okinawa. On such an occasion, Russia with the Sino-Russian defence pact as its pretext, will cross the frontier from Siberia and Mongolia to occupy China, starting at Inner Mongolia and Northeast China. The result will be a confrontation across the Yangtse of the Chinese Liberation Army and the Russian Army . . . It is a mistake to say that in the world today there are war powers and peace powers confronting one another; there only exist revolutionary war powers and anti-revolutionary war powers. World revolution cannot come about by the evasion of war.[38]

Thus it was Mao who suddenly and unexpectedly changed the frame-work of Chinese foreign policy. The other leaders had been adjusting to very alarming circumstances still within a framework of the earlier 1960s. It also makes clear that it must have been at Mao's personal initiative on 20 March 1966 that the decision was made not to send a delegation to the 23rd CPSU Congress which ended party relations between the two countries. As in earlier times Mao (perhaps alone of China's leaders) demonstrated the supreme confidence to act on the basis that 'a resolutely independent and united China could weather any storm.'

This view was soon reflected in formal Chinese pronouncements on international affairs. Thus the Joint Statement of China and Albania issued on 11 May roundly declared: 'The fight against imperialism headed by the United States and its lackey and the fight against modern revisionism with the leading groups of the CPSU as its centre are two inseparable tasks.'[39] Meanwhile, as we have seen, Chou En-lai and the US Secretary of State, Dean Rusk, signalled to each other that neither government sought a war with the other.

Liu Shao-ch'i, however, unlike Chou En-lai for example, did not apparently accommodate himself to the new framework. To illustrate this it is useful to consider again Liu's last public statement. The idio-syncracy of his position in the light of Mao's declared line is best demonstrated by comparing it with that of Ch'en Yi, as outlined in a speech twelve days before Liu's. Liu seems to have mentioned something of his 1963 views, cited earlier, in the sense of affirming a common identity of interests with other socialist countries, and of arguing more narrowly than Mao that the main problems with the Soviet Union arose out of its craven attitude to the United States. Thus Liu's only reference to the Russians is an oblique one in which he regarded Ho Chi Minh's statement of 17 July as a 'telling blow at those monsters who are collaborating with US imperialism to engineer a "peace talks" swindle'. Ch'en Yi, by contrast, claimed that the American bombing of Hanoi and Haiphong was 'entirely the result of collusion of the United States and the Soviet Union', and he went on to demand that 'all countries which genuinely oppose US imperialist aggression must oppose . . . and draw a clear line of distinction between themselves and the Soviet revisionists' united action . . . '

Liu also indicated a far greater determination on China's behalf to help in the Vietnam War against the Americans than Ch'en Yi. Unlike Ch'en, Liu stated that American 'aggression against Vietnam is aggression against China.' He was also alone at this stage in designating China as 'the reliable rear area of the Vietnamese people'. Interestingly, he claimed that the Chinese people were ready 'to take such action at any time and in any place as the Chinese and *Vietnamese* people deem necessary for dealing *joint* blows at the US aggressor' (emphasis added). Quoting a Chinese government statement of 3 July, Ch'en Yi obligated China in a much more limited way and did not suggest any joint decision-making or joint activities of any kind: 'In accordance with the interests and demands of the Vietnamese people, we will at any time take such actions as we deem necessary.'[40] Liu thus asserted that the Vietnamese would take part in determining Chinese decisions and that joint operations might be launched against the Americans. Ch'en Yi, by contrast, spoke only of Chinese decision-making and in no way did he suggest that joint Sino-Vietnamese military action might take place.

Thus, right at the end it is possible to see that although Liu Shaoch'i was critical of Soviet revisionism and shared many of the foreign-policy perspectives of the other Peking leaders, his frame of reference was still the socialist world. One Red Guard source quotes him on some unspecified date in 1965 as saying, 'Only at a time when the Soviet Union loses all hope of making up with US imperialism can we unite.'[41] For Liu the Soviet Union and the United States were very different kinds of actors on the world stage. This was less true for Mao, for whom the Soviet Union had become a counter-revolutionary power. For Liu, in the final analysis, regardless as to how revisionist the Soviet Union had become, China and Russia were still members of the socialist world. Their differences were negotiable. Mao, by contrast, had written off the Soviet leadership and had long since pinned his hopes on a new revolution to overthrow it. There is little or no evidence to indicate that Liu and his associates, however, consciously conspired to promote an alternative foreign policy programme to that of Mao. On the contrary, it seems that the other leaders (the weak-kneed people in Peking) were surprised and out-manoeuvred by Mao, who moved China on to a new stage. Liu seems to have been as unprepared for the enormity of Mao's challenge to the established pattern of operations in foreign affairs as he was in the domestic arena. It is also clear in retrospect that Mao's new position inevitably led to the souring of relations with the JCP and with North Korea. The rationale for the isolationism of the Cultural Revolution was already implicit in Mao's stand.

Notes

1.   For a recent presentation of the Russian view written in a non-polemical tone see O.B. Borisov and B.T. Koloskov, *Soviet Chinese Relations, 1945-1970* (Indiana University Press, 1975).
2.   John Bryan Starr, 'From the Tenth Party Congress to the Premiership of Hua Kuo-feng: The Significance of the Colour of the Cat', *China Quarterly*, No. 67 (September 1976), p. 480.
3.   J. Gittings, *The World and China 1922-1972* (Eyre Methuen, 1974), p. 270.
4.   Mao Tse-tung, 'On People's Democratic Dictatorship', *SW*, Vol. IV, p. 415.
5.   JPRS I, 8 December 1956, address to second session of the First Committee of the All China Federation of Industry and Commerce, p. 37.
6.   See Lung Yun in R. MacFarquhar (ed.), *The Hundred Flowers* (Praeger, 1960), p. 50.
7.   To take but one example, the disagreement as to whether agricultural collectivisation could precede mechanisation — which was contrary to the Soviet model.
8.   It is to this that the Chinese statement referred when in September 1963 it complained that in 1958 the Soviet leadership 'put forward unreasonable demands to bring China under Soviet military control'. The statement went on to say that these demands had been 'rightly and firmly rejected'. *The Polemic on the General Line of the International Communist Movement* (FLP, 1965), p. 77. In his memoirs, Khrushchev refers to Soviet requests for a radio installation to communicate with Soviet submariners, a naval base and to have air squadrons stationed in China. Nikita Khrushchev, *Khrushchev Remembers* (Penguin Books, 1974), Vol. 2, pp. 306-11.
9.   No precise figures are available, but later Chinese accounts have made much out of this Soviet perfidy and of the damage it reflected. Factories and numerous industrial and engineering projects were abandoned uncompleted by departing Russians, who even took away the blueprints with them. China was deprived of much-needed fuel oil and lubricants. The *Work Bulletin* of 1960-1 contains graphic descriptions of the plight of

many agricultural areas as they tried to cope with the legacy of mismanagement in the Great Leap Forward coupled with bad weather for successive years.

10. Ch'en Yun, as cited in the 'Confession of Wu Leng-hsi' (who in 1962 was still head of the New China News Agency) in SCMM 662. Teng Hsiao-p'ing and Wang Chia-hsiang were also said to have held this view; see Byung-joon Ahn, *Chinese Politics and the Cultural Revolution* (University of Washington Press, 1976), p. 192.

11. 'Premier Chou En-lai Reports on the Work of the Government' to the First Session of the Third National People's Congress on 21 and 22 December 1964, *Peking Review*, No. 1 (1965), pp. 12-13. 'The reversal of previous correct decisions' mentioned by Chou En-lai presumably refers to the attempt to have the verdict on Peng Teh-huai reversed. That would have meant that his criticisms of the Great Leap Forward were now seen to have been fundamentally correct and perhaps even more significantly it would have been a severe rebuff for Mao, both personally and in terms of the policies for which he stood.

12. *Collected Works of Liu Shao-ch'i 1958-1967* (Union Research Institute, Hong Kong), p. 361.

13. 'Confession', summer 1967, ibid., p. 367.

14. *Wan Sui*, p. 479. See also JPRS I, p. 345.

15. The three were Wu Han, Liao Mo-sha and Teng T'o. The first was a mayor of Peking, a noted historian and playwright whose play 'Hai Jui Dismissed from Office' was the target for the first blast of the Cultural Revolution in the autumn of 1965, in the form of a criticism by Yao Wen-yuan which had been approved by Mao. Mao had interpreted the play as an allegorical call for the reinstatement of Peng Teh-huai. The most senior of the three was Teng T'o, a former editor-in-chief of the *People's Daily*, who also wrote a column in this period under the heading 'Evening Chats at Yenshan'.

16. These quotations are taken from a selection called 'Teng T'o's Evening Chats at Yenshan is anti-Party and anti-socialist Doubletalk' in *The Great Socialist Cultural Revolution in China* (2) (FLP, 1966), pp. 12-49.

17. These were cited in Yao Wen-yuan's critique 'On "Three-Family Village"' in *The Great Socialist Cultural Revolution in China* (1) (FLP, 1966), pp. 29-69.

18. China's total armed aid commitments for the years 1957 to 1961 respectively are as follows (in US$ millions): 38,51,0, 57 and 125. From Table 2.2 in J. Horvath, *Chinese Technology Transfer to the Third World* (Praeger, 1976), pp. 16-17.

19. Edgar Snow, *The Long Revolution* (Random House, 1972), p. 19.

20. 'Counter-Revolutionary Revisionist P'eng Chen's Towering Crimes of Opposing the Party, Socialism and Mao Tse-tung Thought', published by the Liaison Centre for Thorough Criticism of Liu, Teng, T'ao. *The East is Red Commune*, China University of Science and Technology, Red Guard Congress, 10 June 1967, in SCMM No. 639, p. 15.

21. Snow, *The Long Revolution*, p. 91.

22. Lowell Dittmer, *Liu Shao-ch'i and the Chinese Cultural Revolution: The Politics of Mass Criticism* (University of California Press, 1974), p. 47.

23. For a detailed analysis see S.R. Schram, 'The Party in Chinese Communist Ideology', *China Quarterly*, No. 38 (April-June 1969), pp. 1-26, and his introduction in Stuart Schram (ed.), *Authority, Participation and Cultural Change in China* (Cambridge University Press, 1973), esp. pp. 27-85.

24. See P'eng Chen speech at the Aliarcham Academy of Social Sciences (Indonesia), *Peking Review*, No. 21 (1965), p. 10.

25. *Kommunist* editorial, No. 7 (May 1964), cited in J. Gittings, *Survey of the Sino-Soviet Dispute* (Oxford University Press, 1968), p. 41; and *Pravda*, 7 June 1965, in ibid., p. 230, note 3.

26. Borisov and Koloskov, *Soviet Chinese Relations 1945-1970*, p. 348.

27. See 'The Confession of Wu Leng-hsi', p. 8.

28. Liu Shao-ch'i's Report to the Fourth Enlarged Conference of the Social Sciences section of the Chinese Academy of Sciences (30 November 1963) in *Liu Shao-ch'i Tzu-liao Hui-pian (A Compilation of Materials on Liu Shao-ch'i)*, Tientsin, April 1967. I am grateful to Professor Schram for giving me a copy of this text. While there can be no guarantee that this is the full text of the report, running as it does to the length of nearly 4,000 characters, it is the most detailed and revealing account of Liu's view on the problem of revisionism in international affairs and its consequences for China that is available in the West. Its length ensures that the nature of his reasoning as well as his views on specific topics can be ascertained and compared to those in other contemporary texts.

29. *The Polemic*, p. 295.

30. Liu Shao-ch'i, 'Statement in Support of President Ho Chi Minh's Appeal' of 22 July 1966, *Peking Review*, No. 31 (1966), pp. 9-10. Vice-Premier Ch'en Yi's Speech at the Peking Mass Rally, 10 July 1966, *Peking Review*, No. 29 (1966).

31. See note 24. In fact P'eng was using an image which had appeared earlier in a speech by Aidit, the then leader of the PKI.

32. Yahuda, 'Kremlinology and the Chinese Strategic Debate', *China Quarterly*, No. 49 (Jan.-March 1972), pp. 32-75.

33. Allen S. Whiting, *The Chinese Calculus of Deterrence* (University of Michigan Press, 1975), p. 186. For an authoritative account of China's military moves and their deterrent implications in this period, see generally his Chapter 6, pp. 170-95.

34. Ibid., pp. 291-3.

35. *Peking Review*, Nos. 41 and 52 (1965).

36. The ensuing analysis draws heavily from Yahuda, 'Kremlinology', esp. pp. 66-73.

37. NCNA, 26 March 1966, in SCMP, No. 3668.

38. Cited in Kikuozo Ito and Minoru Shibata, 'The Dilemma of Mao Tse-tung' in *China Quarterly*, No. 35 (July-September 1968).

39. *Peking Review*, No. 21 (1966).

40. See note 30 above.

41. In SCMM, No. 653, p. 13.

7 CHINA AS A BASTION OF SOCIALISM 1966-1968

One of the most distinctive roles chosen for China by its leaders is that of the militant bastion of socialism of the Cultural Revolution period. Although this period is frequently regarded as a time when China turned inward, it had a profound internationalist content as seen from China. Alone of the socialist countries, China was engaged in the struggle to prevent a capitalist restoration from taking place after the socialisation of the economic base. This was regarded as the most important challenge facing the internationalist Communist movement since the Bolshevik Revolution itself. Thus the outcome of the struggles in China was seen as absolutely critical not only for the fate of the revolu tion in China but for the fate of Marxism-Leninism in the world as a whole In this sense the resolution of this struggle was regarded as the most important internationalist revolutionary task for the Chinese people. China's internationalism now turned on the question of carrying on the revolution at home rather than on prolonging an internationalist united front based on the true (as opposed to Khrushchev's) principles of peaceful co-existence. This meant that the prevailing distinction between domestic and international affairs changed considerably. Up until this point China's claims to have become the true centre of Marxism-Leninism involved distinguishing between issues of international significance and those of domestic import only. Thus the famous Nine Comments of 1963 sent to the CPSU sought to outline the general principles of Marxism-Leninism which were universally applicable, while leaving it open to Marxist-Leninists to apply them to the specific conditions of their own countries. In August 1965 Mao Tse-tung Thought was described as 'the application of the universal truths of Marxism-Leninism . . . in the concrete practice of the Chinese revolution'. Now it was argued that, far from being a particularistic manifestation of Marxism-Leninism, Mao Tse-tung's Thought *was* Marxism-Leninism. Thus at the 11th Plenum of the Central Committee of August 1966 it was stated: 'Mao Tse-tung's thought is Marxism-Leninism of the era in which imperialism is heading for total collapse and socialism is advancing to world wide victory.'[1] Earlier references to this alleged new era were now formally enshrined in an authoritative party document. Interestingly, references to this era did not last long into the 1970s. It is also interesting to note that not only was Mao Tse-tung's Thought said to be universally valid but all true revolutionaries were enjoined to carry it out (rather than apply it as they saw fit to the conditions in their countries).

Another of the key phrases of the 11th Plenum was first applied to the international section and was later to be applied to home affairs too: 'All political forces are undergoing a process of great upheaval, great division and great reorganisation.' This had been mentioned before in November 1965 (after the collapse of the AALA united front strategy), and it clearly meant that Peking was anticipating a polarisation of the international scene at all levels. The Communist world was seen as divided between the true Marxist-Leninists and the rest lumped together as revisionists. AALA was regarded as divided between those forces willing to follow Lin Piao's exhortations to carry out armed struggle and the others variously regarded as reactionaries and imperialist stooges. The imperialist camp was seen as riddled with contradictions between the monopoly capitalists and the popular forces in their own countries. The different parts of the world could be seen in this view as being polarised along the same lines into two basic forces: as A.M. Halpern has put it, they constituted 'the popular (revolutionary) and the anti-popular (counter-revolutionary)'.[2]

This generally produced the Sino-centric view of the world revolutionary forces as gravitating around Peking. Likewise the counterrevolutionary forces were seen to be concentrating their activities so as to attack China and revolution. The two were seen as indivisible. Thus the Communiqué of the 11th Plenum depicted the Soviet leadership as 'uniting with US-led imperialism and the reactionaries of various countries and forming a new "Holy Alliance" against communism, the people, revolution and China'.

It would be wrong therefore to view China's foreign policy in this period as simply the spillover of the domestic convulsions of the Cultural Revolution into the foreign affairs area. Although some of the critical struggles in the Cultural Revolution were waged over the Ministry of Foreign Affairs and indeed at one stage in August 1967 it was taken over by a Red Guard faction, China's actual foreign policy did not markedly change in that hot summer.[3] The framework for a foreign policy which turned its back on the accepted norms of international diplomacy had already been established more than a year earlier. Furthermore, the clearest authoritative presentation of the Cultural Revolution view of China's international role was given in November 1967, well after the ultra-leftist group and its high-level supporters associated with the attacks on the Foreign Ministry had been formally disowned and purged.

Lin Piao's speech commemorating the 50th Anniversary of the Bolshevik Revolution and the joint editorial of the *People's Daily, Red Flag* and *Liberation Army Daily* of 6 November 1967 provide the fullest and most clear-cut account of China's international role as a 'bastion of socialism'.[4] The editorial concluded that 'the centre of world revolution', which had been moving steadily eastward over the last hundred and fifty years, 'has since gradually moved to China and Mao Tse-tung's thought has come into being'. In the new era in which, according to Lin Piao, 'the proletariat and the bourgeoisie are locked in the decisive battle on a world-wide scale', Marxism-Leninism had been developed by Mao and 'raised to an entirely new peak'. He went on to declare, 'Mao Tse-tung's thought is the banner of our era,' and he then explained that this was true not only for China but for the people of the whole world. It is well worth quoting him at length to show that it was not a question of adapting Mao's thought to different conditions but rather the different peoples were expected to follow it directly. The word 'grasped' is used repeatedly and with emphasis, and the whole reads like a litany:

> Once Mao Tse-tung's thought — Marxism-Leninism at its highest in the present era — is grasped, the countries that have already established the dictatorship of the proletariat will, through their own struggles, be able to prevent the restoration of capitalism.
>
> Once Mao Tse-tung's thought — Marxism-Leninism at its highest in the present era — is grasped, the people of those countries where political power has been usurped by the revisionists will, through their own struggles, be able to overthrow the rule of revisionism and re-establish the dictatorship of the proletariat.
>
> Once Marxism-Leninism, Mao Tse-tung's thought is integrated with the revolutionary practice of the people of all countries, the entire old world will be shattered to smithereens.

In those heady days of the Cultural Revolution, it was actually argued that Mao had superseded even Marx and Lenin and that if his thought ('the supreme doctrine') were studied, there was no need to read Marx and Lenin. As one Chinese leader asked rhetorically: 'Where can one find theory at such a high level or thought of such maturity, either in ancient times or in the present era, in China or elsewhere?'[5]

According to Lin Piao, the following 'glorious tasks [were] entrusted to the people of our country by history, and they are our incumbent internationalist duty':

> We must raise still higher the great banner of the October Revolution and the great banner of Marxism-Leninism, Mao Tse-tung's Thought, and carry on the great proletarian cultural revolution through to the end.
> We must build our great motherland into a still more powerful base for world revolution.
> We must give ever more vigorous support to the revolutionary struggles of the proletariat and people of all countries.
> We must, together with the revolutionary people everywhere, carry through to the end the struggle against a US-led imperialism and against modern revisionism with the Soviet revisionist renegade clique as its centre.
> We must intensify our efforts in studying and mastering Mao Tse-Tung's thought and disseminate it still more widely throughout the world.

These tasks were predicated on a view in which China was prepared to stand alone if necessary in its revolutionary purity, challenging not only the two superpowers but all those throughout the world who differed significantly from China in opposition to the US or the Soviet Union. The tasks of Chinese diplomats in this view were no more than to support revolutionary struggles (as determined in China) and to disseminate Mao's Thought.

It would be wrong to think that this approach was peculiar to Lin Piao and his associates alone. While Mao may have been unhappy with certain aspects of his personality cult, he himself both publicly and privately committed himself to this view of China's role. Consider this passage from his personal message of 25 October 1966 to the Fifth Congress of the Albanian Party:

> The truth of Marxism-Leninism is on our side. So is the international proletariat. So are the oppressed nations and oppressed peoples. And so are the masses of the people who constitute over 90 per cent of the world's population. We have friends all over the world. We are not afraid of being isolated and we shall never be isolated. We are invincible. The handful of pathetic creatures who oppose China and Albania are doomed to failure . . .
> Let the Parties and peoples of China and Albania unite, let the

Marxist-Leninists of all countries unite, let the revolutionary people of the whole world unite and overthrow imperialism, modern revisionism and the reactionaries of every country! A new world without imperialism, without capitalism and without any system of exploitation is certain to be built.[6]

It is clear that by writing in these terms Mao was fully developing the language and concepts of the Cultural Revolution foreign policy. He disdained the international diplomatic community and the pattern of state relations and proclaimed his readiness to accept isolation in that regard, preferring instead a revolutionary unity with the 90 per cent of the people of the world. Likewise, the desired internationalist united front of barely a year ago was totally ignored in favour of the more profound unity of fellow revolutionaries.

These were the concepts and guidelines under which the Chinese were to casually provoke and encounter diplomatic incidents of varying magnitude with at least 32 countries. In addition to those with whom such trouble may have been expected, others involving friendly countries such as Tanzania, Zambia, Cambodia, Ceylon, etc., showed the utter disregard for normal diplomatic practices and the lack of discrimination between offending countries who had hitherto been friends and those who were more obviously adversaries.[7] Indeed their readiness to allow Sino-Cambodian relations to reach almost a breaking point demonstrated a sublime disregard for even the elementary strategic needs of the Chinese state, not to mention the needs of the Vietnamese revolutionaries. To have forced Prince Sihanouk to sever relations with China would have severely damaged the careful neutrality he had nurtured for Cambodia and would have probably caused him to move Cambodia closer to the American side. In many ways the incidents which led to the confrontation were typical of those which caused trouble with other countries. Elements in the overseas Chinese community, aided and abetted by the Chinese Embassy in Phnom Penh, were claiming the right to express their love for Chairman Mao and to propagate his thought. Sihanouk was provoked into denouncing the 'export' of the Cultural Revolution. This Red Guard type of activity in effect challenged the authority and sovereignty of the local government. In September Prince Sihanouk complained that the Chinese were using the Cambodian-Chinese Friendship Association for subversive activities and ordered its disbandment. Peking, however, encouraged the association by sending a telegram congratulating it on its anniversary the following day. On 15 September Sihanouk declared that

Cambodia's Embassy and staff would be withdrawn from Peking. Hurried assurances from Chou En-lai caused the decision to be rescinded. In October, Chou sent two messages to the Prince in which he let it be understood that China would not interfere in Cambodia's internal affairs.[8] The episode was typical of Peking having to respond to locally engendered disputes. More often than not these were not directed from Peking but rather, in the confused situation in the Ministry of Foreign Affairs and the very narrow parameters in which decision-making could operate, Peking could not but endorse the 'Maoists'. Frequently, as in the case of Hong Kong, the endorsement was rhetorical and consistent with an attempt to contain the local provocations rather than encourage further extremist behaviour.[9] In the case of Cambodia, it took the full authority of Chou En-lai to prevent a serious deterioration of relations.

Mao's attitude in the stormy summer of 1967 seems to have been closer to the leftist Cultural Revolution viewpoint than to the position taken by Chou En-lai. The only available clue to Mao's thinking on these questions is one article in the *Wan Sui* material. It seems very likely that Mao would have had much to say on strategic issues and questions concerning China's role with regard to revolutionary wars, but these statements are unavailable in the West. The one document devoted to these questions is dated 7 July 1967, and it is significantly entitled 'China Must Become the Arsenal for World Revolution.' Mao began by noting with pride that China's rapid pace of nuclear development exceeded that of the other nuclear powers. He then discussed with evident enthusiasm the progress of armed struggle of the Nagas in India and of the revolutionaries in Burma and Thailand. He was particularly impressed with the achievement of the Burmese Party and claimed that 65 per cent of Burma's territory was engulfed in the armed struggle. Mao noted that the rising of Burma and Thailand meant that 'America was being completely dragged around South-East Asia.' At the same time he cautioned, 'of course we must still keep our eyes open for an early and a big war on our territory.' But his next sentence showed a true Cultural Revolution perspective. 'It is still better for the Burmese Government to oppose us and it is to be hoped that they will break relations with us. That would enable us to support the Burmese Communist Party more openly.' Mao then went on to discuss revolutionary movements in AALA, dwelling in particular on Russian alleged perfidy in the Six-Day War in the Middle East. Once again he went on to observe that China was not isolated, but that the fact that China was opposed so sharply showed that its influence was extensive and that those who criticised China were isolated from their own people. 'The more [the American imperialists and the Russian revisionists] oppose China the more they promote popular revolution. The people of these countries realise that China's road is the only road to liberation.' He then went on to make the remarkable observation:

> Our China is not only the political centre of the world revolution but in military affairs and technology it must also become the centre of world revolution. If we give them weapons we should brand them with markings as Chinese weapons (except for those sent to a few special areas). We must indeed support them openly. We must become the arsenal for world revolution.[10]

Mao clearly exceeded even the statements made by Lin Piao. His hope that the Burmese government would sever diplomatic relations and that China should openly send weapons in support of armed revolutionary struggles in south-east Asia accorded very well with the current 'Red Guard diplomacy'. The only point on which Mao departed from the Cultural Revolutionary line was his criticism of the excessive adulation of him and his thought, especially in external propaganda.[11] This criticism seems to have been totally ignored. For example, *Peking Review*, China's main political journal for external distribution, ran a continual weekly series of articles depicting various alleged representatives of peoples from scores of countries in adoring study of Mao and his thought. The series was variously headed, 'The people of the world love Chairman Mao' or 'The brilliance of Mao Tse-tung Thought illuminates the whole world', etc., and it ran from February 1967 to April 1968.

Chinese statements during the period of the Cultural Revolution generally eschewed state to state relations. It was true that cordial relations were maintained with a few countries like Pakistan and Mali. Despite diplomatic irritations the Presidents of Zambia and Tanzania visited China during this period. It seems that these are best regarded as residuary relations which Chou En-lai in particular would have taken care not to have disregarded. In formal lists of its friends China tended to ignore these countries altogether. Thus the aforementioned joint editorial on the 50th anniversary of the Bolshevik Revolution was able to commend only two countries by name, Albania ('the beacon of socialism in Europe') and Vietnam (the 'great example of anti-US armed struggle, of anti-US armed revolutionary struggle for the people of the whole world') and then the *people* of 'Laos, Burma, the Philippines, Thailand, India, Indonesia and other countries [who] are embarking or persisting in the road of revolutionary armed struggle; . . . the national democratic revolutionary movement . . . ' unfolding vigorously in the vast areas of AALA. Finally, not the bourgeois leaders resisting American encroachments, but 'the *proletariat* of Western Europe, North America and Oceania [which] are weakening and plunging into the struggle against US imperialism and monopoly capital in their own countries'.

It should be noted, however, that this period of foreign policy was predicated upon two major considerations, first that the Americans and the Russians were engaged in a counter-revolutionary anti-China holy alliance and, second, that the Cultural Revolution in the words of the joint editorial 'is not merely a revolution within national bounds: it is likewise a revolution of an international order.' Any fundamental change in either or indeed in both of these was bound to have an important impact on foreign policy and on the conceptualisation of China's international role. The events of 1968 were to challenge the accepted domestic and external frameworks. However, in order to be able to analyse satisfactorily the ending of the Cultural Revolution phase of China as a bastion of socialism and the emergence of Chairman Mao's new 'diplomatic revolutionary line' in the early 1970s, it is first necessary to consider the strong leftist or ultra-leftist current in foreign affairs which permeated the Cultural Revolution and which existed as a counter-current thereafter until the fall of the 'gang of four' in October 1976.

The 'Leftist' Current

In the course of the Cultural Revolution there emerged a radical critique of important aspects of China's prevailing foreign policy, the behaviour of Chinese diplomats and the stifling of the Cultural Revolution within the Ministry of Foreign Affairs and the various institutions subordinate to it. The latter was clearly a part of the essentially domestic struggle which affected the Foreign Ministry much as it did all the main organisational structures in China. The fact that it was headed by the blunt-speaking 'scholar-general' Marshal Ch'en Yi, who was a Vice-Premier close to Chou En-lai, gave the struggles here a special flavour. The struggle in the Foreign Ministry was also part of a campaign to dislodge Premier Chou En-lai. The Ministry was also in charge of one of the branches of state interests — namely foreign affairs — to which Mao had always paid close attention and in which he had played consistently the major role as the primary architect of China's foreign policy. The power seizure in the Ministry in August 1967 and the burning of the British mission that month should be seen less in the context of a debate over foreign policy than as the critical point in this essentially domestic struggle. It is clear that at the crucial moment the anti-Chou forces had overplayed their hand and the power seizure failed.[12] The group concerned and its high-level backers were denounced as an ultra-leftist conspiratorial clique.

The concern here, however, is less with the political struggle of the Cultural Revolution than it is with the alternative current in foreign policy thinking. The leftist current stood for a more purist foreign policy line, according to which China would fully support revolutionary movements, distance itself from bourgeois governments whether in AALA or elsewhere, extirpate remaining foreign influence in China, renounce foreign trade and devote itself entirely to the continuation of revolution within and the promotion of revolution outside China. It was a view which ignored or rejected calculations of state interests and the careful analysis of contradictions and balances of forces. Indeed it was a view which betrayed very little understanding of the outside world and the practical dilemmas confronting those who had to guide the Chinese revolutionary ship of state through the hostile waters of more powerful adversaries and of those with whom there were agreements at certain levels and disagreements at others.

Consider, for example, the principal charges against the policy of the PRC towards the overseas Chinese since 1949. Typically these were laid at the door of the head of the Overseas Chinese Affairs Commission, Liao Ch'eng-chih, who in the language of the Cultural Revolution was 'the top party person in authority taking the capitalist road in the Central Commission for Overseas Chinese Affairs' and who was charged with 'betraying the interests of the patriotic Overseas Chinese'. In fact the policies for which he was criticised were those of the government as a whole. Thus Liao was charged with suppressing the revolutionary and patriotic aspirations of the overseas Chinese and with urging them to abjure politics and identify with the interests of the countries in which they resided rather than with those of revolutionary China. He was said to have ordered the disbandment of associations seeking to mobilise overseas Chinese in the active propagation of China's policies on the grounds that these would irritate the local governments and cause them to think that the Chinese were subversive. That would have impaired China's diplomatic standing. The overseas Chinese were instructed, therefore, not to criticise the local governments but to obey the laws and respect local habits and customs. The Red Guard critics clearly wanted the encouragement of a Peking-orientated revolutionary militancy.[13] The criticisms showed a blithe disregard for the implications their alternative path may have had for China's policies of peaceful co-existence in the mid-1950s, and, more seriously, for the fact that there was little that the Chinese government could have done if the overseas Chinese had become targets for persecution and discrimination in their countries of residence as a result of such militancy.

Indeed, confronted with the wholesale slaughter and persecution of the overseas Chinese in Indonesia in the wake of the abortive 30 September 1965 *coup*, the Chinese authorities could only make loud but futile protests. When it came to the crunch they lacked the capabilities to provide protection for the overseas Chinese from a government determined to ignore China's protests. If the leftists were aware of China's limitations in this regard and of the irresponsibility of opening the door to widespread maltreatment of the overseas Chinese they showed no evident sign of this. Similarly no thought had been given to the impact that such a militant policy — which had overtones of Han chauvinism — might have had upon the local governments in south-east Asia. These clearly would have been driven more firmly into the American camp, thus heightening still further the dangers to China's national security. Furthermore, it seems very possible that by urging increased militancy on the overseas Chinese the prospects for local revolutions would actually have been set back: a division on racial lines would have been unavoidable; the native population would have sided with the local governments; and a revolutionary united front would have been unattainable. Finally, it seems likely that had the Red Guard policy been carried through the overwhelming majority of the overseas Chinese in south-east Asia would have repudiated the Peking government.

Red Guard criticism also focused on the top personnel of the Ministry of Foreign Affairs and the diplomats abroad. These were regarded as a 'special privileged stratum of Liu Shao-ch'i . . . in the Foreign Ministry'. These 'ambassadors and counsellors' (who were said to have succumbed to the attractions of the bourgeois way of life) were 'not subject to Party discipline . . . exempted from attending Party conferences [and from] leading an organised life'.[14]

The criticism of the Chinese diplomatic community can be seen as part of the general drive at that time against bureaucratic privilege in China, particularly when this was associated with what was regarded as a bourgeois life-style. Diplomats of course were a prime target for this kind of criticism. The Red Guard critique, however, can also be seen as paralleling general leftist suspicion of the conspicuously privileged life-style of diplomats, the attendant secrecy and specialised professionalism which necessarily keeps diplomats at once removed from their own people and free from supervision of their work by the masses.

To be sure, in their exaggerated way the Red Guards had touched on significant problems of foreign policy. The question of China's commitment to help revolutionary movements abroad and the problem as to the correct conduct of revolutionary China's diplomats abroad and their relationship to the ongoing revolutionary processes at home have continued to be serious issues. Nevertheless they do not really go to the heart of the leftist view of China's proper role in world affairs.

This leftist view has not been fully and coherently spelt out in a single cogent analysis. Therefore it must be culled from various sources. For convenience I shall rely mainly upon the speeches of Mao's former heir-apparent, Lin Piao, and Mao's widow Chiang Ching. Although both are now regarded in China as ultra-rightist conspirators who used a leftist mask for ulterior purposes, their speeches and known political positions before their respective falls from power clearly manifest a 'leftist' current. They can also be shown to have had a leftist impact on policy-making.

The leftist current emerges as a highly Sino-centric one and perhaps paradoxically it should be seen as a nationalist verging on a chauvinistic outlook. Its point of departure was that China alone was the only centre of authentic Marxism-Leninism as displayed in Mao Tse-tung Thought, and that China alone was grappling actively with the problem of preventing a socialist country from being suborned by a capitalist restoration. China alone was continuing the revolution under the dictatorship of the proletariat and it alone was moving towards a genuinely socialist culture and evolving a new socialist political order. It followed therefore that China had nothing to learn from foreign countries and that it was highly desirable that foreign influence, along with old customs, should be extirpated from Chinese social life. In the case of Chiang Ching, this meant that from the early 1960s onwards she was active in the removal of Soviet influence from Chinese arts and in the promotion of new revolutionary dramatic arts to replace the old favoured Chinese operas. I have already quoted from Lin Piao's speech on the 50th Anniversary of the Bolshevik Revolution which proclaimed China as the centre of world revolution and which reduced Chinese diplomacy to the simple propagation of Mao Tse-tung Thought. Another speech of his at this time (November 1967) gives the peculiar nationalistic, not to say Fascist, quality of his outlook:

Progressive ideology is not produced spontaneously by the workers and peasants, but is the ideology of Chairman Mao.

Chairman Mao has incorporated progressive ideology from abroad, such as the theories of Marx, Engels, Lenin, Stalin and others, as well as the progressive ideology of ancient China. He has incorporated it judiciously, so it is the concentrated representation of the most progressive ideology of mankind. Today, the chief task for the army and the nation is to rely on Mao Tse-tung Thought to transform the face of China and of the world, and to continue to transform them.[15]

Thus in Lin Piao's view the inheritance from Marxism-Leninism and the legacy from ancient China are an appropriate basis on which to transform not only China but the world as well. Lin Piao, of course, was the prime mover in the development of the cult of Mao as a genius and of Mao Tse-tung Thought as a universal talisman. It was he who made the celebrated remark to a plenary session of the Central Committee of the CPC that 'We must resolutely carry out Chairman Mao's instructions, whether we understand them or not.'[16] In January 1966 Lin had proclaimed 'Everything [Chairman Mao] says is truth, and every phrase he utters is worth ten thousand phrases.'[17] Perhaps the speech which most typifies Lin's outlook was his extemporary address to the Political Bureau on 18 May 1966. The speech was entirely directed to the problem of political *coups d'état* and the extolling of Mao as a genius. Neither before nor since has a Chinese Communist leader talked in this way about *coups d'état*. It was perhaps a foretaste of what he himself was to attempt five years later. Like a Pentagon analyst he itemised 61 *coups d'état* in AALA since 1960, 'an average of 11 coups per year'. But the overwhelming bulk of his examples were drawn from Chinese history with vivid details of plots and assassinations.[18] Apart from its conspiratorial outlook which was typical of much of the leftist leadership, the Sino-centricism of the speech was characteristic of the Chinese ultra-left.

It was a peculiar and largely unselfconscious paradox that while proclaiming its dedication to eradicating feudal and bourgeois remnants in Chinese social life and its determination to create a new and purer socialist society, the Chinese 'left' drew its examples, metaphors and at times even its inspiration from the Chinese past. Apart from the haloed figures of Marx, Engels and Lenin one can look in vain in the writings of the Chinese ultra-left during the Cultural Revolution for their having drawn inspiration from foreign revolutionary models. Where they did praise foreign revolutionaries it was because they were allegedly following the path of Mao Tse-tung Thought. Even the French revolutionary upsurge of May 1968 was regarded as having been modelled upon the Chinese Cultural Revolution. Interestingly, foreign sympathisers in Peking were not allowed to take part in the huge demonstrations of support for the French revolutionaries.[19]

China of the Cultural Revolution had no place for cosmopolitans of any type. Many of the foreign residents in Peking who had devoted the best part of their lives to the cause of the Chinese Revolution ended up being incarcerated or put under house arrest. Hundreds if not thousands of those Chinese with foreign connections had a very hard time. The very language of the Red Guards was culled deep from Chinese popular folklore and abounded in the use of terms like 'monkey kings', 'bull ghosts', 'snake gods' and other kinds of monsters. Their frequently ritualised political behaviour cannot be understood without reference to China's past history. Much of the attitude to the outside world had xenophobic aspects to it.

Nevertheless from the leftist perspective there was a profound internationalist content to the Cultural Revolution. The future of the world revolutionary movement depended upon·its success. By drawing in its horns and withholding from active participation in international diplomacy China as a bastion of socialism could concentrate upon its internationalist task of continuing the revolution at home unsullied by foreign impurities. It should be noted that the ultra-leftist leadership, unlike Chou En-lai and his associates and indeed some of the displaced leaders like Liu Shao-ch'i and P'eng Chen, were not personally familiar with the outside capitalist world. To be sure, the 'left' was familiar with the Soviet Union. But that was rejected as anathema. Those familiar with the Treaty Ports like Shanghai from the 1930s probably recoiled from the memory with horror and, like Chiang Ching, had been gravely marked by the experience. These Treaty Ports were hardly representative of the modern West or Japan of the late 1960s. From the 1940s onwards China's revolutionary centres had never become the focal point for internationalist foreign revolutionaries in the sense that Lenin's Russia was in its time. Nor had China's revolutionaries had the same internationalist experiences of the early Bolshevik leaders. Thus it is understandable that having rejected the Soviet link and having found the united front with the national bourgeois regimes of AALA collapse in the winter of 1965-6, the Chinese 'leftist' leadership should become nativistic. This is especially true within a context in which China was not only self-reliant militarily and economically, but basically self-sufficient as well.

The basic 'leftist' concern was domestic, and the international dimension of its outlook was a function of that. The values associated with the practice of foreign policy and foreign trade under the aegis of Chou En-lai were hardly those of so-called leftists dedicated to the firm subordination of professionalism to revolutionary will, to the elimination of elitism and above all to placing the demands of revolution ahead of those of production. The 'leftist' current was to manifest itself again in many similar ways in the different context of the mid-1970s. Mao himself, however, should not be identified with the 'leftist' current as described here. He once characterised himself as a centre-leftist, and it was from that position that he began to wind down the 'chaotic' element of the Cultural Revolution in 1968 and, with it, its foreign policy dimension.

The Ending of Exclusive Revolutionary Internationalism

China's international role during the Cultural Revolution as a bastion of socialism appealing to the revolutionary people of the world can be seen as an extension from the domestic themes of the Cultural Revolution to the outside world as a whole. Indeed it can be seen as the blurring of the distinction between the two. At the same time it is useful not to lose sight of the fact that however disrespectful the Chinese were of the national emblems and aspects of the sovereignty of other countries, they paid great attention to the sanctity and inviolability of their own. Moreover the core of the Chinese external revolutionary outlook continued to be the Maoist insistence that revolutions in other countries had to come from within. There was never any question of the export of revolution. Furthermore, Chinese statements repeatedly emphasised China's links with the people of the world rather than with particular sections or classes. There was no sectarianism or 'block thinking' in the Chinese revolutionary perspective.

But China's international role in this period was also predicated upon a particular strategic context. The United States and the Soviet Union, long considered to be in a holy alliance against Communism and against China, were strategically deployed during the Cultural Revolution in a way that did not make China the front line of possible attack. With regard to the Soviet Union, an acceptable (to China) balance of forces seemed to exist in the Sino-Soviet border areas.[20] The United States was seen to be tied down in South Vietnam where its 500,000 troops (by the end of 1967) were failing to defeat the people's war being waged there. The bombings of North Vietnam, it is true, occasionally led to aerial combats between American and Chinese planes.[21] But although there was the continual possibility of an American escalation which would lead to a Sino-American armed conflict, this was not considered probable by the Chinese leadership.[22] According to the Chinese, the Americans had shifted their strategic focus to Asia since 1966 and the Russians had connived at this by easing tensions in Europe to allow US troop transfers to the East.[23] Vietnam was the focal point of the American struggle for imperialism and of its desire to suppress revolution and national liberation in AALA. The great conflict between the Chinese and American world views and strategic interests was being fought out in the Vietnam War. As seen from China, the contradictions in American society, in America's global position as the centre of international capitalism symbolised by the dollar as the major international currency, in America's relations with its smaller capitalist allies, were all becoming more acute as the result of the Vietnam War. But above all, the people's war in Vietnam was a practical refutation of the Soviet position regarding the dangers of armed confrontation with the United States. Thus in the Chinese view it was crucial that Vietnam should not be drawn to the peace talks continually proposed by the Americans and canvassed from time to time by the Russians. That would have led, in the Chinese view, to the subordination of the Viet-namese struggles to the interests of the great power anti-revolutionary collusion between the two superpowers. Whatever tacit understanding had been reached in April 1966 between the Chinese and American leaders that it was in the interests of neither country to attack the other, the Chinese had not sought to subordinate the Vietnamese cause to their own. To be sure, the Sino-Soviet enmity was damaging from the Vietnamese point of view and it constrained them in many respects. But the Vietnamese could hardly complain of domination from the north. As seen from Peking, Vietnam was the major stumbling block in the development of the global duopolistic aims of the Soviet Union and the United States. Developments in 1968 were to change fundamentally both the domestic and the strategic contexts of China's foreign policy so that by the end of the year China's chosen international role as the promoter of exclusive revolutionary internationalism was to be set aside. The ensuing developments led to complex political struggles in-volving both internal and external issues which were to end in the restoration of the Communist Party as the main organisational struc-ture of authority at home, the opening to the United States abroad and the death of Lin Piao, the purging of his associates and the withdrawal of the armed forces from the overt exercise of political power.

From a strategic perspective, curiously, 1968 started off extremely well from the Chinese point of view. The revolutionary successes of the

Tet offensive in South Vietnam were widely acclaimed in China by huge mass rallies. Chinese delight with their Vietnamese comrades, however, was short-lived. On 31 March the American President, Johnson, announced on television yet another bombing pause, a new offer of peace talks and his decision not to run for the presidency. The North Vietnamese accepted the offer. But before they did so a New China News Agency commentary on 5 April denounced the offer as a 'new fraud of inducing peace talks by suspending bombing . . . to win a respite on the battlefields of Vietnam to expand the war further'. The commentary further noted that 'all the signs show that the Soviet renegade revisionist clique has once again played the contemptible role of chief accomplice in Johnson's new plot.' The Chinese press and radio carefully refrained from mentioning afterwards that the Vietnamese had agreed to the talks. Thus China's official media passed in silence over the Peking stopover of the Vietnamese delegation on 8 May *en route* to the talks in Paris. But Chou En-lai reportedly told the head of the Vietnamese delegation that 'in Mao Tse-tung's opinion the talks were a mistake.'[24] The following month demonstrations took place outside the three North Vietnamese consulates in south China and one of them (Nanking) was reportedly ransacked.[25] Through the summer China's leaders publicly criticised the talks to visiting Vietnamese delegations as a fraud and a product of Russo-American collusion.[26] The Paris peace talks, however, did not prevent the Chinese from signing an agreement on 23 July extending further economic and technical aid to North Vietnam.[27]

Apart from the foreign policy setback to China of the Paris peace talks, a very serious change in the strategic situation affecting China had taken place. In terms of the Chinese own analysis, Vietnam had become transformed from an acute stumbling block to Soviet-American collusive interests into an important ingredient of that collusion. It was a collusion which the Chinese believed was directed against them. The fact that Vietnam was in danger of entering that orbit made the Chinese concern about new Soviet overtures to India and to Japan all the more acute.[28] A new diplomatic situation was emerging and it was time for China to return to a more subtle style of diplomacy.

The major change in the global situation from China's point of view, of course, was the Soviet-led invasion of Czechoslovakia on 20 August. Three days later in a speech on Romania's National Day Chou En-lai gave China's response: the Soviet leadership was said to be 'exactly the same as Hitler of the past' (an analogy hitherto reserved exclusively for the American President). 'The Soviet revisionist clique of renegades has long since degenerated into a gang of social imperialists and social fascists.' He then outlined how in China's view the invasion was a function of Soviet-American collusion. Chou argued that it had the 'tacit understanding' of the Americans and linked American acquiescence in the Soviet aggression against Czechoslovakia with Soviet acquiescence in the American aggression against Vietnam. He ended by noting that the Romanian government had ordered the mobilisation of the people to defend the independence and sovereignty of their country. It is interesting to note that neither Chou nor the *People's Daily* commentator on the same day intimated that China itself was in danger of attack. But the commentator made an observation that was later to play a large part in the foreign-policy debates of the ensuing two or three years, namely that because both the American and the Russian leaderships were imperialist their relationship was not only characterised by collaboration but by struggle too.[29]

Ten days later, on 2 September, Chou En-lai in a speech on Vietnamese National Day tried in vain to persuade the Vietnamese authorities that the Soviet-led invasion of Czechoslovakia (which the Vietnamese had formally approved) constituted the final proof that the Soviet leadership had taken the lead in collaboration with the United States, and he listed several examples to try and show that this was so. Chou then went on to declare that 'the Soviet revisionist renegade clique . . . has long since destroyed the socialist camp which once existed.'[30] Curiously, this was a claim which was not to be repeated until spring 1974, nearly six years later. The implications of this formal statement were immense, for it meant, first, that Bulgaria, Czechoslovakia, East Germany, Hungary and Poland were to be seen less as centres of revisionism and more as countries struggling for independence from Russian colonial rule, and, second, that the entire alignment of world forces and the general division of the world had changed fundamentally. There was no consensus among the Chinese leadership and it was not yet ready to draw these implications.

So far the Chinese authorities had given no indication that China itself was actively threatened militarily by the Soviet moves. By October, however, as the Chinese became aware of the Soviet military build-up to the north, and as they digested the possible implications for them of the Brezhnev doctrine of the limited sovereignty of socialist states (which gave the others the right and duty to intervene in a socialist state deemed to be in danger of losing its socialist gains), the Chinese leaders sounded a new note of alarm.[31] Thus Chou En-lai ended his National Day (1 October) address with the warning:

We must heighten our vigilance, intensify our preparedness against war and be ready at all times to smash any invasion launched by US imperialism, Soviet revisionism and their lackeys, whether individually or collectively. Should any enemy dare to invade our great motherland, the 700 million Chinese people who have emerged stronger than ever through the tempering of the great proletarian cultural revolution will definitely wipe them out resolutely, thoroughly, totally, and completely.[32]

The Chief of Staff Huang Yung-sheng spoke to a rally on 4 October welcoming a senior Albanian delegation in which he accused the Russians of having 'of late . . . sent large numbers of troops to reinforce its forces stationed along the Sino-Soviet and Sino-Mongolian frontiers and [of having] intensified [their] armed provocations against China'. Earlier in the speech Huang referred to the massing of Soviet forces in Bulgaria as posing a threat to the security of Albania 'and the other Balkan countries'.[33]

Yugoslavia was clearly meant to be included in this. In fact Chinese Press criticisms of Yugoslavia stopped after the Russian-led invasion of Czechoslovakia,[34] as did criticisms of non-alignment. Before the year was out the Chinese had renewed contact with the Yugoslavs and in February 1969 the first Yugoslav government delegation to visit China for nine years arrived in Peking to negotiate a new trade protocol.[35]

Even more startling adjustments of China's foreign-policy line became evident in November. On the 3rd, the *People's Daily* published without comment the text of President Johnson's speech of 31 October announcing a complete bombing halt over North Vietnam, together with the North Vietnamese government's statement of 2 November. This broke a silence of many months on events in Vietnam and it is indicated that Peking was suspending its hostile public comment on the Paris talks.[36] On 26 November the Ministry of Foreign Affairs issued a statement which, though harsh in tone, in substance called for the resumption of Sino-US ambassadorial talks in February 1969 after the inauguration of President Nixon on the basis of what amounted to pre-Cultural Revolution conditions. The statement declared:

Over the past 13 years, the Chinese government has consistently adhered to the following two principles in the Sino-US ambassadorial talks: first, the US Government undertakes to immediately withdraw all its armed forces from China's territory Taiwan Province and

the Taiwan Straits area and dismantle all its military installations in
Taiwan Province; second, *the US Government agrees that China and
the United States conclude an agreement on the Five Principles of
Peaceful Coexistence* (emphasis added).[37]

As Whiting has pointed out, although the Chinese had mentioned this
second principle in some of the earlier Sino-US ambassadorial talks,
they had not done so specifically in the talks for a long time and they
had certainly not mentioned it in the official Press in the 1960s before.
After all, one of the major points at issue in the Sino-Soviet dispute had
been the Chinese critique of Khrushchev's pursuit of his special brand
of peaceful coexistence with the United States.[38] Indeed this positive
official reference to the Five Principles which applied to countries of
different social systems was among the first (if not the first) since the
Cultural Revolution. It was remarkable that it was applied to the
United States, but it was also a further indication that the PRC was
turning its back on the foreign policy of the Cultural Revolution period
and the special international role claimed·for China.

Once again the orientation of China's foreign policy underwent a
rapid and marked change in response to perceived change in the world
at large, but especially with regard to the disposition of the two superpowers. Henceforth China was to cut back on the various foreign policy
elements associated with the Cultural Revolution and to gradually
restore and indeed develop further in a most rapid way state and trade
relations with a growing number of countries. At the same time, the
Soviet Union had become the major enemy threatening China with war,
so much so that, as we have seen, the Chinese began to try to move
towards a better relationship with the United States. It is also instructive
to note that the ending of the Red Guard phase of the Cultural Revolution (although closely connected with many domestic factors) and
the hurried completion of the setting up of Revolutionary Committees
in the remaining few provinces where they had not yet been established
coincided very closely with the changed diplomatic and strategic outlook. It is also worth noting that China was able to develop state
relations with other countries with relative ease despite the hiatus and
the disregard of diplomatic norms during the previous two years. While
this may suggest an underlying continuity of China's fundamental
international concerns, it is also indicative of the relatively low level of
international interdependency which characterised China's position in
world affairs before, during and after the Cultural Revolution. Few, if
any, countries were damaged by China's withdrawal from the diplo-

matic community and the curtailment of formal international exchanges. At the same time China's role and performance internationally during the Cultural Revolution were disturbing to many countries. Many were alarmed that a country with a fifth of the world's population was behaving in ways domestically which were completely unfathomable and unpredictable. Thus China's return to the prevailing norms of international diplomacy and the ending of the Red Guard phase was welcome to many foreign governments, which accordingly were pleased once again to normalise relations. At the same time, the episode is indicative of China's peculiar position in world affairs as an important influence affecting some of the major issues of world politics and at the same time a country which to a large extent holds the outside world at a certain distance.

Notes

1. Communiqué of the Eleventh Plenary Session of the Eighth Central Committee of the CPC, 12 August 1966. *Peking Review* No. 34 (1966), pp. 4-8.
2. A.M. Halpern, 'China's Foreign Policy Since the Cultural Revolution', in R. MacFarquhar (ed.), *Sino-American Relations 1941-71* (Praeger, 1972), p. 23.
3. For a careful and well-documented account see Melvin Gurtov, 'The Foreign Ministry and Foreign Affairs During the Cultural Revolution', *China Quarterly*, No. 40 (October-December 1969), pp. 65-102. For an account which places the struggles concerned within the revolutionary perspectives of the Cultural Revolution see David and Nancy Milton, *The Wind Will Not Subside* (Penguin Books, 1975).
4. See *Peking Review*, No. 46 (1967), pp. 4-8 (Lin's speech) and pp. 9-16 (the joint editorial).
5. Yang Ch'eng-wu (then Chief of General Staff), 'Thoroughly Establish the Absolute Authority of the Great Supreme Commander Chairman Mao and of his Great Thought', ibid., pp. 17-24.
6. See *Peking Review*, No. 46 (1967), p. 5.
7. See 'Chronicle' in *China Quarterly*, No. 32 (October-December 1967), p. 221, where a list of 32 countries may be found.
8. For brief accounts see ibid., p. 224 and Stephen Fitzgerald, 'Overseas Chinese Affairs and the Cultural Revolution', *China Quarterly*, No. 40 (October-December 1969), esp. p. 124.
9. For a brief account of the Hong Kong episode see Edward E. Rice, *Mao's Way* (University of California Press, 1972), Chapter 22.
10. *Wan Sui*, pp. 679-81. See also analysis by Whiting, 'Mao, China and the Cold War' (in Yōnosuke Nagai *et. al.*, eds. *The Origins of the Cald war in Asia*).
11. Thus Mao excised excessively adulatory references in the statement on the successful detonation of a hydrogen bomb and urged greater modesty, especially to outsiders. See his 'Directive on External Propaganda Work', June 1967, *Wan Sui*, p. 679; JPRS 1, p. 462.
12. For accounts of the episode see note 3 above.
13. Much of this account derives from Stephen Fitzgerald, 'Overseas Chinese

Affairs and the Cultural Revolution'.

14.   *Wai Shih Hung Ch'i (Foreign Affairs Red Flag)*, 14 June 1967: 'Thoroughly Smash the Foreign Affairs Ministry Privileged Stratum', published by the Proletarian Revolutionaries Liaison Committee of the Foreign Affairs System, Peking. Translated in SCMP, No. 4004.

15.   Lin Piao, 'On the Question of "Giving Prominence to Politics"' (November 1967) in *Chinese Law and Government*, Vol. VI, No. 1 (Spring 1973), p. 87.

16.   'Speech at the Eleventh Plenum of the Eighth Central Committee' (1 August 1966), ibid., p. 13.

17.   Ibid., p. 53. Mao was later to complain of these exaggerations, and in his final struggles with Lin Piao in 1970 and 1971 he used these phrases back at his heir-apparent with withering sarcasm. But at the time he did not dissent from them. In a private letter to Chiang Ching on 8 July 1966, which was not released for internal circulation before 1972, Mao complained regarding this: 'It is the first time in my life that I unwillingly concur with others on major questions. I have to do things against my own will!' He went on to refer himself to a saying from the Han dynasty: 'A tall thing is easy to break; a white thing is easy to stain. The white snow in spring can hardly find its match; a high reputation is difficult to live up to.' Ibid., Vol. VI, No. 2, p. 97. But in 1970 Mao told Edgar Snow that he had deliberately built up his own cult at this period as a superior authority with which the masses could beat the revisionist party leaders. Edgar Snow, *The Long Revolution* (Random House, 1972), pp. 69-71.

18.   *Chinese Law and Government*, Vol. II, No. 4, pp. 42-62.

19.   See David and Nancy Milton, *The Wind Will Not Subside*, p. 316. The reasons had to do with problems which had arisen with regard to the participation of these foreigners in the Cultural Revolution up to that stage. Nevertheless here was a revolutionary event in which foreigners above all might have been allocated a role in Peking.

20.   See Thomas W. Robinson, 'The Sino-Soviet Border Dispute: Background Development and the March 1969 Clashes' in *The American Political Science Review*, Vol. 60 (1972), pp. 1175-202. See also Neville Maxwell, 'The Chinese Account of the 1969 Fighting at Chen Pao' in *China Quarterly*, No. 56 (October-December 1973), pp. 730-9.

21.   See Whiting, *The Chinese Calculus of Deterrence*, p. 179.

22.   See, for example, the detailed analysis by the Chairman of the Kiangsi (Province) Revolutionary Committee of early 1968: 'Comrade Ch'eng Shih-ch'ing's Talk on the Vietnam Situation' in *Tzu-liao Chuan Chi (Special Collection of Materials)*, No. 1 (July 1968). Compiled by Kung Ko-lien 'Red Flag News Agency' Reference Materials Unit. In SCMM, No. 623, pp. 1-9.

23.   See *Peking Review*, No. 10 (1966), pp. 3-4 and No. 15 (1966), pp. 6-8.

24.   Quarterly Chronicle and Documentation, *China Quarterly*, No. 35 (July-September 1968), p. 199.

25.   Ibid., pp. 199-200 and K.S. Karol, 'China's Second Revolution', *China Quarterly*, No. 35 (July-September 1968), p. 199.

26.   See, for example, Li Hsien-nien's speech of 10 July (NCNA).

27.   For a detailed account of Sino-Vietnamese relations throughout this period see G.D. Loescher, 'National Liberation War in South Vietnam: The Perceptions and Policies of China and North Vietnam 1954-1969', London University Ph.D. thesis (1975).

28.   See the February comments: 'What Kosygin was up to in India', *Peking Review*, No. 6 (1968), p. 10; 'The Soviet Revisionist Clique is the Vicious Enemy of the Asian People' and 'Japanese Militarists' Yes Men', *Peking*

Review, No. 8 (1968), pp. 28-9. See also the Army Day speech (1 August 1968) speech of Huang Yung-sheng (Chief of Staff) which warned that 'at present' the Americans, Russians and others were 'intensifying their efforts to form a counter-revolutionary ring of encirclement against the PRC', *Peking Review*, No. 32 (1968), esp. p. 13.

29.   *Peking Review,* Supplement to No. 34.
30.   *Peking Review*, No. 36 (1968), pp. 6-7.
31.   This analysis has benefited from the article by Allen S. Whiting, 'The Sino-American Detente: Genesis and Prospects' in Ian Wilson (ed.), *China and the World Community* (Angus and Robertson in association with The Australian Institute of International Affairs, 1973), pp. 70-89.
32.   *Peking Review*, No. 40 (1968), p. 15.
33.   *Peking Review*, No. 41 (1968), p. 9.
34.   The last such criticism in the *Peking Review* was in June 1968. See No. 24 (1968), pp. 9-11.
35.   'Quarterly Chronicle and Documentation', *China Quarterly*, No. 38 (April-June 1969), p. 195.
36.   See ibid., No. 37, p. 169.
37.   *Peking Review*, No. 48 (1968), pp. 30-1.
38.   See Whiting, "The Sino-American Detente', p. 72.

THE INTERNATIONAL RECOGNITION OF CHINA
AS A GREAT POWER 1969-1972

China's international position was totally transformed between 1969
and 1972. Although China had long been regarded as an important
factor in international affairs, it was not until this period that the PRC
received the recognition which allowed it to play an international
diplomatic role commensurate with its importance in world affairs. The
consequent contrast with the chosen role as the 'bastion of socialism'
and the 'centre of world revolution' during the Cultural Revolution
could not have been more marked. The transformation of China's international position coincided with a massive reorganisation of domestic
affairs, and the conjunction of the two occasioned the great political
struggle known as the 'Lin Piao affair'. I shall argue in this chapter that
the struggle involved two alternative views as to how China should be
run and as to what kind of foreign policy it should pursue. In short, the
political struggle can be seen to have turned on the question of what
role was appropriate for China.

Since China's new role was established by the victors in that struggle,
it is appropriate first to consider the dimensions of the changes introduced in this period and the perception of shifts in world forces which
gave rise to them.

Even in retrospect the speed by which China's international role was
transformed is still breathtaking. Within a space of only five years the
Chinese state moved from a position of revolutionary isolation, apparently disdainful of inter-state relations, to one of a fully recognised
great-power participant in a system distinguished by such relationships.
In the process many of the long-standing objectives of the PRC were
achieved almost without effort. Indeed it may be argued that these
constituted deeply felt Chinese national aspirations since the humiliations by the West in the nineteenth century. The Chinese quest for
international recognition as a great country with a distinctive contribution to make in human affairs was finally granted. So much so that
China's leaders were faced with the problem of defining China's new-
found great-power status. It may be convenient at this stage to list some
of the important national objectives achieved during this period.

(1) On its own terms and without the grace and favour of any great

power patron, the PRC was able at long last to take up the China seat in the United Nations as one of the five permanent members of the Security Council. This finally conceded what China's leaders had always maintained, that their voice should be heard in the resolution of major international problems.

(2) The President of the world's most powerful country, the leader of the forces of Western imperialism, came to Peking on his own initiative. China was recognised as one of the very few countries which on its own could exercise a decisive influence in the global strategic balance between the two superpowers. The visit was of immense symbolic significance on many counts. But above all it demonstrated that the West which, since the nineteenth century and particularly since the establishment of the PRC, had been instrumental in attacking the sense of independent dignity of the Chinese people, was henceforth prepared to respect that dignity and accommodate itself to the Chinese sense of self-esteem. President Nixon, by his visit, tacitly conceded that it was a misconceived American policy over the previous twenty-two years which was to blame for the hitherto sterile relationship between the two countries. Furthermore, the improvement in Sino-American relations arose out of the conscious American recognition of the failure of the policy of containment and isolation of China. Indeed its failure was a necessary condition of the Sino-American *détente.*

(3) The PRC normalised relations with most countries in the world largely in accordance with Chinese terms for mutual recognition. This, together with another consequence of Nixon's China visit, meant that by the end of this period the Chinese leadership in Peking had every reason to believe that major progress had been made in de-internationalising the Taiwan issue — a subject which will be discussed more fully later in this chapter.

(4) The establishment of normal state relations with the vast majority of Third World countries on a non-sectarian basis facilitated the emergence of China as an acknowledged leading spokesman for many Third World concerns.

(5) Relations with the medium and small capitalist countries became relatively close for the first time, and this opened the way for a more subtly conceived pattern of diplomacy than had been possible in the

previous twenty years.

(6) China's prospects of gain by international trade became as great as her leaders chose to make them. Any lingering doubts that self-reliance implied self-seclusion were removed. Henceforth foreign trade was no longer regarded as a political tool to evade isolation as had been the case in the 1950s, but was to be viewed more pragmatically as a means to enhance the modernisation of the Chinese economy. At the same time, as we shall see, foreign trade continued to serve political purposes, particularly with regard to Third World countries and in terms of the relations with the small and medium capitalist countries.

These diplomatic successes and dramatic changes were achieved at no cost to the Chinese state. China had not shed even a degree of its sovereignty, self-reliance or powers of self-initiative. China was still a fully independent actor on the world stage, but with an immeasurably enhanced role.

These impressive changes should not obscure, however, the many significant continuities in China's position. Thus China's economic and political system remained insulated from external penetration. No political or economic dependencies were established with other countries. China's principles of self-reliance were not violated by the expansion of its international trade. There can be little doubt that impressive as the growth of foreign trade was, it could have expanded even more rapidly had China's leaders been prepared to modify the principles of self-reliance so as to accept international credits as Lenin had in his day. The continued emphasis on relative autarchy was also reflected in the military sphere, where China remained primarily orientated towards self-defence. It neither sought nor developed an offensive capability which would have enabled China to undertake a sustained military campaign beyond its borders, particularly if opposed by either or both of the two superpowers.

Moreover, many of the themes which underlay the newly dubbed 'Chairman Mao's revolutionary diplomatic line' were far from new in China's approach to the world. For example, the emphasis upon the 'Five Principles of Peaceful Coexistence'; the insistence upon sovereignty based on full political and economic independence; the retention of the capacity for self-initiative; the distinctive aid policies; the call for resistance to the imperialist policies of bullying, manipulation and interference in internal affairs — all date back to the early 1960s and some of them much earlier.

At a deeper level, the mode of analysis and the style of diplomacy on which the new foreign policy was based were traditionally Maoist. The changing patterns of world politics were analysed in terms of contradictions which enabled the drawing of distinctions between lesser and greater (or secondary and primary) enemies and the identification of their respective strengths and weaknesses. Typically, it was a text from Mao written more than thirty years earlier which was circulated in China to provide the people with a proper framework by which to understand the opening to the United States. The text, 'On Policy' of 1940, outlined the need to utilise the differences between the various imperialist powers in order to prosecute the war. Likewise, the basis for conducting negotiations with an enemy was Mao's 1945 piece 'On the Chungking Negotiations' with Chiang Kai-shek. Moreover, the model f the new pattern of inter-state relationships was that of the united front rather than any pattern of alliances.

The new foreign policy nevertheless constituted a decisive break with the previous patterns. In particular the *détente* with the United States raised questions about the revolutionary credentials of China's foreign policy. China's refusal to endorse publicly the revolutionaries in the then East Pakistan (soon to become Bangladesh) as well as those in Sri Lanka (a refusal made 'worse' by Chou En-lai's open letters of support to the leaders of the governments concerned) alienated many of China's erstwhile 'new left' supporters in the West and elsewhere. But much more serious was the attitude of the North Vietnamese, who regarded the prospects of Sino-American *détente* coupled with Soviet-American *détente* as enabling the Americans to bully even further the small countries.[1] Although China's leaders continuously reaffirmed their support and aid for the Vietnamese, Chinese and Vietnamese interests could not but diverge from this point onwards. The starting-point of the Vietnamese position was obviously that the United States should militarily withdraw from south-east Asia (and indeed from Asia as a whole) lock, stock and barrel as quickly as possible. But the essentials of China's new position in this regard were that under the changed conditions of international politics America could still play a useful role in Asia (including south-east Asia, but not Indo-China) as a temporary counterweight to the Soviet Union.

The Perception of a Decisive Shift in World Forces

By the end of 1971 the new view of the changes in world politics had become clear. The United States was seen as unable any longer to

pursue the aggressive expansionist imperial policy which had characterised American international behaviour since the Second World War.
The American experience in Indo-China confirmed the view first
articulated in the wake of the 1968 Tet offensive that various enduring
factors had combined to weaken the American international position.
The American domestic opposition to the Vietnam War had become
increasingly significant, the contradictions in American society had
become more acute, and there was a growing international crisis of the
dollar and America's trading position. Moreover, the importance of
Western Europe in diplomatic and economic terms as an independent
centre was recognised in Peking. The Soviet Union, in the Chinese view,
had begun to emerge as an expansionist imperialist power as signalled
by its invasion of Czechoslovakia and its military threats against China
itself in 1968 and 1969. Moreover, the Chinese argued that America's
continued involvement in Vietnam facilitated the expansion of Russian
influence in Europe, the Middle East and elsewhere. It was therefore a
question of how and when the Americans would withdraw finally from
Indo-China. In short, the general pattern of world politics was seen to
have changed radically since the end of the Second World War. Instead
of a bipolar view of the world, China's leaders now saw the world as
undergoing a profound process of transformation. As the 1972 New
Year editorial of the *People's Daily, Red Flag* and *Liberation Army
Daily* put it, 'The characteristic feature of the world situation can be
summed up in one word "chaos", "upheaval" or "global upheaval".'[2]
'Luan', officially translated as 'upheaval', would have been better translated as 'chaos'. Traditionally, it implied the breakdown of social
harmony in ever-strained conflicts. For Mao it has always had positive
connotations. The world was not just moving into a more complex
multipolar situation, but it was difficult to identify precisely the
emerging new shapes and confrontations of international politics.

America and the Soviet Union were identified as two superpowers
whose relations were dominated by conflict and contention. The references in their press to collusion which was a feature of Chinese analysis
in the 1960s were now fast disappearing. The essential characteristics of
a superpower were defined in behavioural terms as a power which 'wants
to be superior to others and, proceeding from the position of strength,
to lord it over others'.[3] Interestingly, at this stage the Chinese did not
analyse it in the classical Marxist terms of the political economies of the
countries concerned, nor was the concept analysed in the Western
fashion in terms of capabilities.

During this period the Chinese once again reverted to the pre-Cultural

Revolution analysis of the four basic irreconcilable contradictions of world affairs, except that now the United States as an imperial power was joined by the Soviet Union. The new list as outlined to the Ninth Congress read:

> the contradiction between the oppressed nations on the one hand and imperialism and social imperialism on the other; the contradiction between the proletariat and the bourgeoisie in the capitalist and revisionist countries, the contradiction between imperialist and social imperialist countries and among the imperialist countries; and the contradiction between socialist countries on the one hand and imperialism and social imperialism on the other.[4]

It should be noted that these contradictions do not explain the Chinese view of the role of the medium and small capitalist countries. That was explained by reference once again to the two intermediate zones first identified seven years earlier, in 1963.[5] In 1971 this raised ambiguities as to China's precise relationship with both zones. A case could be made that China in certain senses belonged to both. Publications in the official press, of course, spelt out the case for considering China as a member of the first zone of principally the countries of AALA. At the same time, there was clearly an important place for the second intermediate zone capitalist countries in the new internationalist front against imperialism and social imperialism.

There is some tantalising evidence to suggest that in 1971, as China's leaders considered the evolving new patterns of international politics, one view which gained a certain currency for a while was that the world should be regarded in terms of a five-power balance. Thus in a semi-private interview Kuo Mo-jo (then Chairman of the Standing Committee of the National People's Congress and head of the Academy of Sciences — a man who had often been close to Mao), in an analysis of the international situation which may have reflected Mao's own views, described the current state of the world in terms of a 'five pointed star', with the points made up of the US, the USSR, the EEC, Japan and China.[6]

These were the terms of conventional Western balance of power analysis and indeed Dr Kissinger and President Nixon were said to have viewed the world in those terms at that time. There is little that is Marxist about it. Not surprisingly, Chou En-lai did not formally endorse such a view when given the opportunity. His reply was that 'we admit that we can develop in some decades into a strong prosperous country. But we have declared that we will never be a super-power, neither today nor ever in the future.'[7] As we have already seen, the term 'superpower' was at that time defined behaviourally rather than in classical Marxist fashion on socio-economic grounds. In other words, such a power was identified by the character of its activities abroad rather than by the domestic and international structures which gave rise to such behaviour. It may be observed that the attention to behaviour in itself meant that questions of power in international affairs figured very large in the outlook from Peking. Even a refutation of the 'five pointed star' framework by an Assistant Foreign Minister two years later in 1973 focused on the unequal distribution of power between the countries that make up the five points.[8]

Few would dispute that Mao has always been concerned with the nature of effective power and that at times his views have not coincided with Leninist notions.[9] But to describe international affairs in terms of the interrelationships of five powers is to use the language and possibly the concepts of balance-of-power analysis. Such a mode of analysis tends to see an equivalence between the powers involved that is dependent upon their role in international affairs concerning the major questions of the day. A more purely Marxist approach would take as its point of departure the character of the socio-economic systems of the relevant countries. Furthermore, that mode of analysis is out of keeping with the more subtle concepts of contradictions and international united fronts usually employed by Mao. Nevertheless it is worth recalling that in his reported conversation with a visiting French parliamentary delegation in February 1964 following the first introduction of the concept of the second intermediate zone, Mao openly declared that China too was involved: 'France herself, Germany, England on the condition that she ceases to be the courier of America, Japan and we ourselves — there is your Third World.'[10] (This was before the term 'Third World' was formally identified with AALA.) The importance of the formulation of the 'five pointed star' should not be overstressed. As far as can be ascertained, it played a part of little or no importance in the actual operation of policy or indeed in the major foreign policy debate in Peking. The interesting point is that the formulation was even explicitly advanced in Peking and it is illustrative of the uncertainties and ambiguities in the Chinese search for a new role in the changing conditions of world politics.

The critical distinction between the 'balance of power' and the 'intermediate zones' approaches is that in the latter there is still a clear and coherent object of revolutionary struggle around which to orientate a united front. In the 1970s this has been directed against the hegemonic designs of the two superpowers. It constitutes an identifiable ideological line whose application depends upon drawing careful distinctions between primary and secondary contradictions for united front purposes. The 'balance of power' approach lacks such coherence. Even though a revolutionary pattern of development may be projected for the future, the balance of power approach places the revolutionary states on a par with the others, including those ruled by imperialists. There is no continuum linking individual revolutionary struggles with state behaviour. In Maoist terms advocates of 'balance of power' could be regarded as those who promote 'all alliance and no struggle', when in fact both should be pursued. Such advocates would be guilty of a classical 'rightist' error.

The approach to the first intermediate zone of AALA, or as it became increasingly known, the Third World, was also not without ambiguities. In the special conditions of this period as opposed to the mid-1960s the Chinese appeal to the countries concerned was strictly along the line of state relations. This superseded the Cultural Revolution emphasis on the 'people' of the various countries. More interesting, however, was that unlike the mid-1960s no distinctions in public were drawn between revolutionary, progressive or reactionary governments. To be sure, the Chinese still publicly identified certain countries as socialist but they did not go on to draw further distinctions among Third World countries in their public pronouncements. Chinese writers claimed that these countries, amongst whom China was included, were bound together by certain common historical experiences and by common current objectives. It was argued that they all shared a history of struggle against colonialist and semi-colonialist oppression and exploitation[11] and that in the present era they were the true centre of opposition to imperialism (which henceforth the Chinese were to warn included social imperialism too). Furthermore, they all shared the common problem of seeking to build up their economies. In the Chinese view the two struggles were linked because true political independence was inseparable from independence in the economic sphere.[12]

The Chinese attributed the restoration of the UN seat to China after 22 years of exclusion to the Third World countries. Indeed, they maintained that it was because of these countries that the United Nations had ceased to be a tool of the United States or the two superpowers. As Ch'iao Kuan-hua, the chief Chinese delegate, put it to the General Assembly in November 1971, 'profound changes' had taken place in world affairs since the foundation of the UN. Then 'there were only 51 member states and now the membership has grown to 131. Of the 80 members that joined later, the overwhelming majority are countries which achieved independence after World War II.' These had struggled 'to win and safeguard national independence'. He then went on to observe:

> An increasing number of medium and small countries are uniting to oppose the hegemony and power politics practised by the one or two super-powers and to fight for the right to settle their own affairs as independent and sovereign states and for equal status in international relations. Countries want independence, nations want liberation and the people want revolution, this has become an irresistible trend of history.[13]

The distinctive emphasis on statehood has already been noted. But of interest here is the juxtaposition of Mao's new slogan as the last sentence. This suggested two possible interpretations: either that it was an objective fact that each of the collectivities concerned separately sought to achieve these ends, or that the three were linked in a continual dynamic process whereby, once countries obtained full genuine independence, they would necessarily move ever closer to revolution. On balance, the former explanation seems preferable and it is in greater accord with subsequent Chinese practice in foreign affairs. That the 'people' are by definition revolutionary is a Maoist truism. The Chinese have always regarded national liberation struggles as just and as bound to succeed in the end. The stress on countries ('kuo chia'), which could also be translated as 'states', is the new element in the slogan. But here too the Chinese concept of independence as used in the early 1970s is hardly novel in Mao's thought.

The Chen Po-ta, Lin Piao View of China's Role

The wide-ranging implications of the new changes in the official Chinese view of international affairs and of Chairman Mao's new 'revolutionary line' are best seen within the context of the leadership struggle from 1968 until the fall of Lin Piao in September 1971. The concern here is less with the details of the struggle and the political manoeuvring involved than with the theoretical and policy questions around which the struggle took place.[14] These bring out very clearly the complex relationship between China's domestic and external postures and policies.

It should be pointed out at the outset that not all aspects of the following analysis can be fully documented and that much depends upon circumstantial evidence and plausible inference. Compared to the documentary evidence available principally through Taiwan sources (largely confirmed by partial evidence released in Peking) on the Lin Piao affair, the material on Chen Po-ta is very meagre indeed.[15] Chen Po-ta, who had been head of the Cultural Revolution Group of the Central Committee, was purged immediately after the 2nd Plenum of the Central Committee in August 1970. He was later said to have been a key figure in Lin Piao's challenge to Mao's authority and the new policy after the Cultural Revolution.[16] A further problem in identifying the policy position of Lin Piao and Chen Po-ta is that this has to be reconstructed out of the accusations made against them. No texts are available which outline their own views in their own way. There can be no guarantee that the refutations of their alleged proposals represent an accurate or complete summary of the views refuted. At the same time it should be noted that contemporary Peking official publications from late 1968 until the summer of 1971 reflected some aspects of the debate on foreign affairs. The following interpretation and reconstruction of the Chen-Lin position should not be considered as entirely speculative.

Lin Piao and Chen Po-ta opposed many of the changes which Mao sought to introduce at the end of the great upheavals of the Cultural Revolution. Specifically, they were instrumental in delaying the reconstruction of the party apparatus of committees at all levels. They also tried to reintroduce the post of Chairman (or President) of the state.[17] They also opposed the new directions in foreign policy, preferring instead to continue the Cultural Revolution line of a revolutionary policy which sought unity with oppressed and revolutionary peoples.[18] They were unhappy with the way in which the formulation of the 'Five Principles of Peaceful Coexistence' was being used by Chou En-lai to establish relations with a wide range of countries.[19] But above all, they were opposed to the opening of relations with the United States.[20] Right to the end, the Lin Piao group maintained that the United States should be the target of any internationalist united front, and by 1971 it was implied that this was more important than opposition to the Soviet Union.[21]

Chen Po-ta and Lin Piao were accused by Chou En-lai at the Tenth Party Congress of August 1973 of having submitted an unacceptable draft report to the previous Congress in April 1969 which had to be totally rewritten. One of the reasons given for rejecting their draft was that it had incorporated the 'theory of the productive forces'. This was a theory which held that basically the superstructure was socialist and stable, containing few if any class contradictions, and that the main task for advancing socialism was to concentrate upon economic construction. In Maoist terms this was a highly revisionist theory and it constituted one of the main charges hurled against the Russians and indeed against Liu Shao-ch'i during the Cultural Revolution. At first glance it was a strange charge to level against Chen Po-ta in particular. He had been a prime advocate of the Great Leap Forward in 1958, the characteristic feature of which was that changes in the superstructure could unleash stupendous economic development. And more to the point, Chen Po-ta had been the head of the Cultural Revolution group which had argued that the primary task in socialist countries was to carry out revolution in the superstructure. Chou En-lai's accusation was not a charge suddenly made retrospectively several years after the event because it had been made in early 1971 after the fall of Chen but before the collapse of the Lin Piao group.[22]

How then can this apparent paradox be reconciled of a leader being charged with the very thing which he was hitherto known to have opposed? An interesting clue is provided by reference in the Chinese press in the summer of 1971 to a debate as to whether steel or electronics should be the key link in developing China's industry.[23] On 12 August the *People's Daily* published an article called 'A criticism of the theory of making the electronic industry the centre'. Written by the 'revolutionary mass criticism writing group of the electronics industry', it argued that 'Taking steel as the key link to ensure all-round development is the only correct principle for developing industry.' And it took to task 'sham Marxist political swindlers' (i.e. Chen Po-ta) 'who preach that the electronics industry should be made the centre'. The reason for the concentration on steel was that it provided the raw materials for machinery which alone could increase the means of production necessary for the expansion of the economy at all levels. But the article also cited some of Chen Po-ta's arguments:

The development of the electronics industry and electronics technology 'would not only advance the development of the national defence industry but also of the national economy as a whole'. They also said: 'The development of a modern electronics industry will bring about a big leap forward for our industry, and it will be a starting point for a new industrial revolution in the history of China. 'The rapid popularisation of modern electronic technology' will 'make China the first newly industrialised socialist power with first-rate electronic technology'. They did their utmost to convince people that electronic technology is omnipotent.[24]

The interesting point from our perspective is that the Chen Po-ta-Lin Piao argument in favour of electronics was an extension from its importance in the field of national defence. In that regard its main importance was precisely for those sectors of the armed forces in which Lin Piao had active political support, particularly in the air force. Moreover, if the policy of continued opposition to the United States and possibly the Soviet Union too were to be sustained it would be necessary to proceed still more quickly with the development of China's nuclear deterrent. In this regard the electronics industry was obviously more important than steel. Furthermore, it should be noted that the period of Lin Piao's ascendancy from 1967 to 1971 also saw a remarkable expansion in China's defence expenditure and the production of modern weapons systems (i.e. modern in the Chinese context. These were already inferior to their Soviet or American equivalents.).[25]

If the various points of this analysis are pulled together it is possible to reconstruct a plausible account of the Chen-Lin position and of their view as to what China's role should be.

Being still committed to preserving the fruits of the Cultural Revolution, Chen and Lin sought to consolidate the new administrative structures (i.e. the three-way revolutionary committees) which had emerged during the Cultural Revolution and they saw no good reason to restore the party apparatus and the disgraced old cadres. That could only have led to the loss of power and influence by Lin and Chen. Doubtless they argued that such a restoration would have meant almost negating the Cultural Revolution and returning to the *status quo ante*, which in time would once again raise the issue of revisionism. Far better in their view was to regard the new administrative structures as settled and concentrate upon the development of the economy. Likewise, there was no need to do more than modify some of the excesses of the Cultural Revolution foreign policy. In their view, China should still have continued to maintain its revolutionary solidarity with the revolutionary people of the world and with Vietnam. That would have meant continued firm opposition to the United States and it would also have required paying further attention to the development of more advanced means of national defence.

This account does not explain the softening of the Lin Piao group's hostility to the Soviet Union and Lin's abortive flight on 12 September 1971. That seems best explained by the dynamics of the leadership conflict during which Lin Piao was being continually outmanoeuvred by

Mao and driven to more desperate straits. Thus the softening of the hostile attitude to the Soviet Union did not occur until the spring of 1971, which was after the fall of Chen Po-ta and coincident with the beginnings of the plot to oust Mao by a *coup d'état*.[26] These would seem to be the moves of a man with rapidly decreasing options resorting to panic measures. They doubtless reveal a great deal about Lin Piao as a political animal, but these last moves should not be construed as indicative of the more considered Lin Piao-Chen Po-ta view of the role that China should play in world affairs which has been suggested above.

Mao's Turn to the United States

If the Soviet Union wouldn't do (point the way), then [Mao] would place his hopes on the American people . . .

In the meantime, he said, the Foreign Ministry was studying the matter of admitting Americans from the left, middle and right to visit China. Should rightists like Nixon, who represented the monopoly capitalists, be permitted to come? He should be welcomed because, Mao explained, at present the problems between China and the U.S.A. would have to be solved with Nixon. Mao would be happy to talk with him, either as a tourist or as President (Edgar Snow, 12 December 1970).[27]

Mao had effectively signalled his intentions in this regard three months earlier by having Edgar Snow stand with him on the review stand at Tien An Men on National Day, with the resulting photograph displayed prominently in the *People's Daily*. Kissinger's visit in July 1971 and the resulting announcement that President Nixon would visit China the following February in retrospect have lost the sense of shock-waves that encircled the world at the time. The various moves and counter-moves in the complex exchanges and developments from 1968 onwards have been carefully charted by others.[28] Here it is more useful to concentrate upon three issues: the underlying trends identified by Mao and Chou En-lai which led to the opening of Sino-American relations; the Shanghai Communiqué signed by Nixon and Chou En-lai; and the implications for China's role in world affairs which were perceived to follow from this.

As we have seen, much of the Maoist analysis of the changes in the world situation was concerned with power relations, but not in terms of power blocs; rather the analysis sought to identify underlying trends in fluid dynamic shifts of power. In the previous chapter it was argued that 1968 was the critical year for Mao in which the subterranean currents affecting the changing positions of the Soviet Union and the United States finally became manifest. It was perceived as the turning-point in their respective exercise of power in world affairs. The intensifying constraints upon the use of American imperial power in Vietnam finally reached the point at which the American executive had to begin the long road of retreat. It was to be a long road back with many twists and turns along the way which included possible counter-currents. Did the Nixon Doctrine of 1969 followed by the Nixon-Sato (Premier of Japan) Communiqué — which included South Korea and Taiwan as an area of security interest to Japan — mean that Japan was to be rearmed so as to play the US role in East Asia by proxy? Did the American incursion into Cambodia in May 1970 portend a latter-day widening and deepening of the American war in Indo-China? And had Mao mis-read the signs? These were soon to be answered in the negative. By the summer of 1970 it had become clear that the American withdrawal from Indo-China was not being reversed. The waves of vicious American bombing of virtually defenceless Cambodia and Laos in addition to those of Vietnam, though horrendous, did not add up to a reversal of the trend. And despite much Chinese propaganda about the militarisation of Japan, there were precious few signs that Japan's quiescent political and military role in east Asia was being changed in any marked way. In his wide-ranging talks with Edgar Snow in 1970, Mao did not even refer to this once. By 1970/1 both Mao and Chou En-lai were sufficiently confident of their judgement that the days of US expansionism were over that they freely confided to Western visitors their view that the American people would no longer allow it.

As for the Soviet Union, Mao and Chou maintained that the changes wrought by the 'usurpation of power by a bourgeois clique' finally bore fruit in the Soviet readiness to use force and power politics to advance its great-power interests in world affairs. Czechoslovakia was the turning-point. The thinly veiled nuclear threats and the concentration by the early 1970s of 40 highly modernised divisions to the north of China as well as, of course, the skirmishing on the border (including the highly publicised but still obscure battles in March 1969 over an island in the Ussuri River border) had an immediate impact on China. Thereafter, under Mao's slogan of 'dig tunnels deep, store grain everywhere and be prepared for war and natural disasters', the Chinese people in their spare time literally dug an amazing series of underground tunnels under the big cities, linking them with communes many miles away. It is difficult to judge how serious and immediate the Russian threat was. But it clearly had an immediate impact on the Chinese people. Whether or not it was a factor in the ongoing leadership struggle can only be a matter of speculation since no information has been revealed on this aspect. It is difficult to believe that the Soviet factor did not figure largely in a situation in which the future domestic and international orientation of China was in dispute. At the same time, the presence of superior modern Russian military power on the borders was real enough. Peking is within easy reach of highly mobile Russian armour across the North China Plain from the Mongolian border several hundred miles away. For their part the Russian leaders' discussion of a potentially aggressive and expansionist China mentioned only in whispers in the 1950s had by now grown very loud. So pervasive was the talk and preparations for war that the experienced and noted American journalist Harrison Salisbury, who toured Soviet Asia in the late 1960s, wrote a book on his experience simply titled *The Coming War Between China and Russia*. Yet despite — or perhaps because of — the preparations, neither side seriously made moves to attack the other. The Chinese side in any case lacked the necessary capabilities to launch a strategic attack. That did not preclude the option of taking local tactical initiatives. But the broad strategic Chinese posture was that as applied to the United States in earlier years. China would not attack but it would defend itself if attacked.

The atmosphere on both sides arising out of the border skirmishes became much more embittered. China's popular defence preparations were obviously undertaken with the Soviet Union in mind; while in the Soviet Union the Ussuri River incidents, apart from inflaming anti-China passions which were never far below the surface, also revived long-standing fears of the 'Yellow Peril' going back several hundred years to the Mongol invasions of Genghis Khan.[29] The Russian poet Yevtushenko captured and inflamed the racialist mood in a long poem on the affair of which the following five lines capture the essence:

> You can see in the murky twilight
> The new Mongol warriors with bombs in their quivers.
> But if they attack the alarm bells will ring
> And there will be more than enough fighters
> For a new battle of Kulikovo.

Amidst the intensity of mutual recrimination and preparation for armed conflict, the Sino-Soviet leaders in fact did seek negotiations. In September 1969, following the funeral of Ho Chi Minh, Soviet Premier Kosygin broke his journey back home from Hanoi to fly to Peking via

Calcutta. It was then agreed to resume the border negotiations, and it was on this occasion that Mao made his famous comment to Kosygin that while it was possible to improve Sino-Soviet state relations the struggle on the ideological level would continue. Mao told Kosygin that he (Mao) used to say that the struggle would continue for 10,000 years if necessary, but now that Kosygin had come Mao would take off 1,000 years.[30]

Despite the sense of crisis in 1968/9 Mao's concern regarding the Soviet Union seemed more long-term than immediate. Brezhnev's proposal of an Asian Collective Security system in June 1969 suggested to the Chinese that the Soviet Union was engaged on a long-term encirclement of China.[31] It seemed that the Soviet Union had inherited the mantle of the late John Foster Dulles. Much to the alarm of the Chinese, the Soviet leadership was cultivating relations with the Japanese government of Prime Minister Sato.[32] The ubiquitous Soviet emissary and journalist Victor Louis visited Taiwan and Soviet ties with south-east Asia were increasing.

At the global level Mao and Chou En-lai argued that the United States was bound to respond to the new Soviet challenge. Their relationship was characterised by both collusion and contention. It was now argued that the former was superficial and transitory while the latter was substantive and permanent. The focal points of their contention were Europe and the Middle East rather than East Asia. Part of the reason for the American withdrawal of troops from Indo-China and the Nixon Doctrine was that by being bogged down in the hopeless quagmire of Vietnam the United States had made it easier for the Russians to invade Czechoslovakia. If the Americans were to continue the hopeless endeavour, perhaps even greater opportunities would arise for the expansion of Soviet influence in the more critical areas of Europe and the Middle East. The Americans, therefore, were bound to become less directly militarily active in Asia. The Soviets, by contrast, would become more active. This general analysis was confirmed by their respective roles in the war which led to the dismemberment of east Pakistan and the establishment of Bangladesh.

Thus it made sense not only to exploit the contradiction between the two superpowers, but to do so by extending an opening to the United States. In a confidential briefing in December 1971 Chou En-lai advanced as one of the primary reasons for Nixon's interest in coming to China the following explanation:

when the U.S. got stuck in Vietnam, the Soviet revisionists embraced the opportunity to extend vigorously their sphere of influence in Europe and the Middle East. The U.S. imperialists cannot but improve their relations with China to combat the Soviet revisionists.[33]

The Shanghai Communiqué and China's New Role

President Nixon's visit to China in February 1972 signalled the acceptance of China as a great power in world affairs, but the Shanghai Communiqué signed by Nixon and Premier Chou En-lai on 27 February spelt out the terms in which the great-power role was to be carried out.[34] Both sides made separate statements of their respective views on international relations and made specific comments on Asian trouble-spots. They agreed to base their mutual relations on what amounted to the 'Five Principles of Peaceful Coexistence'. Progress towards normalisation of relations between the two countries was judged to be 'in the interests of all countries'. Then followed three key positions which reflected in particular the Chinese outlook and which provided the basis for co-operative great-power diplomacy between China and America:

> neither should seek hegemony in the Asia-Pacific region and each is opposed to efforts by any other country or group of countries to establish such hegemony; and neither is prepared to negotiate on behalf of any third party or to enter into agreements or understandings with the other directed at other states. Both sides are of the view that it would be against the interests of the peoples of the world for any major country to collude with another against other countries, or for major countries to divide up the world into spheres of interest.

The first provision was clearly directed at any possible attempt by the Soviet Union to become militarily dominant in the region. The second from a Chinese perspective was designed to assure their revolutionary friends, in particular the Vietnamese, that unlike past Russian attempts to improve relations with the United States the Chinese attempt would not be at their expense. Moreover, it also reflected the long held Chinese theoretical and practical adherence to the significance of the independence and sovereign equality of all states. The rejection of the principles of classic great-power diplomacy by which the great settled the affairs of the small was the corollary of the Chinese rejection of any notion that revolution could be exported. Just as revolutions had to come from within the countries concerned and could not be determined from the outside, so in international relations problems should be settled by the countries directly involved. The third principle too was a rejection of the classic great-power tendency to divide the world into various spheres of interest and to conspire together against third parties.

The Chinese side's earlier statement of its view of international relations provided a succinct summary of the general principles which still underlay the new diplomacy. This provided, too, China's main claims to be still carrying out a foreign policy based on revolutionary principles. As such, it deserves quoting at length:

> Wherever there is oppression, there is resistance. Countries want independence, nations want liberation and the people want revolution — this has become the irresistible trend of history. All nations, big or small, should be equal; big nations should not bully the small and strong nations should not bully the weak. China will never be a superpower and it opposes hegemony and power politics of any kind. The Chinese side stated that it firmly supports the struggles of all the oppressed people and nations for freedom and liberation and that the people of all countries have the right to choose their social systems according to their own wishes and the right to safeguard the independence, sovereignty and territorial integrity of their own countries and oppose foreign aggression, interference, control and subversion. All foreign troops should be withdrawn to their own countries.

These principles reflected the experience of the Chinese Revolution and the emergence of China as a socialist self-reliant great country on the world stage. In effect they represent the universalisation of that particular experience which combined both the struggle for nation independence from alien control and external penetration and the struggle for revolution. The two are seen to be linked in the outside world too. In the Chinese experience the popular drive for independence led inexorably to and became inextricably linked with the popular demand for social change and revolution. Thus in the Chinese view by opposing great-power politics and the two superpowers in its foreign policy, China is necessarily helping forward the prospects for eventual revolutionary change. By the same token, however, by stressing so much the importance of sovereignty and independence China's leaders were also by implication arguing that the Chinese people should concentrate within their own borders upon revolution and socialist construction in their own distinctive way without foreign interference or diversion by the claims of other socialist countries. In other words, implicit in these new formulations was the concept of China pursuing a variant of socialism in one country. Unlike Stalin's approach, however, the Chinese did not call upon Marxist-Leninists to subordinate the interests of revolutionary prospects in their own countries to those of the Soviet Union. On the contrary, the Chinese variant was self-reliant and it has been consistently argued in China that the genuine revolutionary struggles of other countries are mutually supportive. The Chinese also committed themselves to firmly support 'oppressed peoples and nations'. Obviously, the extent and nature of that support would depend as always upon China's capacities and the view taken of the struggles concerned. But as the Chinese statement and subsequent Chinese practice made clear, the Chinese did not intend to mark China's entry into the world of power politics by acting as a conventional great power, even for revolutionary purposes.

The remaining aspects of the Shanghai Communiqué dealt with Asian trouble-spots, where it may be observed that because of geographical contiguity China was influential in conventional great-power terms. More importantly, however, there were still outstanding problems over which the Chinese and the Americans had clashed over the previous 22 years.

The problem which attracted most interest, however, was the question of Taiwan. For reasons of space the full complexities of the problem cannot be analysed here. But some observations regarding its impact on China's role in international affairs are in order. The fact that the opening to the United States took place at all without the simultaneous resolution of the Taiwan question is important. It suggests that the significance of the Taiwan problem ever since 1950 has been two-fold. The first was and continues to be that it is seen as part of an uncompleted civil war in which outsiders have intervened, thus threatening China's sovereignty over the island and dangerously supporting a rival government. The second, which was hitherto largely obscured from sight, was that the American presence in Taiwan was also seen as part of the general policy of American imperial expansion in Asia during the 1950s and 1960s. Thus once America was perceived to have begun the process of decline and withdrawal from Asia, the Taiwan problem from the perspective of Peking acquired reduced significance. Therefore, what China's leaders required from President Nixon was a formal recognition that Taiwan was a part of China and a formal commitment in principle to withdraw the American forces from the island. This was in fact written into the communiqué. The American side then declared that it 'will progressively reduce its forces and military installations on Taiwan as the tension in the area diminishes'. As Chou En-lai later indicated to Sihanouk and the North Vietnamese, this meant that China had implicitly consented to delay the resolution of the Taiwan issue until after the conflict in Indo-China had been settled. It was a clear affirmation of the principle that China would not damage the cause of the revolutionary armed struggles in Indo-China in pursuit of major power accommodations.

As a result of the opening to the United States China's international position had been transformed. The situation in which China had been relatively isolated from the international diplomatic community and subject to the twin pressures of the two superpowers was gone for ever. To be sure, China was still under major threat from the Soviet Union in the north. But China had now established an understanding with the United States which could go a long way to neutralise that threat. The Soviet threat, however, was more than just a military threat. There remained the possibility that it could subvert the Maoist order in China or that a faction in the Chinese leadership might, like Lin Piao, turn to it for support. Moreover, there was also the threat that the Soviet Union might seek to establish its influence and even detach some of China's border provinces like Sinkiang where it had once been extremely influential. The ability to withstand these pressures depended (as they had always done) on how well the Chinese people managed their internal affairs. Meanwhile China had made important diplomatic breakthroughs and these had been achieved without surrendering its long-standing vital principles. Moreover, the way was now open for further diplomatic successes. Perhaps the most important of these was the recognition by Japan.[35] This of course had a vital bearing on the Taiwan problem since the condition of recognition was the severance of all formal governmental relations with the island.

It now remained for China's leaders to clarify various outstanding problems regarding China's new-found role. New opportunities had arisen for Chinese diplomacy. How would they be handled? How would the prospects for revolutionary change in world affairs be identified now? What would be the elements of continuity and of change in China's foreign policy now that China was to be drawn into the more complex multilateral bargaining of international diplomacy? And underlying these questions, if the old shape of international politics had gone what had replaced it? And how would China seek to use its new position to reshape the changing international order? In Chinese terms, what was to be the new pattern for the 1970s, given the Chinese description of the situation?

Today in the 70's, the medium-sized and small countries are uniting against hegemony and this situation is developing; the revolutionary struggle of the world's people against imperialism and colonisation has been mounting as never before; the basic contradictions in the international arena are sharpening and all the political forces are re-grouping in a process of great upheaval, great division and great reorganisation.[36]

Notes

1. See, for example, speech by Truong Chinh, broadcast on 1 February 1972. BBC SWB FE/3907.
2. In *Peking Review*, No. 1 (1972).
3. The New Year editorial in ibid., No. 1 (1971).
4. Lin Piao, 'Report to the Ninth National Congress of the Communist Party of China', 1969. *Peking Review*, No. 16 (1969); c.f. Lin Piao, 'Long Live the Victory of People's War!', ibid., No. 36 (1965).
5. *People's Daily,* 21 January 1964.
6. Reported interview by G. Rowbotham, *East is Red*, October 1971 (York SACU), pp. 6-10, cited by John Gittings, 'China's Foreign Policy: Continuity or Change?' in *Journal of Contemporary Asia*, Vol. 2, No. 1.
7. Interviewed by Neville Maxwell in *Sunday Times*, London, 19 December 1971.
8. See interview by a delegation from the Australian National University cited as appendix in J.D. Armstrong, 'The United Front Doctrine and China's Foreign Policy', Ph.D thesis, Australian National University, Canberra (July 1975),pp. 330-40.
9. See the analysis in S.R. Schram, *The Political Thought of Mao Tse-tung* (Penguin Books, 1969), pp. 90-110 and 134-8.
10. *New York Times,* 21 February 1964. See the discussion in Chapter 5, pp. 149-54.
11. See the articles by Shih Chun (pseudonym) on Studying World History, *Peking Review*, Nos. 21, 24 and 25 (1972).
12. See for example, the first speech to the General Assembly by the Chairman of the Chinese Delegation on 15 November 1971 after the restoration of the China seat in the United Nations in *Peking Review*, No. 46 (1971).
13. Ibid.
14. For an account of that struggle, see Philip Bridgham, 'The Fall of Lin Piao', *China Quarterly*, No. 55 (July-September 1973), pp. 427-49.
15. The documents on the Lin Piao affair are conveniently assembled together in *Chinese Law and Government* ,Vol. 5, Nos. 3-4 (Fall-Winter 1972-3). No such documents exist with regard to Chen Po-ta.
16. For the most authoritative condemnation of the two see the 'Press Communiqué of the Tenth National Congress of the CPC', and Chou En-lai's Report in *Peking Review*, Nos. 35 and 36 (1973).

17. For brief analyses see Jaap van Ginnekan, *The Rise and Fall of Lin Piao* (Penguin Books, 1976), pp. 253-5; and Edward E. Rice, *Mao's Way* (University of California Press, 1972), pp. 499-505.

18. See,for example, *Peking Review*, No. 1 (1969), which carried two contrasting views of the world. The New Year editorial called for an internationalist united front which included 'oppressed nations' and used a quotation from Mao which referred to the need to 'engage in great struggles which have many features different in form from those of the past'. The other article, entitled 'The World Revolution has Entered a Great New Era', continued the themes from the Cultural Revolution and referred neither to a united front with 'nations' nor to new forms of struggle. Instead it warned against wavering, compromising and even surrendering in the ups and downs of the development of the revolution.

19. The National Day speeches of October 1969 by Lin Piao and Chou En-lai were very similar except that Chou referred to the 'Five Principles' and Lin did not. *Peking Review*, No. 40 (1969). Although the New Year editorial of 1970 affirmed the importance of these principles, the long article of 22 April 1970 on the centenary of Lenin's birth which also touched on foreign policy did not. *Peking Review*, No. 17 (1970).

20. In June 1970 Huang Yung-sheng (Chief of General Staff, member of the Political Bureau and key associate of Lin Piao) spoke to a rally in Pyongyang attended by leaders of the liberation movements in Indo-China, in which he specifically ruled out Sino-US relations on the basis of the Five Principles because of US interference in internal Chinese affairs by maintaining armed forces in Taiwan. *Peking Review*, No. 27 (1970).

21. See the formulations of the editorials for May Day (*Peking Review*, No. 19 (1971)) and for the first anniversary of Mao's 20 May statement on the American attack on Cambodia (*Peking Review*, No. 21 (1971)), which mentioned only the United States as the target for the united front. Indeed as late as 1 and 18 August 1971 (after Kissinger's visit to Peking in July) Huang Yung-sheng was still making speeches which opposed the new line. See NCNA, 1 and 18 August.

22. See *Red Flag*, No. 2 (1971) for articles on economic affairs, pp. 39-62. Also *Peking Review*, No. 4 (1971), 'Struggle in Philosophy and Class Struggle'; ibid., No. 17 (1971), 'Theory of "Combine Two Into One" is Reactionary Philosophy for Restoring Capitalism'; and ibid., No. 25 (1971), 'Guiding Principle for Knowing and Changing the World'.

23. For a brief summary of this still largely obscure debate, see *China News Analysis*, 854 (10 September 1971).

24. In BBC SWB FE/3766.

25. Sydney H. James, 'The Chinese Defense Burden, 1965-1974' in *China: A Reassessment of the Economy*, a compendium of papers submitted to the Joint Economics Committee, Congress of the United States, 10 July 1975.

26. See notes 21 and 15 above.

27. Edgar Snow, *The Long Revolution* (Random House, 1972), pp. 171-2.

28. For American views, see for example the two special issues of *Problems of Communism* with more than a dozen contributions by various writers; G.T. Hsiao (ed.), *Sino-American Detente and its Policy Implications* (Praeger, 1974); Francis O. Wilcox (ed.), *China and the Great Powers: Relations with the United States, the Soviet Union and Japan* (Praeger, 1974); A.S. Whiting, 'The Sino-American Detente: Genesis and Prospects'; in Ian Wilson (ed.), *China and the World Community* (Angus and Robertson in association with The Australian Institute of International Affairs, 1973); Harold C. Hinton, *The Bear at the Gate: Chinese Policy Making Under*

Soviet Pressure (Washington, American Enterprise Institute and Stanford, Hoover Institution, 1971), and *Three and a Half Powers: The New Balance in Asia* (Indiana University Press, 1975). For other perspectives, see John Gittings, 'China's Foreign Policy: Continuity or Change?'; my own 'China's New Foreign Policy' in *The World Today* (January 1972); the account by Ross Terrill in *800,000: The ɪ.   ɪinemann, 1972); and, of course, that by Edgar Snow in *The Long Revolution*.

29. It is interesting to note that Soviet scholarship regards Genghis Khan as a retrogressive figure in history and the Mongols in the Mongolian People's Republic have perforce followed suit with regard to their traditionally accepted great national hero. The Chinese, by contrast, evaluate him as having played a progressive role in world history.

30. Snow, *The Long Revolution*, p. 175.

31. See, for example, 'Trap is the Word for so-called Asian "Regional Economic Cooperation"', *Peking Review*, No. 29 (1969), pp. 23-4; and 'Another Step in New Tsars' Expansion in Asia — expose expansionist essence of so-called "Asian Collective Security System"', ibid., No. 37 (1969), pp. 18-20.

32. 'Reactionary Sato Government is Following Tojo's Road', *Peking Review*, No. 29 (1969), pp. 24-5 and 32.

33. 'Chou En-lai's Report on the International Situation, December 1971' in *Issues and Studies* (Taiwan) (January 1977), p. 116

34. For a succinct account of the Presidential visit and a clear presentation of the main documents see the 'Quarterly Chronicle and Documentation' in *China Quarterly*, No. 50 (April-June 1972), pp. 390-402.

35. For an account of this see G.T. Hsiao, 'Prospects for a New Sino-Japanese Relationship', *China Quarterly*, No. 60 (December 1974), pp. 720-49.

36. *Peking Review*, No. 4 (1972), p. 16.

9 CHINA AS A SOCIALIST MEMBER OF THE THIRD WORLD: 1973 ONWARDS

In my view, the United States and the Soviet Union form the first world. Japan, Europe and Canada, the middle section, belong to the second world. We are the third world. The third world has a huge population. With the exception of Japan, Asia belongs to the third world. The whole of Africa belongs to the third world, and Latin America too.[1]

China belongs to the third world. For China cannot compare with the rich or powerful countries politically, economically, etc. She can be grouped only with the relatively poor countries (Mao Tse-tung, 22 February 1974).[2]

China's new-found status in 1972 as an acknowledged full participatory member of the international diplomatic system in the view of China's leaders was the result of 'Chairman Mao's revolutionary diplomatic line', which emerged out of his appreciation of the profound changes taking place in the structure of international politics. The above quotations are the first available reference by Mao to the three worlds. They show that it was not until 1974 that he decided the international processes 'of great upheaval, great division and great reorganization' he had identified as beginning in the 1960s had finally ended in a new coherent pattern. Only then did it become possible to identify more clearly China's chosen place in world politics as a socialist developing country and a member of the Third World.

On the surface that is a comparatively modest role. But a fuller consideration of the three worlds theory and the way it has provided operational guidelines for the actual conduct of China's foreign policy will show that China's self-chosen role is of greater significance than may be appreciated at first.

As was argued in the previous chapter, in 1972 China had become a full member of the international community largely on its own terms. The essential conditions of membership such as acceptance of statehood, sovereignty, etc. had long been an integral component of the Chinese Communist viewpoint so that no fundamental challenges were posed to China's leaders by entry into that community. Moreover, even the taking up of China's permanent seat in the United Nations Security Council has not really brought China into a very different diplomatic style of wheeling and dealing by which high principles become whittled down through multilateral diplomacy in the interests of passing favoured resolutions. To be sure, China's Ministry of Foreign Affairs has been drawn into more complex processes of diplomacy and organisational politics. But the United Nations has basically provided China with a convenient international platform from which to enunciate its views, appeal to the Third World countries, and expose what it considers to be the nefarious policies of the two superpowers and especially those of the Soviet Union. It has also provided Peking with a clearer window on the world and a meeting place where its senior officials can sometimes meet with their counterparts from countries like Indonesia, which as yet do not have diplomatic relations with the PRC. Although China has joined most of the special agencies of the United Nations, she does not draw on their services as do the vast majority of the countries of the Third World.

China has carefully avoided becoming closely identified with any of the major voting blocs in the United Nations. Moreover, China's essential view of the United Nations has not really altered. China's leaders do not regard it as a supranational body with an objective viewpoint above the fray of states. They have consistently regarded it as a body which reflects the balances of world forces. Thus in the years after the Second World War, they regarded it as a tool of the Americans. Later it was regarded as one of the international structures where the superpower politics of collusion and contention were played out. Still later they saw it as an important forum in which principally the Third World countries struggled with the superpowers to establish a more equitable basis for the rules of international politics and for a better international economic system. Thus the Chinese have consistently opposed any attempt to have the United Nations override the sovereignty of any state. They have also opposed the institution of UN peace-keeping forces.

But the Chinese have never voted against enabling resolutions when these have been presented to the Security Council. The problem here has been that the relevant sovereign states — such as Cyprus or countries in the Middle East — had already indicated their approval, so that rather than foist their views on unwilling states the Chinese chose to state their views and then withdraw altogether from the vote. Even abstention could have been regarded as implicitly accepting the framework of UN peace-keeping forces. Indeed, if the Chinese have contributed institutionally to the UN it has been by making the procedural innovation of taking no part in the vote. The only time the PRC has actually used its power of the veto was fairly early on after entry into the UN, when it turned down the first applications of Bangladesh for admission to the UN. Arguably, had the Chinese been more experienced in the processes of the UN they might have been able to have attained their objective without recourse to the veto. But the Chinese regretted the use of the veto and they have taken care never to use it again. Indeed they have frequently sided with those who have called for the reform of the United Nations so as to enable it to reflect more adequately the importance of the Third World and to remove the built-in preferential position of the great powers as symbolised by their veto power in the Security Council. The Chinese would like to see the principle of the sovereign equality of states enshrined even further in the procedures and processes of the UN.[3]

It would be wrong to suggest, however, that the changes in international politics and China's fully fledged entry into the international community of states did not bring China into a more complex series of relationships and even a degree of interdependency. Interestingly, this became truer of China's relations with her more immediate neighbours in east and south-east Asia, with whom she had always had closer relations.

Sino-Japanese relations, for example, which have always been special, henceforth became marked by a delicate economic relationship involving current actualities and future potentialities. This was particularly so with regard to the complex mix of oil economics and politics. The importance to China of advance technology transfers from Japan was more than counterbalanced by the subtle but very real Chinese involvement in domestic Japanese politics, especially on issues affecting Japan's relations with the two superpowers and with Taiwan. Moreover, the Chinese have made it progressively clearer that they favour a continued security link between Japan and the US, and indeed that they even would welcome a limited expansion of Japan's military power. In the Chinese view both countries share a common interest in limiting Russian penetration into the area. But China's diplomacy suggests that Peking has accepted the necessity of a certain degree of interdependence with Tokyo if it is to succeed in this goal.

With a similar objective in mind, China's leaders not only supported the growing sense of regional solidarity as shown by the countries of the Association of South East Asian Nations (ASEAN), but they have also encouraged the settlement of inter-state conflict by peaceful consultations. The Chinese believe that such conflicts provide the Soviet Union with opportunities to establish deep footholds in the area. Given that the Chinese have eschewed the power politics of establishing spheres of influence and dominance over smaller neighbours, China has become dependent to a certain extent upon the will and the capacity of these countries to hold the Soviet Union at bay from areas close to China's national security concerns.

At the same time, the Chinese in early 1974 gave the other governments in the region much food for thought by a suitable display of an effective resort to force when challenged for control of territory claimed to be within Chinese sovereignty. A task force of the Thieu regime of South Vietnam was quickly overwhelmed in a struggle for control over islands in the South China Sea. The target for the Chinese attack was what they considered to be an illegitimate regime. Doubtless other governments would not be dealt with so severely. Nevertheless, as we shall see later in this chapter, the fact that many islands in the area are disputed between China and other states and the fact that the vital continental shelf which China shares with many other countries is still undemarcated means that China has considerable bargaining strength at its disposal in its relations with those countries. That this bargaining power is not used overtly does not mean that the states concerned are unaware of it nor does it mean that it is entirely absent from the calculations of policy-makers and executives in Peking.

Even though it can be argued, as just suggested above, that China's full entry into the international political system has modified and complicated China's practice of diplomacy, it still remains true that China's relative detachment from the outside world continued. Thus the main theme which I have advanced in this book, that China's foreign policy is best understood within China's own frame of reference, still holds good.

The Emergence of the Theory of the Three Worlds

It was not until two years after President Nixon's visit to China that the Chinese leaders finally outlined their considered view as to the new structures which had emerged in world politics. Up to 1974 their favourite term for describing the character of the international system was 'upheaval', or turmoil. To be sure, they had been able to identify confidently certain trends. In particular, these concerned the relative decline of the United States and the emergence to the front line of the Soviet Union as among the imperialist superpowers. Also China's leaders had become more confident about Third World countries who on the state level were beginning to play a more positive role in advancing the interests of their people in opposing the encroachments of the two superpowers. It was, however, the unfolding of events in 1972 and 1973 which seems to have persuaded Mao and his colleagues that new patterns had definitely taken shape.

China's leaders attached a great deal of importance to the Paris Agreements between the United States and the Democratic Republic of Vietnam, signed on 27 January 1973. In many ways it was a vindication of their assessment of the situation which had led to their opening up to the United States a year earlier. The Chinese regarded the agreements as 'a great victory won by the Vietnamese people through self-reliance, arduous struggles and perseverance in a protracted people's war'.[4] In their private assessments China's leaders regarded the new situation as one which would require about a year and a half's healing, consolidation and preparations before the struggle for reunification could be resumed by the revolutionary forces of Vietnam. They felt that the United States would not be able to return again in strength because of Soviet pressures elsewhere in the world, but primarily in Europe and the Middle East; and also because of the opposition that would certainly arise from wide sections of the American people. Thus China's leaders felt that the die had finally been cast in Indo-China and that, although there were many struggles which lay ahead, the victorious outcome for the revolutionary forces in all three countries was at long last in sight.[5]

Other events of significance from a Chinese perspective concerned the Middle East and Europe. The expulsion of Soviet military personnel in 1972 from Egypt followed by the October 1973 Arab-Israeli war was regarded by the Chinese as evidence that Third World countries were beginning to resist Soviet attempts to control them and that they were realising that they could be masters of their own fate.[6] This progressive aspect of the Third World was confirmed in Chinese eyes by the oil boycott followed by the trebling of oil prices by the oil-producing and exporting countries (OPEC) acting in unison. The intervening period between President Nixon's visit to Peking in 1972 and the enunciation of the three worlds theory two years later also witnessed the enlargement of the EEC to include Britain, Denmark and Ireland in addition to the original six. A Chinese commentary observed: 'Intensified contention and collusion in Europe between the two superpowers, the United States and the Soviet Union, in the past few years have increasingly threatened the West European countries' vital interests. This promoted their unity in resisting the two superpowers.'[7] Thus the National Day editorial of 1 October 1972 resurrected Mao's 1964 concept of the 'second intermediate zone', which had not been mentioned in the Chinese Press for more than seven years. The editorial declared:

More and more countries in the first as well as the second intermediate zone are joining forces in different forms on a varying scale
to engage in struggles against one or two superpowers. The third
world is playing an increasingly important role in international
affairs. Even some countries under fairly tight control of Soviet
revisionism or US imperialism are striving to free themselves from
their dictates.[8]

China's leaders' view about the emerging new structure of the international political system crystallised in early 1974. Significantly, the
occasion chosen for enunciating the three worlds theory was a special
session of the UN General Assembly, called at the insistence of the less
developed countries to voice demands for a new international economic order. It was an example of the kind of positive moves by Third
World countries to confront imperialist forces and to try to assert
greater control over their own situations which China's leaders had identified as a major factor in changing world politics.

Vice Premier Teng Hsiao-p'ing, as Chairman of the Delegation to the
Sixth Special Session of the UN General Assembly, delivered on 10
April 1974 perhaps the most important speech on China's foreign policy
since the Sino-Soviet split.[9] At the outset Teng declared that, as the
result of the transformation of the Soviet Union into a social imperialist
superpower (that is, an imperialist power masquerading as a socialist
one), 'the socialist camp which existed for a time after World War II is
no longer in existence'. This meant that most of Eastern Europe was
under Russian imperialist domination.

Elaborating further, Teng argued that 'owing to the law of uneven
development of capitalism, the Western imperialist bloc, too, is disinte-
grating.' A new analytical division of the world was called for and Teng
immediately provided it:

Judging from the changes in international relations, the world today
actually consists of three parts or three worlds, that are inter-
connected and in contradiction to one another. The United States
and the Soviet Union make up the First World. The developing
countries in Asia, Africa and Latin America and other regions make
up the Third World. The developed countries between the two make
up the Second World.

The implications of this analysis were considerable. The Chinese
were in effect asserting that the orthodox Communist view of the world

which had obtained since Lenin's day was now out of date. The world was no longer seen as fundamentally divided structurally and ideologically into socialist and capitalist camps. In the Chinese view the most important conflict in the world which is likely to determine change in the immediate future is no longer in the first instance the conflict between the forces of socialism and those of capitalism. Rather Teng maintained that the most significant conflict was that of the two superpowers' struggle for world hegemony and the struggle of other countries in the world to resist them. Teng described the 'Three Worlds' as follows:

> The two superpowers are the biggest international exploiters and oppressors of today. They are the source of a new world war. They both possess large numbers of nuclear weapons. They carry on a keenly contested arms race, station massive forces abroad and set up military bases everywhere, threatening the independence and security of all nations. They both keep subjecting other countries to their control, subversion, interference or aggression. They both exploit other countries economically, plundering their wealth and grabbing their resources. In bullying others, the superpower which flaunts the label of socialism is especially vicious. It has despatched its armed forces to occupy its 'ally' Czechoslovakia, and instigated the war to dismember Pakistan. It does not honour its words and is perfidious; it is self-seeking and unscrupulous.
>
> The case of the developed countries in between the superpowers and the developing countries is a complicated one. Some of them still retain colonialist relations of one form or another with Third World countries . . . At the same time, all these developed countries are in varying degrees controlled, threatened or bullied by one superpower or the other. Some of them have in fact been reduced by a superpower to the position of dependencies under the signboard of its so-called 'family'. In varying degrees, all these countries have the desire of shaking off superpower enslavement or control and safeguarding their national independence and the integrity of their sovereignty.
>
> The numerous developing countries have long suffered from colonialist and imperialist oppression and exploitation. They have won political independence, yet all of them still face the historic task of clearing out the remnant forces of colonialism, developing the national economy and consolidating national independence. These countries cover vast territories, encompass a large population and

abound in natural resources. Having suffered the heaviest oppression, they have the strongest desire to oppose oppression and seek liberation and development. In the struggle for national liberation and independence, they have demonstrated immense power and continually won splendid victories. They constitute a revolutionary force propelling the wheel of history and are the main forces combating colonialism, imperialism and particularly the superpowers.

Teng went on to dismiss the notion that the present world situation is characterised by *détente* and by the relaxation of tensions: 'the contradiction between the two superpowers is irreconcilable.' So long as they exist there could not be peace. 'Either they will fight each other, or the people will rise in revolution.' Their policies and practices had already aroused increasingly successful struggles against them in the Third World which have 'exposed the essential weakness of imperialism and particularly the superpowers'. The countries of the Second World too were roused to 'strong dissatisfaction'. Teng was lavish in his praise for those Arab countries which had made use of the oil weapon: 'What was done in the oil battle should, and can, be done in the case of other raw materials.' This was of great importance in Teng's view as 'control and protection of their resources by the developing countries are essential, not only for combating superpower arms expansion and war preparations and stopping the superpowers from launching wars of aggression.'

Teng then outlined the programme of action which the Chinese hoped Third World countries would undertake. This involved first of all securing genuine political independence from overt and covert external controls, primarily through recognising that without economic independence political independence was lacking in substance. Thus it was essential to pursue economic development based upon the principle of self-reliance and full control over all aspects concerning the production and sale of their raw materials. To these ends there should be greater stress on the need for political unity, mutual economic help and co-operation between Third World countries. They should seek together to change the unequal international economic system. Equality and mutual benefit should be the yardstick of their trade and aid. Practical proposals were made to ensure that the principles of aid should work in favour of the recipient and not the donor.

Finally, Teng classified China as 'a socialist country and a developing country. China belongs to the Third World . . . China is not a superpower nor will she ever seek to be one.' Moreover, should she one day become one, 'the people of the world should identify her as social imperialism, expose it and work together with the Chinese people to overthrow it.'

The speech as a whole provided a completely fresh theoretical framework for Chinese foreign policy. It was by no means comprehensive as it did not address itself to the question of 'proletarian internationalism' (i.e. relations with socialist countries and revolutionary movements), or to China's operational policies with regard to the two superpowers, or indeed to the strategic and foreign trade context of China's foreign policy both regionally and globally. Nevertheless it did provide a broad framework within which much of China's foreign policy is conducted.

Teng's analysis explained coherently and fairly accurately the Second and Third World dimensions of China's foreign policy. It explained why China had placed so much stress on state-to-state relations in its dealings with these countries, and it also showed that these should not be seen simply as being dominated by anti-Russian reflexes. The analysis also brought out very well why China sees the 'Third World' as 'the motive force of world history' at the present time. Teng's speech, however, did raise new problems. For example, although China could declare the socialist camp to be at an end and proclaim itself a socialist developing country of the Third World, it was doubtful whether its socialist allies could equally do so. For a while in 1974 the leadership of the Democratic Republic of Korea described their country as a member of the Third World;[10] but, presumably to avoid antagonising the Soviet Union, they soon stopped doing so. The Democratic Republic of Vietnam, however, rejected the three worlds thesis and continued to maintain that the socialist camp still exists.[11]

Unlike the Vietnamese, the Albanian leadership endorsed China's view of the Soviet Union, but, as was made clear in the summer of 1977 after the death of Chairman Mao in September 1976 and the overthrow of the 'gang of four' a month later, the Albanian leadership was sharply critical of the three worlds theory. In particular the Albanians objected to the theory's rejection of the view that the main division of the world was between socialism on the one hand and capitalism on the other. They argued that, just as within domestic socialist society the principal contradiction was a class struggle between the proletariat and the bourgeoisie, so this was true of international society as.a whole. The Albanians rejected China's policy of differentiating between the two superpowers as an unprincipled policy of regarding 'my enemy's enemy as my friend.' They also attacked China's views of the Second and Third Worlds: the former because it was capitalist and the latter because it made them bedfellows with reactionary regimes like those of the Shah of Iran and Pinochet of Chile.[12]

In response to these criticisms the Chinese eventually came up with a lengthy coherent explanation of the Marxist-Leninist credentials of the three worlds theory.[13] The *People's Daily* explained that it was only in 'appearance' that Chairman Mao's theory involved only relations between countries and nations, but 'in essence, it bears directly on the vital question of present-day class struggle on a world scale.' The article went on to cite many examples from the writing of Marx, Engels, Lenin and Stalin to show that they too had differentiated between the struggles of various non-socialist states and that they had often taken sides in these struggles. The Chinese argued that in differentiating between the three worlds Chairman Mao had identified who were the friends with whom genuine Marxist-Leninists should unite and who were to be opposed, and finally who constituted the middle ground to be won over. In this they suggested that Mao was very much in line with Lenin. Indeed the article was able to quote Lenin analysing the divisions of the world in 1920 in terms remarkably similar to those of Mao in 1974. In his report to the Second Congress of the Communist International, Lenin explicitly divided the countries of the world into three categories and made that division his basic point of departure for determining the strategy and tactics of the international proletariat. By Lenin's account, Soviet Russia was included in the category of the colonies or else placed in equivalent positions (this list also included the vanquished countries of the First World War); the second category was of countries who had retained their pre-war positions but had become economically dependent on America; and the third were those countries whose upper stratum had actually benefited from the post-war partition of the world.

The Chinese stated repeatedly that any analysis of the differentiation of the political forces at work in the world could not be done in the abstract, but had to be done only on the basis of a careful enquiry into the actual situation. As for the question of uniting with those who might otherwise be considered to be reactionaries, the *People's Daily* referred to a passage by Mao in his celebrated article 'On New Democracy' of 1940, which was one of his programmatic articles for the period before the establishment of socialism in China. The passage goes right to the heart of Mao's strategy of united fronts:

> No matter what classes, parties or individuals in an oppressed nation
> join the revolution, and no matter whether they themselves are

conscious of the point or understand it, so long as they oppose imperialism, their revolution becomes part of the proletarian-socialist world revolution and they become its allies.

This was the basis on which under Mao's leadership the Chinese Revolution had prospered by winning over the middle ground and isolating the enemy, and this helped to explain how socialist China could make common ground with countries of vastly different social systems whose governments from other points of view could be regarded as reactionary or in league with one or other of the two superpowers.

- The *People's Daily* noted the antecedents in Mao's writings for the three worlds theory, citing in particular his observations in 1946 regarding the vast intermediate zone between the Soviet Union and the United States which the latter was seeking to dominate under the slogan of an anti-Soviet war (see Chapter 2), and his observations in 1957 of the two contradictions and three forces at work in the Middle East following the Suez incident (see Chapter 4). The article could also have mentioned Mao's analyses of the emergence of the second intermediate zone in 1964 (see Chapter 6). But the paper argued that it was the vast change which had occurred in the 1960s which led to a new historical situation:

> For a time US imperialism remained the arch enemy of the people of the world. But many countries in its camp were no longer taking their cue from it and most of the countries in Asia, Africa and Latin America won independence. Meanwhile the Soviet leadership betrayed socialism, restored capitalism at home and the Soviet Union degenerated into a social imperialist country. Then, after a succession of grave events, the Soviet Union not only turned into an imperialist superpower that threatened the world as the United States did, but also became the most dangerous source of another world war.

The *People's Daily* continued that the betrayal of the revolutionary movement caused many splits and difficulties. And the paper later declared that:

> Generally speaking and for the time being, as a result of the Soviet ruling clique's betrayal, the spread of revisionist ideology and the splits in the ranks of the working class, the workers' revolutionary

movement in the developed capitalist countries cannot but remain at the stage of regrouping and accumulating strength. In these countries there is as yet no revolutionary situation for the immediate seizure of state power.

The Chinese could not have been clearer in explaining why they think there are no immediate prospects for socialist revolution in Europe.

Under these circumstances, the Chinese argued that to divide the world into the few remaining socialist countries and the relatively weak Marxist-Leninist organisations on the one side and a capitalist world on the other would not only serve no useful purpose, but would be counter-productive as well. The main danger in the world today came from the hegemonic ambitions of the two superpowers and the main way ahead lay in uniting the Third World against them and in seeking to win over the Second World. The *People's Daily* then explained why in attacking the two superpowers it was essential to focus upon the Soviet Union. The arguments about the relative decline of the United States were repeated. It was now said to be on the defensive. The Soviet Union as a younger imperialist power was on the offensive and, just as historically such powers tended to be more ambitious and rapacious, so it was true today. Second, because it was economically comparatively weaker it has to spend proportionately more of its total national income on military equipment and it necessarily has to rely more on its military power to achieve its aims. Third, as a monopoly capitalist country it is far more centralised than its rival and it is therefore more able to militarise the economy and imbue its people with militarism and great-nation chauvinism. Fourth, the Chinese argued that, precisely because it still dons the cloak of socialism and the mantle of Lenin, the Soviet leadership can use the prestige of the Soviet Union having been the first socialist country so as to effectively deceive others as to its true character. These were the main reasons why it would be wrong to fail to differentiate between the two superpowers.

The First World

Instead of proceeding with a close analysis of this theoretical article I now propose to examine China's foreign policy within the framework of the three worlds theory. As indicated above, the Chinese regard both superpowers as imperialist countries and, although initially they defined superpower in behavioural terms only, by the time of the enunciation of the three worlds theory they had come to define it in full accord with Lenin's five pertinent criteria for identifying a capitalist country at the imperialist stage.[14] As we have seen, the Chinese identify the Soviet Union as the more aggressive of the two superpowers and as the main source of war in the world today. It is this which has provided the theoretical rationale for having better relations with the Americans than with the Russians and for regarding the American forces in the Far East as principally a countervailing power against the Russians. In fact, however, as the Russian military presence in the Soviet Far East stabilised at between 40 and 45 divisions, or about a quarter of their military might, in 1973 the Chinese began to claim that they no longer thought that the Soviet Union was about to attack China. They argued that the main Russian military threat was to Europe. This line was first advanced in public by Chou En-lai at the Tenth Party Congress in the summer of 1973.[15] Still later the Chinese leaders claimed that even in the Far East the Russian forces in the first instance were directed against the Americans and the Japanese, and only secondarily against China. This was partly because the Chinese held that the principal Russian adversary was America, and partly because they were well prepared to fight a popular war of defence. At the same time in their domestic propaganda the Chinese continually stressed the danger of possible Soviet military intervention in China's border provinces such as Sinkiang, Inner Mongolia and even Manchuria.[16]

Chinese publications hardly ever discuss questions of defence openly, but in the context of the campaign to discredit Lin Piao they discussed in 1974 his alleged mistakes in handling the main forces in the large-scale battles of the civil war in 1948-9 in terms which suggested that these had a contemporary significance. These analyses of the civil war campaigns could be seen as implying that a conventional Soviet military attack would be met not by military withdrawal so as to fight a people's war (although that was not excluded), but by early engagements with the main forces, especially while the Soviet force was on the move and before it had stabilised itself.[17] Presumably this would apply particularly to any possible Soviet attempts to detach territory from China. It is not without significance in this regard that the Chinese have purchased at the cost of £100 million advanced aircraft engines from Britain to be manufactured in China under licence. They have also purchased helicopters from France and West Germany. Typically, the Chinese have purchased this advanced weaponry from Second World countries rather than the United States.

China's leaders, however, have continually stressed both privately and publicly that the focal point of Soviet imperial interest is Europe, and linked with that is the Middle East, Africa and the Indian Ocean. In

China's view it was the Soviet Union which was taking the strategic initiative by continually increasing its forces in Europe while seeking to assuage the Europeans with talk of *détente*. The Chinese have therefore not only energetically encouraged measures towards West European unity and greater self-defence, but they have also come to regard NATO in a positive light too. The Chinese recognise that the West European countries could not hope to defend themselves without the United States, but they maintain that the effectiveness of the American military presence will only be credible if the West Europeans display a certain capacity of self-defence.

Some have argued that there are obvious reasons for the Chinese to emphasise the dangers allegedly posed by the Soviet Union in Europe. The greater the tensions in Europe, the more difficult it is for the Soviet Union to concentrate its military might in the Far East against China. While in one sense this may be true, it would be wrong to assume *a priori* that this is the only reason for China's concern. As we have seen, the Chinese regard the Soviet Union as an imperialist predator with a global appetite that is not limited by geography. Moreover, in the Chinese view the principal adversary of the Soviet Union is the United States. Europe is perhaps more vital to the two superpowers than any other region. Europe is central to the global balance between them and indeed to the continued viability of their own domestic systems. But militarily Europe is weak, even though the EEC controls more than half the world's trade. These are the kinds of considerations which the Chinese have taken into account rather than their own parochial security concerns.

One problem which has preoccupied China's leaders from 1973 onwards was the extent to which successive American leaders have been prepared to give way to Soviet pressures in their bilateral relations. Thus the former American Secretary of State, Dr Kissinger, was known to have regarded *détente* as a means by which the changing power relations between the two superpowers, in which the Americans were conceding their post-war position of superiority, could be managed without conflict. Thus the Chinese were particularly critical of the so-called Sonnenfeldt Doctrine, by which the former counsellor to the US State Department reportedly argued that the Americans should seek to strengthen Soviet dominance in Eastern Europe so that the relationship would become a more 'organic' one. In Sonnenfeldt's view (which was said to 'faithfully reflect' that of Kissinger), such an 'organic' relationship would strengthen stability in Europe. The Chinese regarded this as a manifestation of appeasement.[18] Chinese commentaries in the latter half of 1977 continually stressed the dangers of a new Munich type of appeasement. Their strictures have not been confined to any particular American administration.

These doubts about American firmness began to surface in 1973 and they were also related to Chinese suspicions that the Americans were taking the Chinese position for granted in the complex relationship which was emerging between the three great powers. The most vivid indication of America's relative strategic disdain for China was the agreement of the newly nominated President Ford and his Secretary of State Kissinger to resume the SALT summit with the Soviet leaders in Vladivostok in November 1974. 'Vladivostok' in Russian means 'Star of the East' and it was the chief port in the Far East by which the Russian Tsars had sought to dominate north-east Asia. It has an older Chinese name and it is one of the strategic sites in the vast area of the Soviet Far East which was taken by the Russians from the Chinese Empire in the nineteenth century by imperialist unequal treaties. A more sensitive site for Chinese nationalistic sensibilities could not have been chosen. The fact that the leaders of the two superpowers were to resume their bilateral SALT negotiations — an aspect of their relationship much hated and feared by the Chinese, as it emphasised their general strategic dominance — only added insult to injury. After the summit Kissinger visited China for the seventh time, but this was the first occasion on which he did not meet Chairman Mao. His explanations on SALT did not convince the Chinese leaders. A month later the *People's Daily* dismissed the new agreement as simply 'new emulation rules for their next round of nuclear arms race'. The paper even suggested that 'this scrap of paper' involved self-deception. In other words, the Chinese leaders were implying that the American leadership was naïve.

Related to this is the Chinese view of the inevitability of war. With impeccable Leninist logic the Chinese have consistently maintained in the 1970s that because of their imperialist nature the contention between the two superpowers is 'absolute and protracted, whereas collusion is relative and temporary'.[19] Short of a revolution in America and Russia this coming war can only be postponed but not averted. In all their statements and communications with the leaders of other countries the Chinese have consistently warned that internationally the situation is marked by heightened tension. Therefore the only way ahead in the Chinese view is to be vigilant and to be prepared for a war that may be unleashed by the Soviet Union. The pursuit of *détente* and the making of concessions towards the Soviet Union in the Chinese view is counter-productive and is nothing more than appeasement. As the

Chinese never tire from pointing out in any forum, the Soviet Union, like the United States, is a paper tiger and it is necessary to stand up to it and expose what they consider to be its true essence. The Chinese have been delighted by the expulsion of Soviet personnel and influence from Egypt, the Sudan and Somalia as examples of countries who had accepted Soviet aid in a big way only to throw it out as they discovered that the aid did not work to their advantage and that their independence was under threat. The Chinese have also noted that many influential voices in the West have been alerted to the danger of the Soviet military build-up. Nevertheless, as we shall see, the Chinese have not generally been successful in persuading Western and Third World political leaders that war is inevitable and that the pursuit of *détente* is a dangerous illusion.

The Soviet Union

The bilateral relationship between the two countries has been more complex than the Chinese theoretical view of the Soviet Union might suggest at first sight. For one thing, as Mao told Kosygin when he saw him for the last time in 1969, it is possible to improve their state-to-state relations but the ideological conflict will continue for ever. And indeed their mutual trade has increased considerably, although it is still only a tiny proportion of their respective overall figures for foreign trade. Thus the value of total two-way trade, which in 1970 stood at only 42 million roubles, had increased by 1973 to 224 and in 1976 to about 400 million roubles. Peking-Moscow flights were inaugurated on 30 January 1974 under the terms of a July 1973 agreement. More interestingly, the two sides have been able to reach temporary agreements regarding navigation on the boundary rivers. Their negotiations in this regard have often ended in deadlock but from time to time agreement has been reached; a case in point is that reached on 6 December 1977.[20]

With regard to the disputed border itself, no real progress has been achieved. Despite repeated negotiations, even of a protracted nature, the deadlock has been unresolved. Notionally the framework for a settlement exists as both sides have indicated their readiness to sign a non-aggression pact and a treaty along the lines of the 'Five Principles of Peaceful Coexistence'. Moreover, the dispute is recognised by both sides as a border one rather than a dispute over sovereignty over large tracts of land. At present the Chinese have suggested that, as a prelude to an agreement and to give substance to a non-aggression pact, both sides should withdraw their military forces from the disputed border areas.

The Soviet side has consistently rejected this. The Chinese have also proposed that any agreement should incorporate a Soviet declaration that the previous basis for the border was unequal treaties imposed on China by Tsarist Russia. This too has been rejected by the Soviet side. Following the death of Chairman Mao (whom the Russians have consistently regarded as personally responsible for the deterioration in Sino-Soviet relations), a new set of border negotiations began amid rumours from East European sources that a breakthrough was imminent within a month. The Chinese, however, let it be known on 16 December 1976 that the talks were bound to fail and in consequence Sino-Soviet relations would deteriorate even further.[21] The Chinese revealed to a visiting Japanese delegation in Heilungkiang (the most northerly province in Manchuria) that in that section of the border alone there had been 9,000 Soviet violations and attacks on Chinese citizens in the area during the fifteen-year period 1960 to 1975. And in the period January to August 1976 there had been 150 violations. Soviet manoeuvres were said to be continually being held along the border.[22]

Sino-Soviet bilateral relations, however, take place within a global and a regional context, but especially within a trilateral framework which includes the United States. The Chinese are obviously aware of Western appreciations which identify an interrelationship between the European and Far Eastern theatres of the confrontation with the Soviet Union. The Chinese have always reacted sharply to what they perceive as Western moves to stabilise the European sector through concessions so as to encourage the Soviet Union to move eastwards.[23] But they are also aware of Western apprehensions lest China and the Soviet Union should improve their relations to such an extent as to alter the current balance of power. Of greater concern to the Chinese leaders is that China should be placed in a disadvantageous situation as a result of collusion between the two superpowers and should be used as a pawn in the struggle between the two. One example of this has already been referred to, namely the SALT agreements in Vladivostok. Indeed it was precisely after that occasion that Leonid Brezhnev went to Ulan Bator to celebrate the 50th anniversary of Mongolian independence from Chinese rule, and there rejected Chinese proposals for reaching a border agreement. A further example was the flurry of Soviet moves after Mao's death to suggest that Sino-Soviet relations were on the point of breakthrough. The Chinese openly revealed to Western correspondents in Peking that these, accompanied by the Soviet-inspired rumours on the border talks, were no more than another gesture designed to win concessions for Russia from the United States by making Washington fear a Sino-Soviet *rapprochement*.[24]

The complexity of the power relations should not be seen, however, as negating the significance of the framework of analysis with which the Chinese understand international politics and the place of the Soviet Union within it. Even if the Chinese were to judge that the Americans were conceding too much to the Soviet Union there is no sign that the Chinese would seek to reactivate the Sino-Soviet alliance. But they may in such a situation look for alternative ways of containing Soviet expanding power. Since the Chinese are fond of drawing analogies between the present international situation and that of the late 1930s, they must have paid attention to the Soviet-Nazi Non-Aggression Pact of 1939. It is possible to envisage a situation in which the Chinese might despair of American pusillanimity to such an extent that they may seek such a measure. In this context it is worth noting that the 1939 pact ended two years later with an invasion of the Soviet Union.

In reflecting upon the pattern of Sino-Soviet relations, it is important to consider the peculiarity of the threat posed to China by the Soviet Union. It is different from that posed by the Americans in the 1950s and 1960s. The main political threat was that the United States might seek to reinstate Chiang Kai-shek in China proper. The last time China's leaders genuinely felt threatened by such a possibility was in 1962. Since that time the main issue has not been how to deal with an attack from Taiwan but rather how to 'liberate' the island. Basically the main fear of the United States arose from its military might and its ability to inflict damage upon China. At the same time the United States and China did not have basic clashes of fundamental strategic interests. They did not share common boundaries. The United States in the Far East is basically a maritime power while China is a continental one. Neither need be the principal adversary of the other. In many respects they share common interests in the Far East, at least in the short term. They both oppose any further increase in Soviet influence in the area; they both favour the emergence of a local regional balance of forces in south-east Asia; they both favour the prospect of a continued independent and prosperous Japan. America's continued intervention in Taiwan (which in China's view originally arose from a period of offensive imperialism now past) is the major stumbling block to the normalisation of relations between China and the United States. While China would like to see American troops vacate South Korea, China's leaders have encouraged the Japanese to maintain the American military presence in Japan — at least for the present.

The Soviet Union, by contrast, represents a very different challenge.

China and the Soviet Union share a common disputed border. There is a long history of conflict between the two countries going back to the seventeenth century. Regionally in the Far East they have long been strategic adversaries. The Russian people and government have deep forebodings about the emergence of a strong China and as we have seen there have been times of encouragement of a yellow peril myth about China. Their ideological differences have long reached the point where they may be said to espouse two distinctly separate and different ideologies. Nevertheless these two ideologies stem from the same roots and claim the same founding fathers. Therefore as seen from Peking the danger from Russia is both a military and a political one. The military threat involves the possibility of armed attack at many levels from all-out war through to limited armed incursions. This can only be met by continually ensuring that China is militarily prepared to deal adequately with the variety of military threats presented by the Soviet side. To this end the Chinese have displayed a readiness to purchase advanced military equipment from the West Europeans. The political threat as seen from Peking is of helping China to change colour and turn revisionist along similar lines to the Soviet Union. Moreover, there is a danger of Soviet subversion, most obviously in the border regions but also through association with disaffected leaders in Peking. The Chinese point to the major political struggles in Peking since 1949 as having a Soviet connection. Moreover, it is only by attacking Soviet practices that the Chinese have been able to clarify the operative distinctions between revisionism and true Marxism-Leninism.

It seems unlikely, however, that the Chinese would seek to turn to the Soviet Union in the way that there is a tacit reliance upon the United States as a countervailing power to the other superpower on the basis of identifying common points of interest while acknowledging differences on other issues. This does not exclude, however, the possibility of improving state relations to such an extent that there may be a relaxation of tensions on the Sino-Soviet border.

The United States

The bilateral relationship between the two countries from a Chinese perspective is a complicated one. As we have seen, the Chinese readiness to develop a limited *détente* was based upon their appreciation of American relative strategic decline to a fundamentally defensive position as compared with a more offensive and assertive Soviet threat. It was also based upon a mutual recognition that, especially in East Asia, they had certain points in common. At the same time, the Chinese have consistently opposed America as an imperialist superpower on a global scale. When on the basis of interviews in Peking William Hinton wrote that the Chinese sought to 'neutralise' the United States, this was quickly denied by the Chinese authorities. The Chinese explanation is still that advanced in 1971, namely that it is a question of exploiting the contradictions between the primary and the secondary imperialist power. Chou En-lai conceded the difficulties in distinguishing on the surface between Soviet-American and Sino-American talks. But he nevertheless asserted the importance of doing so, when he reported to the Tenth Party Congress:

> We should point out here that necessary compromises between revolutionary countries and imperialist countries must be distinguished from collusion and compromise between Soviet revisionism and US imperialism. Lenin put it well: 'There are compromises and compromises. One must be able to analyse the situation and the concrete conditions of each compromise or of each variety of compromise. One must learn to distinguish between a man who gave the bandits money and firearms in order to lessen the damage they can do to facilitate their capture and execution, and a man who gives money and firearms in order to share in the loot.'

On a global level the Chinese have repeatedly denounced American imperialism, but with less frequency, intensity and harshness than with regard to the Soviet Union. The point of Chinese criticisms is directed against essentially Soviet military expansionism. Even the acquisition by the United States of naval base facilities in Diego Garcia in the Indian Ocean — a development much criticised by other Asian states — was turned into an occasion for more of an anti-Soviet polemic. The main thrust of the Chinese argument was that, given the superpower contention for hegemony, the United States was bound to respond to the strong expansion of Soviet naval forces in the Indian Ocean.[25]

As we have seen, strategically at both the regional and the global level China's leaders regard the United States as primarily a countervailing power to the Soviet Union. In this regard the Chinese have had occasion to feel disquiet by what they have identified as appeasing tendencies on the American side. As a result, from 1974 Chinese attitudes towards the United States have noticeably cooled. In the first flush of enthusiasm after the first Nixon visit the two sides soon agreed to establish liaison offices in their respective capitals and trade blossomed. In 1973 it reached the value of $800 million and in 1974 it even exceeded the $1,000 million mark, to reach about the same level as Soviet-American trade. But the trade was badly imbalanced since Chinese exports barely reached a tenth of that figure. It was inevitable, therefore, that the value of trade would decline after that. But although the trade gradually became better balanced it is at a much lower level and there are no immediate indications that it is likely to rise. With regard to agricultural products, the Chinese have since preferred to import from Australia and Canada, and in advanced technology the West Europeans and Japan have preference.

Another stumbling block is Taiwan. The Chinese argue that the Americans have repeatedly reneged on their commitment to withdraw militarily from the island. They claimed that Kissinger had promised to do this within two years when the Shanghai Communiqué was first signed in February 1972. They later claimed that former President Ford had committed the United States to withdrawal after the November 1976 Presidential elections.[26]

There appeared to be two conflicting interpretations of the terms of the Shanghai Communiqué. The Chinese side evidently saw it as a self-fulfilling agreement by which the Americans committed themselves to withdraw altogether from Taiwan. Apart from the question of troop withdrawals, the American side appears to regard itself as free of the kind of commitment specified by the Chinese. China's leaders have repeatedly stated that the Americans must withdraw all their military forces and installations, abrogate the 1954 Security Treaty and sever all formal state relations with the island. That would bring to an end American intervention in Chinese sovereign affairs. The Chinese have suggested that the Americans could follow the Japanese solution by which effective trade relations have been maintained and consular functions are performed by an unofficial body. The American leadership, however, has maintained that it has a moral responsibility to the people on Taiwan and it has sought to persuade Peking to undertake to liberate the island by peaceful means only. To concede that would be to formally accept a limitation upon Chinese sovereignty. The Chinese have refused to yield at all on such an issue of principle since the 1950s and they are hardly likely to yield now.

The issue was joined in the visit to Peking by the US Secretary of State, Cyrus Vance, in August 1977. The Chinese side may have been prepared to agree yet again that American withdrawal could be further postponed, provided that the essential principles of their position were not challenged. But Vance asked for flexibility on the Chinese part and presented various possible options. Teng Hsiao-p'ing, China's chief negotiator, turned these all down and declared bluntly that Sino-American relations had suffered a setback. When assured by Vance that America was strategically superior to the Soviet Union, Teng simply told him: 'We Chinese people do not believe it.'[27] Thus Sino-American relations have declined since their high watermark of 1972 and 1973. Nevertheless the essential political-strategic evaluations that initially led to the Nixon visit still apply. Despite the repercussions of the Vance visit the American administration still claims that Sino-American relations are based on the Shanghai Communiqué. Although there is a possibility that these relations might founder on the Taiwan question, that stage had not yet been reached by the end of 1977. It does seem, though, that now the issue has been brought into the limelight, Sino-American relations are unlikely to improve until the American side accepts China's principles for its final withdrawal.

The Second World

As Ten Hsiao-p'ing put it in his UN speech, 'the case of the developed countries in between the superpowers and the developing countries is a complicated one.' In the Chinese view these countries are dominated by their own monopoly capitalists but at the same time they are struggling against superpower controls, threats or bullying. Yet some others are dependencies of the Soviet Union struggling for independence. In many ways they still seek to exploit Third World countries, but they are not the main force doing so and quite frequently in their own interests they are compelled 'to make certain concessions to Third World countries or to give some support to the Third World's struggle against hegemonism or to remain neutral'.[28] In the Chinese view, the Western countries in the last three decades have moved out from US domination. They cite the development of the EEC, the passive or critical attitudes of these countries to the American war in Indo-China, the collapse of the dollar-centred monetary system and other examples to illustrate this. To be sure, the Chinese recognise 'the thousand and one ties' which still exist between these countries and the United States; likewise they acknowledge the need of the West Europeans and the Japanese to rely on the American protective umbrella. But in the Chinese view, 'so long as the United States continues its policy of control they will not cease in their struggle against such control and for equal partnership.'[29]

As we have seen, the Chinese do not think there are any imminent prospects for revolution in the Second World. Accordingly they regard the primary task at the present time as the defence of the national independence of such countries, especially in Europe.

The Chinese themselves have greatly expanded their trade with Second World countries in the 1970s. It virtually quadrupled in the five years after 1971. Moreover, the trade with the countries of Western Europe, Canada, Australasia and Japan takes up more than 50 per cent of China's total foreign trade. It is from these countries primarily that China has imported advanced technology and it is from them too that China has purchased components for advanced weapons systems.[30]

Extended political contacts with the leaders of these countries have become a feature of China's foreign policy in the 1970s. There are but few Western European countries whose Ministers and leading politicians have not visited Peking. The Chinese have paid particular attention to the EEC. They look forward more ardently than the most committed European Federalist to the day when political union will take place and when the EEC will also become an effective self-defence community. China's leaders, however, have come to appreciate some of the difficulties involved in the process and accordingly embarrass their European friends less. A greater problem has arisen from the fact that not one of the West European governments has accepted the Chinese view of the Soviet danger to Europe or of the probability of war.

Periodically official Chinese commentaries in the 1970s have pointed to the capitalist nature of West Europe and to the operation of class conflict in European countries. Their rulers, monopoly capitalists, were said to be shifting the burdens of the economic crisis on to the backs of the masses of the working people. The Communist parties of Western Europe were dismissed as revisionist organs which would be repudiated by the people in time. The Chinese have continued to reject the proposition that the transition to socialism could be effected without armed struggle. The changes in Portugal in 1974-5 were accordingly regarded with grave suspicion. Since the Chinese regard the social-democratic labour parties in the West as thoroughly bourgeois, they do not as a rule allow for much difference between them and the Conservative parties, even on ideological grounds. But on balance the Chinese seem to prefer to deal with governments led by conservative leaders. It is not only that they tend to be more solidly against the Soviet Union and to prefer more defence preparedness, but it is also because in the Chinese view they are more reliable and predictable. Most of the Labour social-democratic parties have powerful elements within them who since the days of the Cold War have tended to regard the Soviet Union as not wholly an antagonistic power and have regarded the possibility of closer relations with the Soviet Union as preferable to strengthening defence alignment with the United States. Indeed, many of them feel antipathetic to the United States and oppose many aspects of the capitalist system under which they live. As a result many of the West European leaders most liked by the Chinese have tended to belong more to the right wing of the political spectrum.

Thus, politicians like Mr Heath and Mrs Thatcher of Britain or Franz Joseph Strauss of West Germany, and generals from both France and West Germany, have been particularly welcome visitors to Peking. This, coupled with Chinese support for NATO, the EEC and its line in the Third World countries, which has not led to a disassociation from reactionary regimes, has not enhanced China's popularity among the left in Europe. Membership of Chinese-supported Marxist-Leninist groups has been tiny and entirely marginal to the working class in Europe.

In sum, the Chinese attitude to the Second World is complex. In a sense the Second World is identified as playing a role analogous to that of the petit bourgeoisie and the national bourgeoisie in the four-bloc united front which Mao held to be of such importance in the liberation of China. Like all analogies, this too is not entirely appropriate, but it does give a better understanding of the Chinese point of view than any attempts at the seemingly more purist Marxist analysis which would stress the domestic socio-economic systems as fundamentally determining the external roles of the countries concerned. The Chinese view of the Second World as a middle ground to be won over makes sense only if the two main contradictions of the First World are regarded as the most important in world affairs. This is particularly true if one regards the contradiction between the two superpowers (but especially the Soviet Union) on the one hand, and the people of the world on the other, as the principal contradiction in the world today. That is the contradiction to which all the others are subordinate.

The Third World

China's policies towards the Third World countries reflected its long-standing declaratory positions. Their common identity has been continually stressed, as has been their putative revolutionary international role. The Chinese view has already been described in this and previous chapters so that here will be developed only those analytical points which help to clarify China's view of the world and her place within it.

In his UN speech Teng outlined this view succinctly:

The numerous developing countries have long suffered from colonialist and imperialist oppression and exploitation. They have won political independence, yet all of them still face the historic task of

cleaning out the remnant forces of colonialism, developing the
national economy and consolidating national independence. These
countries cover vast territories, encompass a large population and
abound in natural resources. Having suffered the heaviest oppression,
they have the strongest desire to oppose oppression and seek liberation and development. In the struggle for national liberation and independence, they have demonstrated immense power and continually won splendid victories. They constitute a revolutionary motive
force propelling the wheel of world history and are the main force
combating colonialism, imperialism and particularly the superpowers.

In addition to AALA countries the Chinese also include the three
Balkan countries, Albania, Romania and Yugoslavia, in this category.
While acknowledging that many of the governments of the states concerned which cover a whole range of social systems are reactionary and
even compradors of one or other of the two superpowers, the Chinese
have consistently opposed any attempts to differentiate them into the
more or less reactionary and the more or less progressive. Such distinctions only divide Third World countries against each other and provide
opportunities for Soviet penetration. Likewise the Chinese have rejected
any moves to subdivide the Third World into yet a poorer 'Fourth
World'. As the former Chinese Foreign Minister Chiao Kuan-hua
observed to the 1975 Session of the UN General Assembly:

> It is true that among the developing countries some are in greatest
> need. Other countries should give them more help, and they have
> already begun to do so. The neediest and other developing countries
> share common experiences and face common tasks. To call the
> neediest countries the 'fourth world' is groundless or ill-intentioned.[31]

He went on to observe tersely,

> There are no saviours in the world. To develop the national
> economy, a country must persist in independence and self-reliance.
> Political independence is not won easily, so it is essential to give play
> to state sovereignty to eliminate gradually but firmly the forces of
> imperialism and all forces of colonialism and neo-colonialism.

The Chinese view as to the future path for Third World countries is
simple and straightforward. Basically they should stress independence,
control of their own resources, self-reliance, especially in agriculture,

mutual help and aid that is both practical and in accordance with the perceived needs of the recipient. In particular they stress the need for unity. To this end, the Chinese support the attempts at regionalism, such as the Association of South East Asian Nations or the Organization of African Unity, and they also support the attempts of Third World commodity producers to unite together on the model of OPEC. This would help to break through even further 'the international economic monopoly long maintained by imperialism'. As we shall see, however, there has never been any suggestion that China itself would join such an association. That would compromise China's autonomy as a socialist country.

In many ways China has emerged as the most important articulator of Third World needs and aspirations. This has been true of China's performance in the United Nations and the major UN Conferences on the Law of the Sea, on Population, on Food, etc. China has long held most of the principles recently taken up by Third World countries. Furthermore, an increasing number of Third World countries are coming round to accepting some elements of the Chinese view of the two superpowers. The Chinese have also found vindication for their view that even when Third World countries are seduced by Soviet blandishments these countries frequently end up by resisting them because quite simply these blandishments come to be seen to be so oppressive and demanding in their implications. The examples of Egypt, Sudan and Somalia are frequently cited in this regard. Chinese commentators have been able increasingly to identify even in India signs of dissatisfaction with the Soviet relationship.[32] As against this China's policies in Angola, which at one stage seemed to place them on the same side as the Americans and the South Africans, did some damage to China's revolutionary image among the more radical African countries. Yet it may be doubted whether this will have long-lasting effects. The Chinese have avoided establishing a dominant influence in any single African country. They have also indicated that they are unlikely to follow up the successful conclusion of the TanZam railway with any other similar huge aid projects. The Chinese thus pose no threat to any African country, but they have been and will continue to be a useful source of disinterested and effective supportive aid. The implications of all this for China's new role in world affairs will be examined more closely in the final chapter.

The Asia Pacific Region

From a Chinese perspective the changes which had occurred in the world balance of forces and indeed in the structure of world politics affected this region in a number of important ways. The relative decline of American global dominance since the Second World War was marked first in this area. After all, this decline was proved on the battlegrounds of Indo-China. And the first apparent alignment of China and America occurred over the 1971 war on the Indian subcontinent, when Nixon prevailed over his State Department bureaucracy to order the 'tilt' against India. Likewise it was Nixon's visit to China which brought in its wake Japan's recognition of Peking and still later recognition from Australia and New Zealand.

But perhaps the deepest and most subtle repercussions were felt in south-east Asia. The Paris Agreements of January 1973, followed two-and-a-half years later by the total defeat of America's client regimes in Indo-China, indicated not only American decline in the area but the removal of this region (or at least that substantial part of it which was west of the Pacific rim) in the American view from the arena of its central balance of power conflicts with the Soviet Union. Locally, this meant that the externally derived Cold War alignments were removed from the region. While Westerners speculated about the possible new balances of power which might emerge in the region, the Chinese warned the countries in the area lest in seeing out the American tiger from the front door they let in the Russian wolf through the back door. These changes also meant the emergence of what the Chinese call 'problems left over from history'. In other words the trends, conflicts and problems which were taking place before the colonial interventions in the previous century would now reappear.[33] This reappearance, however, would take place in modern circumstances and with due allowance for the changes which had occurred at the domestic, regional and global levels. The basic Chinese position was that, as the countries concerned were all members of the Third World, any resulting conflicts should be settled through negotiations rather than by military means; the latter would only work to superpower advantage.

Until this period one of China's principal concerns in south-east Asia was to prevent American dominance and the establishment of offensive military bases in countries actually bordering China. But as the result of perceived changes in America's global and regional position, China's views changed. Meanwhile the governments in the area also had to respond to these changes, even though they were not necessarily perceived in the same way as by China.

It was thus seemingly paradoxical, but not really unexpected, that among the last countries to normalise relations with China should be her neighbours, the member states of ASEAN. These largely anti-Communist states with significant Chinese overseas minorities and with ongoing insurgency problems had been suspicious and antagonistic to China for nearly twenty years. But the changes in China's foreign policy, its international recognition as a full participatory member of the diplomatic community, the relative decline of the United States marked especially by its defeats in Indo-China, and the general changes in international affairs meant that here too changes would occur. The pace was necessarily slow. But the ice was broken with Malaysia in 1974, followed by the Philippines and Thailand in 1975. The Prime Minister of Singapore visited China in 1976, where he found understanding of Singapore's special position as a city-state with a population of 97 per cent ethnic Chinese, so that recognition would be delayed. Indonesia had still not reopened diplomatic relations by the end of 1977, but the Chinese have made known their desire to do so and the two countries are gradually moving in that direction.[34]

Some of the difficulties in the new relationships could be discerned when privately China's leaders disclaimed involvement with the insurgents in these countries while at the same time China's media continued to endorse the activities and declarations of these movements. This became most apparent on China's National Day of 1 October 1974. The foreign guests listed as seated at the main table of Chou En-lai's National Day reception included two Burmese Communist Party leaders (ranked second in the list after Prince Sihanouk and before the Vietnamese), and a leader of the Indonesian Communist Party (fourth). This unusual distinction was followed by the prominent publication of messages of greetings on National Day from the Central Committees of the Communist parties of Malaya (N.B. not Malaysia), Ceylon (not Sri Lanka), Indonesia and Thailand. The Chinese could hardly claim that this was exclusively a question of party-to-party relations since the occasion of the celebrations was a state rather than a party one.

This was the one area in the world where revolutionary movements were following the Maoist way of engaging in armed struggle in the countryside under the leadership of genuine Marxist-Leninist parties. As self-conscious Marxist-Leninists the Chinese were necessarily bound to support them. At the same time, China's support was largely moral and ideological. China's relations with the countries of Indo-China and with North Korea continued to follow a strictly correct policy of total commitment and support. All these countries were independent of China and there were no attempts to cajole or dragoon them into strictly following the Chinese line.

   The victories of the revolutionaries of Indo-China, however, brought about a new situation. As we have seen, Vietnam has largely followed the Soviet line in international affairs and Soviet aid, which had played a primary role in the war, began to play an important role in Vietnam's plans for economic rehabilitation. Nevertheless, as Mao pointed out, 'the Vietnamese had not been fighting the French and then the Americans for thirty years only to be run by the Russians.'[35] At the same time it should be recognised that among 'the problems left over from history' were Vietnamese fears of being controlled from China. After all, many of the great heroes celebrated in Vietnamese history had won fame by acts of resistance to invading Chinese from previous eras. Likewise the new Cambodian revolutionary leaders suspected that the Vietnamese Communists were still motivated by traditional Vietnamese expansionist ambitions to dominate the whole of Indo-China. Moreover, the Cambodian-Vietnamese border had been settled by the colonial French over and against contemporary Cambodian protests. The Chinese in 1972 had let it be known that they were opposed to a situation in which Indo-China would be dominated by any single country (in practice Vietnam).[36] Given the fact, too, that after the 1970 *coup* the Soviet Union had given recognition to the Lon Nol regime, thereby incurring the enmity of Prince Sihanouk and the eventual victors, the Khmer Rouge, it was hardly surprising that China developed close relations with Cambodia (or Kampuchea as it preferred to be called after the revolutionary victory in 1975).

   Thus China has acted as an important (though not necessarily decisive) influence on Cambodian foreign policy. It was instrumental in getting the Thai and Khmer governments to reach certain agreements despite continuous border skirmishes. The border conflict and the major fighting between Cambodia and Vietnam raised more serious problems for China, as the Cambodians charged it carried with it implications of possible Vietnamese dominance of their country and hence of Indo-China as a whole. There were also the ramifications of bringing the Sino-Soviet conflict more deeply into the region. The Soviets had good relations with Vietnam and none at all with Cambodia; whereas there were irridentist claims between China and Vietnam and the Vietnamese supported the Soviet position on many international issues on which the Chinese held diametrically opposed views. And as we have seen, Chinese-Cambodian relations were close, partly because of the Vietnamese and Soviet factors. On the other hand, Sino-Vietnamese relations were not antagonistic. In 1977, for example, apparently cordial visits to Peking were paid by the famous war hero

Marshal Giap in the early summer and then later in the year by the General Secretary of the Party, Le Duan. To be sure, important differences between the two sides continued to exist, but there were also important areas of common understanding. The Chinese, therefore, had a clear interest in trying to get the two countries to settle their differences. But having eschewed the great-power practice of establishing spheres of influence near their borders by dominating their smaller neighbours economically, politically and militarily, this is no simple task for Chinese statesmanship. Nevertheless, armed inter-state conflict in Peking's view can only have the effect in the long run of paving the way for Soviet interference and intervention.

In some ways this may be regarded as a role normally played by a great power in its own region. As was pointed out early in this chapter, the impressive use of force by the Chinese in early 1974 to dislodge the intruding forces of the Thieu regime of South Vietnam from the Hsi Sha (Paracel) Islands was an example to all governments in the area that the Chinese were capable of resorting to the use of overwhelming power if challenged on questions of sovereignty. Many of the countries in the area are familiar with the great-power role China had played in the past and they are all conscious of China as the permanent great power present in south-east and east Asia. Yet as we have seen, the Chinese have not sought to act as a conventional great power, demanding exclusive spheres of influence on its periphery. Nor has China sought to dominate the lesser countries on its borders. Thus with regard to the disputed islands in the South China Sea (concerning principally the Nan Sha or Spratly Islands group), which are variously claimed by the PRC, Vietnam, the Philippines and the Taiwan authorities, the Chinese have indicated a readiness to negotiate.

China's relations with Japan have continued to be determined by special factors. In addition to the historical experience of the 1930s and the 1940s, notice should be taken of the fact that China's trade with Japan continued to be greater than with any other single country, and that regularly the number of Japanese who visit China easily exceeds the total from the rest of the world combined together. The strategic considerations and the question of Taiwan have already been discussed in this chapter. Fortunately, from a Chinese perspective the Russians have made it exceedingly difficult for the Japanese to approach their two great neighbours on an even-handed basis. For example, after a certain prevarication the Japanese had indicated their willingness to participate in the development of Siberia through capital loans and technical assistance, but the Russians placed so many practical difficulties in their way that very little progress was made. Also, by taking a hard line on the four islands south of the Kurile Islands (which in any case had not been granted the Soviet Union by the terms of the 1945 Yalta Agreements), the Russians have made it impossible for the Japanese leaders to make progress in improving their relations.

Sino-Japanese relations have made considerable progress. As the result of complex negotiations agreements have been reached on aviation, fishing and shipping. All these constituted setbacks to the right-wing pro-Taiwan lobby in Japan. Moreover, Sino-Japanese relations have been marked by great complexity and subtlety regarding the question of oil supplies from China, the transfer of oil exploration and downstream technology to China, and above all the potential allocation of rights to the continental shelf.[37]

Thus, despite the long delay in effecting an agreement on a treaty of peace and amity because of the controversial anti-hegemony clause insisted upon by the Chinese, Sino-Japanese relations, now that China is firmly embarked upon a programme of economic modernisation, are likely to get even closer.

The Chinese categorisation of the three worlds has provided a framework and a key with which to understand China's new foreign policy. The issues posed by the two superpowers have provided a clear connecting thread between the various facets of China's foreign policy. The different levels of China's foreign policy from orthodox Marxist-Leninist encouragement of revolution, through support of the Third World, the Second World and through to the strategic and tactical usage of power politics, are all bound together by the complex Maoist interpretation of the trends of world politics and by Mao's views of the Soviet Union and the United States.

The main problem which affects the conduct of China's foreign policy arises from its relative weakness as a global power. It is this which leads to the continued sense of marginality which China has in the international system. China's lack of capabilities and the industrial infrastructure necessary to transform it into an effective global power has meant that it has been powerless to make effective contributions in support of its friends and to back up the political line which it has taken in a number of areas in the world such as the Middle East and Africa. As a result its views are often ignored or discounted. Moreover, it can be argued that since the high-water mark of Sino-American relations in 1972-3 the American leadership has progressively come round to the view that its main global issue is the bilateral strategic adversary relationship with the Soviet Union, and China has become of periphery importance.

Nevertheless, China has chalked up a number of significant successes in the Second and Third Worlds, and it could be argued that the Chinese characterisation of the world as dominated by superpower conflict rather than by *détente* and the relaxation of tensions has found increasing support.

Notes

1.   Cited publicly for the first time on 1 November 1977 by the Editorial Department of the *People's Daily* in a 35,000-word article entitled 'Chairman Mao's Theory of the Differentiation of the Three Worlds is a Major Contribution to Marxism-Leninism'. For the official translation see *Peking Review*, No. 45 (1977); the quote is on p. 11. The article simply stated that Chairman Mao had said this in a talk with a leader of a Third World country. An interview with a senior Chinese official (Wang Ping-nan) in *China Now* (November-December 1977) (the journal of the Society for Anglo-Chinese Understanding) revealed that the leader in question was President Kaunda of Zambia. At the time the official New China News Agency stated that President Kaunda, who was then on a visit to China, met with Chairman Mao on 22 February. This occasion was the first time in which a Chinese leader is known to have articulated the theory of the three worlds. It is also interesting to note that this is the only known statement by Chairman Mao espousing the theory. Its publication at this late stage (i.e. more than three-and-a-half years after he made the statement) was obviously the result of the ideological dispute with the Albanians who in the summer of 1977 openly criticised the three worlds theory. Indeed some of their European supporters even questioned whether Chairman Mao himself supported the theory.
2.   Ibid., p. 28.
3.   See for example the speech by China's Foreign Minister of 26 September 1975 to the UN General Assembly, *Peking Review*, No. 40 (1975). For accounts of China and the United Nations see Byron S. Weng, *Peking's UN Policy: Diversity and Change* (Praeger, 1972); Samuel S. Kim, 'The People's Republic of China in the UN: A Preliminary Analysis', *World Politics*, Vol. XVIII, No. 3 (April 1974); William R. Feeney, 'The PRC and the UN, 1971-75', *Current Scene* (H.K.), Vol. XIV, No. 2 (February 1976); William R. Feeney, 'Sino-Soviet Competition in the United Nations', *Asian Survey* (September 1977); and Samuel S. Kim, 'Behavioural Dimensions of Chinese Multilateral Diplomacy', *C.Q.* No. 72 December 1977.
4.   See the congratulatory message of 29 January signed by Mao, Tung Pi-wu, Chu Teh and Chou En-lai in *Peking Review*, No. 5 (1973).
5.   See 'Chou En-lai's Report on the International Situation, March 1973', *Issues and Studies* (Taiwan) (January 1977), pp. 120-7; and 'Outline for Education on Situation for Companies', *Issues and Studies* (Taiwan) (January 1974), pp. 90-108. These documents were allegedly captured by Taiwan sources and as they were published in Taiwan their authenticity cannot be regarded as beyond doubt. Nevertheless, both in terms of their style and content these particular documents seem to be genuine. Hence the

reliance upon them here for identifying Chinese calculations that one would have assumed in any case.

6. See the discussion in Y. Shichor, 'The Middle East in China's Foreign Policy', London University Ph.D. thesis (1976), pp. 387-90.

7. *Peking Review*, No. 45 (1972), p. 22. See also Dick Wilson, 'China and the European Community', *China Quarterly*, No. 56 (October-December 1973), pp. 647-66.

8. *Peking Review*, No. 40 (1972).

9. *Peking Review*, Special Supplement to No. 15 (12 April 1974).

10. See *China Quarterly*, No. 60 (December 1974), Chronicle and Documentation, p. 841, and ibid., No. 63 (September 1975), p. 597.

11. *China Quarterly*, No. 60, Chronicle and Documentation, p. 852.

12. *Zeri i Popullit*, 7 July 1977 editorial, 'The Theory and Practice of Revolution'.

13. Editorial Department of *The People's Daily*, 1 November 1977, 'Chairman Mao's Theory of the Differentiation of the Three Worlds is a Major Contribution to Marxism-Leninism' in *Peking Review*, No. 45 (1977), pp. 10-41.

14. 'If it were necessary to give the briefest possible definition of imperialism we should say that imperialism is the monopoly stage of capitalism.' But for a fuller picture, 'we must give a definition of imperialism that will include the following five of its basic features: 1) the concentration of production and capital has developed to such a high stage that it has created monopolies which play a decisive role in economic life; 2) the merging of bank capital with industrial capital, and the creation on the basis of this "financial capital", of a financial oligarchy; 3) the export of capital as distinguished from the export of commodities acquires exceptional importance; 4) the formation of international monopolist capitalist combines which share the world among themselves; and 5) the territorial division of the whole world among the biggest capitalist powers is completed.' (V.I. Lenin, *Imperialism, The Highest Stage of Capitalism* (FLP), pp. 105-6.) Two substantive Chinese articles have applied this analysis to the Soviet Union, the first by the 'gang of four' writing group 'Liang Hsiao', 'The Economic Base of Social Imperialism' in *Peking Review*, No. 45 (7 November 1975); and after the fall of the 'gang' that by the Institute of World Economy of the Chinese Academy of Social Science, 'Soviet Social-Imperialism − Most Dangerous Source of World War', *Peking Review*, No. 27 (1975). Although there were some differences between the two articles, they both agreed that Lenin's analysis was entirely appropriate.

15. Chou En-lai, 'Political Report to the Tenth National Congress of the CPC', *Peking Review*, Nos. 35-6 (1973).

16. For the clearest statement of China's fears in this regard see Saifudin, 'Sinkiang Advances Triumphantly Under the Guidance of Chairman Mao's Revolutionary Line', *Red Flag*, No. 10 (1975). Abridged in *Peking Review*, No. 42 (1975). In addition to local nationalism which he did not regard as involving an antagonistic contradiction, Saifudin referred to 'national splittists' who were both 'objectively and subjectively' in league with the Soviets across the border. The *People's Daily* editorial on the thirtieth anniversary of the setting up of the Autonomous Region of Inner Mongolia on 31 July also warned of Soviet 'aggression' and 'subversion' and cautioned the armed forces to work with the people and 'be ready at all times to wipe out any enemy who dares to intrude. Inner Mongolia is an inalienable part of our great motherland.' See *Peking Review*, No. 33 (1977), p. 35.

17. See the 1972-4 criticisms of Lin Piao's alleged military strategy at the critical battles of the Civil War in 1948-9, which suggested a contemporary

significance for these observations. See, for example, the articles in *Peking Review*, No. 46 (1972); *Peking Review*, Nos. 38 and 39 (1974). For an analysis see my paper 'Towards a New Strategy: The Military Aspects of the Criticize Lin Piao Criticize Confucius Campaign' prepared for the Toronto Conference 'Another Past, Another Future' of August 1976. Foreign diplomats in Peking at the time also sensed a change in China's strategy; see 'Chinese Debate Ways of Confronting Threats from Russia', *The Times* (London), 31 October 1974.

18. The sharpest Chinese observation in this regard is in the article on the three worlds theory, note 13 above. Also see accompanying note.

19. Chou En-lai, 'Report to the Tenth National Congress of the CPC'.

20. See *The Times* (London), 24 December 1977.

21. *Daily Telegraph*, 17 December 1976.

22. BBC SWB/FE/5394.

23. See Chou En-lai's 'Report to the Tenth Congress of the CPC' and that of Hua Kuo-feng to the Eleventh Congress four years later, *Peking Review*, No. 35 (1977).

24. *Daily Telegraph*, 17 December 1976.

25. New China News Agency, 23 and 27 March 1974.

26. See *China Quarterly*, No. 72 (December 1977), Chronicle and Documentation section on US.

27. Ibid.

28. See *People's Daily* article cited above, note 13, p. 30.

29. Ibid.

30. Joint Economic Committee, Congress of the United States, *China: A Reassessment of the Economy*, 10 July 1975, p. 631, Table 1 and pp. 649-50, Table A6.

31. *Peking Review*, No. 40 (1975).

32. See, for example, 'Soviet Social Imperialism is the Root Cause of Unrest in South Asia' in *Peking Review*, No. 12 (1976).

33. For an analysis of some of these see Milton Osborn, *Region in Revolt* (Pergamon Press, 1970).

34. For example, following a visit to Peking, Premier Somare of Papua New Guinea later visited Indonesia where he revealed on 14 January 1977 that he had been entrusted with a message to the Indonesian leadership that the Chinese leaders desired to establish diplomatic relations if its leaders were prepared to do so. (BBC SWB/FE/5413).

35. Mr Heath's report of his conversations with Chairman Mao, Quarterly Chronicle and Documentation, *China Quarterly*, No. 64 (December 1975), p. 813.

36. See Chou En-lai's observation to a European ambassador cited in Ross Terrill, *800,000,000, The Real China* (Penguin, 1975), p. 235: 'We don't want to see any one country of Indochina dominate the others.'

37. For the best account see Selig S. Harrison, *China, Oil and Asia: Conflict Ahead?* (Columbia University Press, 1977), especially Chapter 7, pp. 146-88.

10 CHINA'S NEW WORLD ROLE

Having described China's new foreign policy within the context of China's new view of the structure of international politics, it is appropriate to consider the implications of this for the ways in which China has come to play a new and distinctive role in world affairs. The theory of the differentiation of the three worlds, however, is more than an attempt to define the main operative characteristics of international politics, and can also be seen as a programmatic doctrine which seeks to establish nothing short of a new world order. It is only within this grand design that China's new chosen role in international affairs can be discerned and any attendant problems identified.

Towards a Transitional New World Order

The Chinese hold that in the long term capitalism and its imperialist manifestations will be replaced by socialism and ultimately by Communism. The three worlds theory is regarded as a framework for analysis and action which will help to accelerate this eventuality. Although the theory deals primarily with struggle at the national or state level, the Chinese argue that 'in the final analysis national struggle is class struggle.' Thus the penultimate paragraph of the *People's Daily* 35,000-word theoretical analysis of the differentiation of the three worlds of 1 November 1977 states:

> Victory in the world wide struggle against hegemonism and victory in the international proletariat's struggle for Socialism and Communism are identical as far as fundamental interests are concerned. Capitalism has reached the stage of imperialism which is moribund and decaying, and the two superpowers, their hands dripping with blood, are already inextricably caught in the net they themselves have cast over the world. The day is not far off when the international proletariat, the grave diggers of the bourgeoisie, together with their close ally, the oppressed people and nations, will shake off their chains and win the whole world for themselves.[1]

At the same time the three worlds theory applies to an international situation which is perceived to be overhung by the clouds of a new world war. The character of world politics at present, therefore, may be seen as transitional in two senses which are closely related: first, 'the day is not far off' when it will be replaced by socialism; and second, it will be undermined by an inevitable world war.

The present epoch in the Chinese view is characterised by the two principal contradictions surrounding the superpowers and their relationship to the rest of the world. The first contradiction the Chinese assert will inevitably lead to a new world war between the Soviet Union and the United States. Ultimately, this can only be prevented by revolutions in both countries. The Chinese have not specified any time frame for these developments, but from the urgency of their admonitions and from the frequent analogies they draw between the 1930s and the 1970s it may be surmised that they feel war is probable in the near future rather than in the distance of several decades away. Although the Chinese do not welcome the advent of such a war, they believe that people should not be filled with despair by the prospect. In this regard it is worth quoting at some length from the *People's Daily* article of 1 November 1977 which best explains the Chinese position:

The people of China and the people of the world firmly demand peace and oppose a new world war. Faced with the gigantic task of speeding up our Socialist construction and modernising our agriculture, industry, national defence and science and technology, we in China urgently need a long period of peace. Like us, most countries in the world are against war. Except for a few war maniacs who vainly attempt to dominate the world, nobody wants a new war, which undoubtedly will bring humanity widespread disaster. As Chairman Mao consistently stated, our attitude towards a world war is: 'first we are against it; second, we are not afraid of it.' We say we are not afraid of war not because we like it or fail to see the devastation it will cause but because fear solves no problem whatsoever. Moreover, we firmly believe that man will definitely eliminate war rather than the other way round.

The *People's Daily* then proceeded to outline the familiar argument about the inevitability of imperialist war and to draw attention to the enormous war preparations made by both the superpowers, and especially by the Soviet Union. The article continued:

However, it will not be easy for them to achieve their [hegemonist] war. They are bound to come up against serious difficulties and road-blocks. Compared with wars in the past, a large-scale modern

war is even less a purely military question. Its preparations cannot but be closely interwoven with such factors as domestic, financial and economic affairs and external relations. As each frenziedly strengthens its costly war machine, the Soviet Union and the United States are bound to intensify their oppression and exploitation of the people at home and thus aggravate contradictions – their economies and the internal contradictions between the different classes and nationalities. In carrying out aggression and expansion everywhere and stepping up their global strategic deployment, they are bound to encroach upon the sovereignty and interests of other countries and thus aggravate their contradictions with these countries and people. Therefore it is only natural that, as they prepare for war, the Soviet Union and the United States should experience a sharpening of their internal and external crises. All this will inevitably upset their timetable for launching a war.

This was the classic Maoist argument that the more aggressive an imperialist power became, the more irresolvable problems and difficulties it created for itself. Not surprisingly, the *People's Daily* went on to cite the late Chairman Mao's paper tiger thesis. The United States was said to have

so much to protect and its battle fronts are so far-flung that it is trying to catch ten fleas with ten fingers, as Chairman Mao put it. As a result it has landed itself in a passive position strategically. Today Soviet social-imperialism is on the offensive, but 'in its offensiveness lies defeat' . . . the Soviet Union finds that 'its strength falls short of its wild ambitions', and it is 'unable to cope with Europe, the Middle East, South Asia, China and the Pacific Region'.

As a result of this analysis, the *People's Daily* argued that it was in fact possible to postpone the war. But this could only be done by concentrating upon necessary defence preparedness.

On the possibility of fighting a major war sooner rather than later. The key to putting off war lies not in holding talks and concluding agreements, as is vociferously preached by some people, but in the united struggle of the people of all countries against hegemonism.

The article warned against all forms of appeasement as being counter-productive. Any proposals to concede Soviet control of certain areas or to buy it off through co-operative economic endeavours or to divert it eastwards would only result in the same consequences as the policies of Chamberlain and Daladier in the late 1930s.

Instead the *People's Daily* urged:

> The people of every country must work hard and step up their preparations materially and organisationally against wars of aggression, closely watch the aggressive and expansionist activities of the two hegemonist powers and resolutely defeat them. The people must see to it that these two superpowers do not violate their country's or any other country's sovereign rights, do not encroach on their country's or any other country's territory and territorial seas or violate their strategic areas and strategic lines of communication, do not use force or the threat of force or other manoeuvres to interfere in their country's or any other country's internal affairs; moreover, both powers must be closely watched lest they resort to schemes of subversion and use 'aid' as a pretext to push through their military, political and economic plots. The people must also see to it that they do not establish, enlarge, carve up and wrest spheres of influence in any part of the world. So long as all this is done, it will be possible to hold up the timetable of the two hegemonists for launching a world war, and the people of the world will be better prepared and find themselves in a more favourable position should war break out. To this end, all the countries and people of the third and second world that are threatened by the two hegemonists must first of all foster a dauntless spirit and strengthen the conviction that no matter how the superpowers huff and puff, they can be defeated. They must not give in to intimidation and never allow themselves to be taken in. They must persist in safeguarding their independence, interests and security mainly by relying on themselves, redouble their efforts to support each other on the basis of equality and unite with all the forces that can be united to carry the struggle against hegemonism through to the end.

Thus in China's view what is required is that the countries of the Second and Third World should co-operate more together on the basis of vigilance and preparedness against the two superpowers by emphasising sovereignty and independence. Judging from China's practice and other statements the Chinese also endorse the entry into agreements with the United States because of its strategically passive situation on the basis of clearly perceived shared interests. Such agreements should not entail illusions as to the essential character of the United States as a superpower, but they are possible in certain situations, as in east Asia or in Western Europe, so as to utilise American countervailing power against the Soviet Union. In the Chinese view such arrangements should not become a substitute for defence preparedness but to the contrary, they can only work if independent defence work is carried out.

A necessary corollary of the Chinese view is that participants in local or regional conflicts, particularly in the Third World, should seek to find solutions without bringing in the two superpowers. The Chinese have consistently maintained that imperialists make use of such conflicts for their own purposes. In recent years China has encouraged Third World countries to settle their inter-state disputes without recourse to superpower or even UN intervention. Thus, for example, the Chinese commented approvingly on the border agreement reached by Iran and Iraq through the good offices of Algeria.[2] More controversially perhaps, the Chinese noted without criticism President Sadat's visit to Jerusalem. The Chinese had long held that the fundamental reason for the failure to settle the conflict in the Middle East was external intervention by the superpowers. Thus here was an occasion on which two of the local countries sought to resolve the problem essentially by themselves. President Sadat announced in Jerusalem his commitment to resolve the conflict without sacrificing the three basic Arab principles long supported by China: the return of all Arab territory seized in the 1967 war; justice for Palestinian national rights; and no separate peace. This facilitated what amounted to open Chinese support.[3] The objections of the rejectionist Arab states (including the PLO) were not mentioned at this time in the Chinese public media.

With similar considerations in mind the Chinese have welcomed the various moves towards united groupings in the Third and Second Worlds, whether it be on regional levels like the EEC and ASEAN or on a shared economic basis, like OPEC and the putative cartels of copper producers, etc. Such developments, in the Chinese view, offer the best way for such countries to co-operate together so as to better withstand the pressures from imperialism and social imperialism.

The Chinese have also opposed all attempts to subdivide the Third World countries. As we have seen in the previous chapter, China's Foreign Minister rejected the categorisation of the poorest such countries as a 'Fourth World'. In the 1970s the Chinese have scrupulously avoided drawing distinctions between more or less progressive and more or less reactionary regimes in the Third World. Such distinctions in the current era only serve superpower objectives of utilising divisions in the

Third World so as to be able to penetrate them more effectively. In particular, the Chinese object to Soviet-inspired attempts to fix 'progressive' or 'reactionary' labels on regimes or political movements and leaders as having the effect of serving Soviet superpower interests.

In the Chinese view the Third World countries are the main force in opposition to superpower politics and economic exploitation. Accordingly, the Chinese have vociferously supported in international forums all the attempts to establish a new international economic order. This forms an integral part of the Chinese conception of a new transitional world order. As we have seen in the previous chapter, the Chinese have spelt out a coherent programme for Third World countries by which their political independence can be sustained by an independent economic development which stresses self-reliance. Obviously, few countries are endowed with the extensive resources and capabilities of China. But the Chinese argue that by emphasising agriculture in an all-round way, intermediate technology, mutual self-help, political control of the transfer of technology (preferably from the Second World), radical reform of the terms of international trade, etc., it is possible for Third World countries to move towards a more self-reliant position.

This Chinese view of a transitional world order is predicated upon the primacy of state sovereignty and independence. The basis of their relations with each other ideally should be the Five Principles of Peaceful Coexistence. The new order is bound to be transitional in their view not only because of the ultimate inevitability of war but because it is bound to be superseded by more thoroughgoing revolutionary activity. As the Chinese put it, the 'objective trend' in the world is that 'countries want independence, nations want liberation and people want revolution.' Nevertheless, until the onset of a more overt revolutionary stage, the Chinese preferred pattern of developments constitutes in a sense a plan for a new kind of world order.

Two major sets of questions arise from this view of a transitional world order affecting China's role in international affairs. The first concerns China's capacity to push world politics along the desired pattern. To a large extent China's leaders have deliberately eschewed the policies traditionally associated with great-power politics. Thus China has not sought to establish special spheres of influence. Nor have China's leaders pursued the diplomatic style of 'wheeling and dealing' by which such capabilities and influence as China possesses could have been used to penetrate and pressurise other countries to act in ways other than those which they would prefer. (This has been generally true except where issues of Chinese sovereignty have been involved.) It follows, therefore, that China's leaders will be engaged in a massive 'educational' exercise to persuade the leaders of Second and Third World countries of the correctness and wisdom of the Chinese view. Given that any attempt to use great-power sanctions would be self-defeating, a great deal of the success of this didactic enterprise will depend on the perceptions of China held by the leaders of these countries. The second series of questions concerns China's role as a socialist country and the revolutionary dimensions of its foreign policy. It is this second question which will be considered first because analysis of China's larger world role is to a large extent conditional upon this.

Socialism in One Country

In many ways the Chinese position can be regarded as a variant of socialism in one country. China's leaders undoubtedly feel that they stand at the forefront of the development of Marxism-Leninism at the present time. Since going its own way in socialist construction from the late 1950s, China has vigilantly maintained the principles of self-reliance and of keeping the initiative within its own hands. The Chinese people have developed a unique political system which is self-generating and which is deliberately kept apart from penetration from outside forces. More important, however, is the fact that in the Chinese view they were the first to point to the emergence of revisionism in the Soviet Union and that theirs is the socialist system which has undertaken the most thoroughgoing measures to prevent a possible regression to capitalism. Thus China in this view is the centre of revolutionary socialism and the main bastion against superpower imperialism. In the imagery of the Chinese revolution, China may be considered as the reliable base area of world revolution. In this sense China could be regarded as playing an international role similar to that which Mao held that the Soviet Union played in Stalin's day. The continued existence of the Soviet Union as a socialist bulwark in the era of imperialism was of inestimable benefit for the revolutionary forces in China. It was this, coupled with the example of the Bolshevik Revolution, which in the end transcended by far the significance of Stalin's catalogue of erroneous acts and advice. Thus China's most important contribution to the world revolutionary process may be regarded as simply to continue the struggles for socialist construction as a bulwark against imperialism. This view of China's revolutionary role is enhanced by consideration of the criterion by which the Chinese have designated the Third World as a 'revolutionary motive force propelling forward the wheel of history'. From a Marxist perspective only two criteria are possible: first, that based on a country's *internal* class struggle; and second, that based on the country's objective position in the *external* balance of world forces relevant to the principal contradiction of the particular period of world politics. Clearly the criterion with regard to the Third World is the external one. At the same time, considered from a larger historical perspective, the ultimate struggle is between the revolutionary forces of socialism and their allies on the one side and those of imperialism on the other. The continued existence of China as a genuine socialist country can be seen as ensuring that the link between the internal and external criteria of the revolutionary process will be sustained.

Before analysing the further implications of China's position as a variant of socialism in one country, it is important to distinguish this from Stalin's version. In the first place China is not the only socialist country in the world. Even though theirs is the only socialist country which has undergone a cultural revolution in the struggle to prevent a capitalist restoration, and which upholds the three worlds theory, the Chinese do recognise that other genuine socialist countries exist in the world. Second, the Chinese do not insist upon laying down the ideological line for other Marxist-Leninist organisations or socialist countries, nor do they display any signs of seeking to establish a new Communist International; and third, the Chinese do not require of other Marxist-Leninists that they subordinate their own national interests for the sake of defending the Chinese socialist state.

Since the break with the Soviet Union the Chinese have consistently regarded the defence of the Chinese socialist state to be purely a matter for the Chinese people. To be sure, they have always maintained that independent revolutionary activity by other peoples and any genuine resistance to imperialism by others is helpful to China's own struggles. Likewise, China's leaders have consistently acted upon the principle that revolution cannot be exported and that any revolutionary movement must rely primarily on its own resources and only secondarily and minimally upon external aid. Nevertheless the Chinese leaders have always argued that they do have external revolutionary duties and obligations and it is to consideration of China's proletarian internationalism that we now turn.

Although the Chinese have identified a number of other Third World countries as being socialist they have not recognised them as a special sub-group. As the *People's Daily* Editorial Department put it, 'True, there are China and the other Socialist countries, but what was once the Socialist camp no longer exists, nor do historical conditions necessitate its formation for a second time.'[4]

The fact that not a single country designated by Peking as socialist has fully accepted China's new theories has not caused the Chinese to alter their public designations of these countries. Vietnam, for example, has even rejected China's three-world analysis and its leaders take a fundamentally different view of the Soviet Union and the United States. Moreover the Vietnamese hold that the socialist camp is very much alive. These and other differences between China and Vietnam have not caused the Chinese to reclassify Vietnam or to stop their economic aid, much of which until the final revolutionary victory in April 1975 was provided free of charge.

China's party and state constitutions and the programmatic statements of China's leaders all claim that China's foreign policy is based on proletarian internationalism. Thus the 1977 Party Constitution stated in the only passage devoted to foreign affairs:

> The CPC upholds proletarian internationalism and opposes great-nation chauvinism; it unites firmly with the genuine Marxist-Leninist Parties and organisations the world over, unites with the proletariat, the oppressed people and nations of the whole world and fights shoulder to shoulder with them to oppose the hegemonism of the two superpowers, the Soviet Union and the United States, to over-throw imperialism and modern revisionism and all reaction, and to wipe the system of exploitation of man by man off the face of the earth, so that all mankind will be emancipated.[5]

The practical manifestation of proletarian internationalism in China's foreign policy may appear at first sight to belong purely to the declaratory and symbolic level. Thus China's leaders set time aside from their busy schedules to meet with representatives of the minuscule and politically insignificant self-styled Marxist-Leninist organisations of various countries.[6] It may be regarded that that serves the purpose of demonstrating that on the ideological level China is still a part of a world-wide internationalist movement. On a more politically significant level China extends propaganda support and perhaps limited material aid to various Communist parties in south-east Asia which are actually engaged in leading revolutionary armed struggles against the incumbent local regimes. These parties all espouse Maoist ideology and their struggles are modelled to a large extent on the experience of the Chinese Revolution. In this regard the Chinese can claim a consistency of outlook. Since the establishment of the People's Republic and indeed ever since Mao became leader of the Chinese Revolution, the Chinese have always argued that a socialist revolution cannot be won except as the result of armed struggle led by a Communist Party following correct Leninist principles.

By emphasising the *external* criteria of identifying the revolutionary motive force in the world it should not be thought the Chinese have set aside the general principles they have specified regarding the *internal* criteria for making revolution and the carrying out of national liberation struggles. The application of the two criteria to concrete situations can be seen from two examples which have caused many leftists outside China to doubt the revolutionary credentials of China's practice of foreign policy: the liberation of Angola and the rightist *coup* in Chile.

It is as well first to recall the Maoist principles which were advanced in the selection of united front allies during the War of Resistance against Japan and which have recently been applied on a global basis to explain how socialist China can seek allies among regimes which internally are radically anti-socialist. In 1940 Mao argued explicitly:

> No matter what classes, parties or individuals in an oppressed nation join the revolution, and no matter whether they themselves are conscious of the point or understand it, so long as they oppose imperialism, their revolution becomes part of the proletarian-socialist world revolution and they become its allies.[7]

Angola

The Chinese are frequently criticised in leftist circles outside China for having supported the CIA-backed FNLA and the South African-aided UNITA movements against the more genuinely progressive MPLA in the Angolan civil war. China in these criticisms stands condemned for allowing anti-Soviet considerations to lead it into alignment with American imperialist and South African interests which most African black nationalists (especially the radical variety who used to count as China's closest friends on the continent) regard as their main enemy. The Chinese reject these criticisms as malicious or ill-informed.[8] First, they argue that in the years before the *coup* in Portugal in April 1974 and the subsequent Portuguese decision to grant Angola independence in 1975 the Chinese extended aid and support to all three liberation movements, including the MPLA. Indeed the Chinese had given military training to MPLA guerrillas. Neto, the MPLA leader, visited Peking twice. Although the three sets of leaders separately complained to the Chinese about the other two, the Chinese consistently urged them to unite. (It may be noted that this is the general line the Chinese follow with regard to liberation movements. For example, China's leaders have consistently recognised the more widely representative Fatah and the PLO as the leaders of the Palestinians rather than any more radical group sympathetic to Marxism-Leninism.) Following the Portuguese decision to grant independence to Angola, the three movements agreed to a form of unity. The OAU also formally urged them to unite. The Chinese supported these moves. It was at this point that the Chinese argue that the Soviet Union suddenly designated the MPLA as progressive and the other two as reactionary. It then proceeded to send in a massive arms supply and a few thousand Cuban troops (formally labelled as 'mercenaries' by the Chinese). In the Chinese view the Russians are principally to blame for the ensuing civil war. With the outbreak of the civil war which also brought in the intervention by other external powers, the Chinese ceased all aid to the warring three movements.

In the Chinese view, the MPLA government of Angola is not independent. The Cuban 'mercenaries' are still present in Angola. Angola is now regarded as serving Soviet imperialist strategic designs on Africa which are largely concerned with attempts to outflank Europe and also with attempts to gain access to African mineral resources. The Chinese assert that by relying upon the Soviet Union black African nationalists are making a grave mistake. The Chinese note that a guerrilla war is still taking place in the country and that there are some signs of contradictions emerging in the MPLA-Soviet relationship. As for the question of recognition, the Chinese draw the analogy with Bangladesh, where Chinese recognition followed after the country became independent from Indian dominance which was then seen as a kind of proxy for the Soviet Union. Meanwhile the Chinese urge African countries to draw the appropriate lessons from the expulsion of the Russians from Egypt, the Sudan and Somalia. Whether or not the Chinese explanation is regarded as satisfactory it can be seen as principled from a Chinese perspective. On the other hand, it is a measure of the distinctiveness of China's policies that the more radical African regimes which used to have a close relationship with China in earlier years take a very different attitude.

Chile

Many find inexplicable the Chinese reaction to the CIA-aided *coup* which overthrew the Allende government and the Pinochet regime which proceeded to slaughter all kinds of leftists in their thousands. Not only have the Chinese continued to extend recognition to the regime but they have also developed trade relations with it. By way of reply the Chinese essentially make three points: first, Allende was regarded as a particularly friendly personage. He was a former head of the Chile-China Friendship Association and his was the first South American government to extend diplomatic recognition to the PRC. Chou En-lai personally sent a message of condolence to Allende's widow on his death. Second, the fundamental reason for the *coup*, the Chinese assert, was Soviet influence and the pernicious doctrine of peaceful transition. This meant that after his coming to tenuous power the major class enemies remained undefeated, and moreover there was a lack of clarity as to who were friends, who were enemies and which were the middle forces to be won over. So, instead of concentrating upon foreign monopoly capitalists and their local agents, the Allende government focused upon dispossessing and nationalising the property of the small businesses. At the same time wages were increased and the government undertook social security responsibilities far beyond its capacity to discharge. This was a product of ultra-leftism and the Chinese urged Allende against this course in vain. As a result of these policies the base of support of the government weakened and it excited the hostility of the petit bourgeoisie, so the government with Soviet support, called in generals to become members of the Cabinet. By following Soviet precepts the Allende government lacked a solid Marxist-Leninist line and it veered widely between ultra-leftist and rightist policies which finally left it without organised mass support by the broad sections of the people when the militarists struck. Third, with regard to recognition (or its withdrawal) the Chinese argue that they follow the five principles of peaceful coexistence. Otherwise doubtless they would have withdrawn recognition from the Soviet Union long ago. For as seen from China, whatever the horrors of the Pinochet regime, those of Brezhnev are worse.

Whether or not these explanations are regarded as satisfactory by leftists, they point up the harsh realities of the application of China's revolutionary principles to foreign policy. Although the Chinese deliberately eschew the policy of charting the principles for others to follow and they do not 'wave a baton' over other socialist countries, revolutionary movements or national liberation movements, their own specific policies are determined by priorities derived from their analysis of the principal contradictions in world affairs. Beyond that, China lends general moral support to those movements whose cause is considered just on the basis of China's revolutionary principles. But the degree of specific aid and the enthusiasm of the support given will depend to a large extent upon general Chinese foreign-policy considerations and the extent to which the movement concerned is regarded as carrying out its political and armed struggles in a correct way.

It follows from this that China's revolutionary role in world affairs is as a kind of revolutionary base area whose continued existence as a correct socialist entity is vital to the long-term prospects of the revolutionisation of the world along the lines quoted above from the Party Constitution. This is a role which conforms fully with China's own revolutionary experience. Although Mao's successful leadership of the revolution to the seizure of state power may be said to have been despite actual Soviet activity there can be no doubt, as he himself repeatedly pointed out, China's revolutionary struggles were successful precisely because of the Russian Revolution and the continued existence of the Soviet Union as an example and as a bulwark against imperialism. In this sense China's primarily revolutionary role is to persevere with the struggle to keep the country on the socialist road and to carry on successfully with socialist construction. Thus the commitment to modernise the country so that by the end of the twentieth century China should become a powerful modernised socialist state has a revolutionary significance.

China's New World Role: Problems and Prospects

It is appropriate now to return to consideration of the questions arising from China's attempt to encourage a new pattern of international politics. As mentioned earlier, having deliberately chosen not to follow the path of great-power politics in an era which by virtue of its imperialist character (in the Chinese view) is necessarily governed by these considerations, the Chinese necessarily have few alternatives but to pursue a didactic role. Thus in so far as China is a leader of the Third World it is not as a leader of a bloc, but as a country which gives a lead by example and exhortation. Meanwhile, the PRC as a state which is following the policy of 'Socialism in one country' (as suggested earlier) necessarily reserves the right to carry out such measures as it deems desirable for its self-defence, as, for example, the use of American countervailing power against the Soviet Union.

One major problem confronting China in the Third World is that, while China is generally regarded as a member of this world, many Third World countries consider it as a rather idiosyncratic one which differs from the rest in many important respects. China is freely regarded as one of the great powers in world affairs. Its nuclear programme is well advanced and although it may seem of small significance in comparison with the nuclear capabilities of the two superpowers, it is nevertheless fast approaching the stage of having a limited second-strike capability. Indeed some analysts are already beginning to credit China with the capacity to absorb a first nuclear strike (from, say, the Soviet Union) and still have the ability to strike back in a small way.[9] (That is, the so-called 'bee-sting' deterrent). No other Third World country could hope to aspire to reach such a stage for the foreseeable future. Furthermore, unlike any other country in the world, China is in the position to claim that by resorting to a people's war it could survive and defeat a full invasion force launched by either of the two superpowers. In the international economic arena too, China stands apart from all other countries, but especially those of the Third World. China's domestic economy is practically insulated from the forces at work in the world's international economic system. To be sure, China's foreign trade is affected by these forces. But even though that trade has trebled in value since the Cultural Revolution,[10] the total amount is still only 5-6 per cent of China's gross national product,[11] and its total impact on the economy is at best very marginal indeed. China's abundance of natural resources, coupled with its unique system of self-reliance and virtual self-sufficiency, separate it very clearly from all the other developing countries. Thus China's interest in the establishment of a new international economic order is necessarily different from the overwhelming majority of the other Third World countries for whom this may well be a question of survival. Politically, too, China is seen by the majority of the regimes in Third World countries as very different from them. They see China as having experienced perhaps the deepest and most profound revolution of the epoch. Many are impressed by China's determination to continue along a revolutionary path of development. They suspect that the Chinese regard them often as comprador bourgeoisie and at best as national bourgeoisie and that, therefore, they are regarded as transitional leaders. They suspect that (Chinese protestations to the contrary) the Chinese are appealing to revolutionary forces within their societies and that the Chinese connection for them in the long term may be a highly destabilising one. While there is nothing but admiration for China's achievements and indeed for the Chinese model, very few Third World countries have seriously attempted to emulate the Chinese example.

The Chinese, for their part, do not seek to impress their model upon others. Unlike the practice in the Soviet Union, the Chinese do not publish books and pamphlets for foreign consumption which explain systematically and clearly the main features of their model and how others may copy it. The Chinese approach is to let others come to China so that they can observe and perhaps study the Chinese experience and then it is left to them as to how best they may wish to apply any of the lessons learnt. The Chinese message has always been that the primary sources for change, innovation and development must come from within the society or country concerned. The external factors should always be secondary, and this applies to economic development as much as to the practice of revolution.

China's bilateral relations with Second World countries have developed considerably in the 1970s. Trade in particular has greatly expanded and to a certain extent the Western European countries and Japan share elements of the Chinese concern regarding the Soviet Union. But not a single government of these countries believes with China in the inevitability of a world war or that *détente* is a dangerous illusion to be equated with the appeasement policies of the 1930s. In this regard China is widely seen as being engaged in a case of special pleading. Moreover, there are few signs that the Second World countries identify their economic interests with those of Third World aspirations for a new international economic order. To be sure, most of these countries have demonstrated a preference for conciliation as opposed to confrontation with the Third World. But then this has become largely true of the United States. On the major issue of the 'North-South dialogue' the Second World countries share American perspectives and indeed are so perceived by most of the Third World.

The prospects of Chinese success in persuading Second and Third World countries to pursue the roles allocated for them in China's projected new world order do not seem bright. The difficulties are further compounded if the various actual and incipient conflicts between Third World countries are taken into account. Examples drawn from China's immediate periphery alone are sufficient to illustrate the problem. Witness, for example, the animosities between Kampuchea (Cambodia) and Vietnam which have deep historical roots, or indeed the clashes of sovereignty and interests between China itself and many of its maritime neighbours over claims to islands in the South China Seas and the resources of the sea bed.

From a long-term perspective, however, China might yet have greater success than is immediately apparent. The three worlds theory may indeed prove to be prescient in its characterisation of the dynamics of the rather fluid international situation. But paradoxically, if the modernisation of China on the variant of socialism in one country should prove successful, this would have immense consequences in shaping the balance of world forces — more in terms of power relations than in the promotion of revolution. For the success of revolutionary forces elsewhere is independent of Chinese activities, except perhaps if China were to emerge sufficiently strong to deter external intervention in a revolutionary situation. But such prospects belong to the distant rather than the immediate future. Meanwhile the primary tasks set for the Chinese people are the domestic goals of modernisation on the basis of independent self-reliance. China's chosen role within the 'three worlds' is still one of considerable importance, but it is one that enables China to continue to set itself apart from the interdependencies of others. This means that China's foreign policy will continue to be based on the politically determined 'grand strategy'. In this sense the 'three worlds theory' will provide both a basis for analysing the international situation and for specifying the main determinants of China's foreign policy.

In the final analysis, China's international significance may be said to stem from its impermeability to external controls and damage short of actual invasion. In practical terms, this means that so long as China can continue to be held at one remove from the outside world, China will be able to determine its own priorities and role in world affairs independently of the pressures of seemingly more powerful and technologically more advanced countries than China itself. In practical terms this also means that China will continue to be an important and independent factor in the balance of world forces and that the key to China's actual role in world affairs will depend upon essentially two factors: first, upon self-generated ideas as derived from the synthesis of China's history and revolutionary experience; and second, upon the degree of success achieved in the programme of modernisation which could transform the capabilities by which China's impact as a great power is actually felt by other countries. At the same time, China's main preoccupation continues to be the relations with the more militarily powerful superpowers, as has been the case since the foundation of the People's Republic. Ultimately this will depend upon how well and how quickly the Chinese people achieve what Chairman Mao once called the 'main task' of economic construction within a 'genuine socialist' framework.

Notes

1. 'Chairman Mao's Theory of The Differentiation of the Three Worlds Is a Major Contribution to Marxism-Leninism', *Peking Review*, No. 45 (1977).
2. See the statement of 28 February 1974 by Huang Hua, then China's perma-

nent representative in the United Nations to the Security Council, in *China Quarterly*, No. 58 (April/June 1974), Chronicle and Documentation, pp. 427-8.

3. See *Peking Review*, No. 49 (1977), pp. 28-9.
4. See Note 1.
5. 'The Constitution of the Communist Party of China', *Peking Review*, No. 36 (1977). The quotation is from p. 17.
6. Thus in the course of 1977 Chairman Hua himself found time to receive and hold discussions with no less than eight such delegations.
7. Mao Tse-tung, 'On New Democracy', *SW*, Vol. II, pp. 346-7.
8. The ensuing discussion on Angola and Chile is based upon my understanding of talks with Chinese officials in Peking.
9. See Jonathan Pollack, 'Peking's Nuclear Restraint', *International Herald Tribune*, 16 April 1976.
10. Joint Economic Committee, Congress of the United States, *China: A Reassessment of the Economy*, 10 July 1975, p. 645, Table A1.
11. Ibid., p. 25.

Armstrong, J.D. *Revolutionary Diplomacy*. Berkeley: University of
California Press, 1977

Borisov, O.B. and Kolokov, B.T. *Soviet Chinese Relations 1945-1970*.
Edited with introduction by Vladimir Petrov, Indiana: Indiana
University Press, 1975

Bowie, R.R. and Fairbank, J.K. (eds.). *Communist China 1955-59:
Policy Documents*. Cambridge, Mass.: Harvard University Press, 1962

D'Encausse, H. Carrere and Schram, Stuart R. *Marxism and Asia*.
London: Allen Lane, 1969

Doak, A. Barnett. *Uncertain Passage: China's Transition to the Post
Mao Era*. Washington: Brookings Institution, 1974

Fairbank, J.K. (ed.), *The Chinese Traditional World Order*. Cambridge,
Mass.: Harvard University Press, 1968

Fitzgerald, Stephen. *China and the Overseas Chinese: A Study of
Peking's Changing Policy 1949-1970*. Cambridge: Cambridge University Press, 1970

Friedman, E. and Selden, M. *America's Asia*. New York: Pantheon,
1969

Gittings, John. *The World and China 1922-1972*. New York: Eyre
Methuen, 1974

Gittings, John. *Survey of the Sino-Soviet Dispute*. London: Oxford
University Press, 1968

Gurtov, M. *China and South East Asia: The Politics of Survival*.
Lexington, Mass.: Heath Lexington Books, 1971

Halpern, A.M. (ed.). *Policies Toward China: Views from Six Continents*.
New York: McGraw-Hill, 1965

Hinton, Harold C. *Communist China in World Politics*. London:
Macmillan, 1966

Hsieh, Alice Langley. *Communist China's Strategy in the Nuclear Era*.
Englewood Cliffs, N.J.: Prentice-Hall, 1962

Huck, Arthur. *The Security of China*. London: Chatto and Windus,
1970

Klein, Donald W. and Clark, Anne B. *Biographic Dictionary of Chinese
Communism 1921-1965*. 2 vols. Cambridge, Mass.: Harvard
University Press, 1971

Lamb, Alastair. *The China-India Border*. London: Oxford University

Press, 1964

Larkin, Bruce D. *China and Africa 1949-1970.* Berkeley: California University Press, 1971

MacFarquhar, R. (ed.). *Sino-American Relations 1949-1971.* New York: Praeger, 1972

MacFarquhar, R. *The Origins of the Cultural Revolution: Contradictions Among the People.* Vol 1. London: Oxford University Press, 1974

Mao Tse-tung. *Selected Works, Vols. I-V.* Peking: Foreign Languages Press

Mao Tse-tung. *Miscellany of Mao Tse-tung Thought.* 2 vols. Washington: Joint Publications Research Service, 1974

Maxwell, Neville. *India's China War.* London: Pelican, 1970

Ogansanwo, Alaba. *China's Policy in Africa 1959-1971.* Cambridge: Cambridge University Press, 1974

Ojha, I.C. *Chinese Foreign Policy in an Age of Transition: The Diplomacy of Cultural Despair.* Boston: Beacon Press, 1969

Schram, Stuart R. *The Political Thought of Mao Tse-tung* (revised edition). Harmondsworth: Penguin, 1969

Schram, Stuart R. (ed.). *Mao Tse-tung Unrehearsed.* Harmondsworth: Penguin, 1974

Schurmann, Franz. *The Logic of World Power.* New York: Pantheon, 1974

Schwartz, Benjamin. *Communism and China: Ideology in Flux.* Cambridge, Mass.: Harvard University Press, 1968

Simmonds, J.D. *China's World: The Foreign Policy of a Developing State.* Canberra: Australian National University, 1970

Simon, Sheldon. *The Broken Triangle: Peking, Djakarta and the P.K.I.* Baltimore: Johns Hopkins University Press, 1968

Snow, Edgar. *The Long Revolution.* New York: Random House, 1972

Van Ness, Peter. *Revolution and Chinese Foreign Policy: Peking's Support for Wars of National Liberation.* Berkeley: University of California Press, 1970

Wang Gung-wu. *China and the World Since 1949: The Impact of Independence, Modernity and Revolution.* London: Macmillan, 1977

Whiting, Allen S. *China Crosses the Yalu.* Michigan: Michigan University Press, 1960

Whiting, Allen S. *The Chinese Calculus of Deterrence.* Michigan: University of Michigan Press, 1975

Wilson, Ian (ed.). *China and the World Community.* Melbourne: Angus and Robertson, 1973

Zagoria, Donald S. *The Sino-Soviet Conflict 1956-1961.* Princeton: Princeton University Press, 1962

INDEX

298 *Index*

Since the completion of the book in December China's foreign relations
have entered a new phase. Beginning in 1978 China began to side
openly with Kampuchea (Cambodia) in its conflict with Vietnam.
In April a deep conflict between China itself and Vietnam surfaced in
public as tens of thousands of ethnic Chinese refugees began to stream
across the border into southern China. By the time of writing, July
1978, more than 150,000 ethnic Chinese had fled to China over the
previous three months. Mutual recriminations between the two
countries have reached such a pitch that open armed clashes between
the two sides can no longer be ruled out. Moreover the Chinese leaders
have charged that the Vietnamese actions were instigated by the Soviet
Union. In early July Vietnam joined the Soviet dominated Council for
Mutual Economic Assistance (Comecon) and a few days later the
Chinese finally cut off all economic aid to Vietnam. In late June
Albania took the Vietnamese side of the dispute and for good measure
it charged the Chinese with imperialism. Chinese aid to Albania then
came to an end too.

Chinese fears of Soviet encirclement have been greatly intensified.
Communist newspapers in Hong Kong which normally reflect the
thinking in Peking have identified a pattern of Soviet strategic encirclement of China which stretches from the expansion of Soviet influence
in the Horn of Africa to an alleged growing military presence in
Vietnam. China began to meet this intensified challenge with a more
outgoing and active diplomacy than at any time since the beginning of
the Cultural Revolution more than twelve years ago. China's most
senior leaders including Chairman Hua Kuo-feng himself undertook a
series of goodwill visits to neighbouring countries.

The domestic drive towards rapid economic modernisation has made
the Chinese leadership appreciate even more keenly the enormous
technological gap between China and the advanced levels in the outside
world. Foreign trade is now recognised to have an important part to
play in the realisation of the ambitious economic targets set by China's
leaders. This is particularly true of what might be regarded as the need
to obtain so-called 'turn key' plants which would set the tone for whole
new projects in China.

The conjunction of the sharpened awareness of the need for foreign advanced technology with the greater immediate fear of Soviet strategic encirclement in the light of the Sino-Vietnamese conflict has begun to make China more openly and directly globally engaged than hitherto. Nevertheless the difference is still one of degree. China continues to hold the outside world at one remove while focusing primarily upon the domestic tasks of modernisation within a socialist framework as set out by the post Mao leadership.